FREE AND NATURAL

NATURE AND CULTURE IN AMERICA

Marguerite S. Shaffer, Series Editor

Volumes in the series explore the intersections between the construction of cultural meaning and perception and the history of human interaction with the natural world. The series is meant to highlight the complex relationship between nature and culture and provide a distinct position for interdisciplinary scholarship that brings together environmental and cultural history.

FREE AND NATURAL

Nudity and the American Cult of the Body

Sarah Schrank

UNIVERSITY OF PENNSYLVANIA PRESS

PHILADELPHIA

Published by
University of Pennsylvania Press
Philadelphia, Pennsylvania 19104-4112
www.upenn.edu/pennpress

Printed in the United States of America on acid-free paper
10 9 8 7 6 5 4 3 2 1

Library of Congress Cataloging-in-Publication Data

Names: Schrank, Sarah, author.
Title: Free and natural: nudity and the American cult of the body /
    Sarah Schrank.
Other titles: Nature and culture in America.
Description: 1st edition. | Philadelphia: University of Pennsylvania Press,
    [2019] | Series: Nature and culture in America | Includes bibliographical
    references and index.
Identifiers: LCCN 2018053108 | ISBN 9780812251425 (hardcover)
Subjects: LCSH: Nudism—United States—History. | Nudity—Social
    aspects—United States—History. | Human body—Social aspects—
    United States—History.
Classification: LCC GV450.S325 2019 | DDC 613/.194—dc23
LC record available at https://lccn.loc.gov/2018053108

For my family

CONTENTS

ON BEING
FREE AND NATURAL

In 1916, the prolific journalist George Wharton James, famous for his colorful accounts of Native American life in the Southwest and florid Southern California boosterism, self-published a memoir entitled *Living the Radiant Life: A Personal Narrative*. Featuring a swirl of modern Christian thought, praise for Whitman's and Twain's portrayals of America, shameless name-dropping, and references to his own Western adventuring, the book is most remarkable for James's extolling the body beautiful and his quest for a liberated experience in nature. From his opening line, "Everything in Nature is radiant," James explored his theory that if human beings could just marry mind, body, and soul through encounters with nature, we all could achieve longevity and vigorous health.[1] *Living the Radiant Life* developed contemplations on the physical self that James had introduced in his earlier writing, including his conviction that it would be far better to "know the sanctity of nudity, rather than to cover the body."[2]

In prose startlingly reminiscent of today's New Age lingo, James described ideal health as emanating from the body in straight, parallel lines, invisible to everyone but the occultist's eye, but experienced personally as charisma, vigor, and joy. The healthy body was a radiant body full of energy and "life-force."[3] This life-force might also be described as a series of auras that in a healthy body were experienced as strong pulsing waves. In a sick body, however, the auras lost power, pulsed weakly, and created a "confused direction."[4] For James, such feelings of malaise were evidence that mind and body were deeply connected and optimal health meant lining up one's psyche with one's corporeal being. Unlike medical practitioners of the late nineteenth and early twentieth centuries who understood the body as a battleground upon which to fight illness, James believed the body to be a container of experiences, some good, some bad, but with infinite possibility for happiness. As he asked his readers, "I want to radiate spiritual health. Do you?"[5]

The key to the radiant health James held dear was the life lived outdoors, and so he instructed his readers first to emulate the American Indian: "Learn of him and be wise. He is a believer in the virtue of the outdoor life, not as an occasional thing, but as his regular, uniform habit. He lives out of doors; and not only does his body remain in the open, but his mind, his soul, are ever also there."[6] Native Americans, however, were not the only guides to radiance. In extolling the physicality of the outdoor life, James also exposed a profound, and possibly homoerotic, fetishism of the working man's body: Fishermen had "brawny arms and shoulders and backs"; sea captains were "brave, powerful, massive men"; and loggers "[swung] their axes or handled the huge logs with an ease and power that stagger the ordinary city man."[7] Three weeks spent riding with real cowboys turned James from a "dyspeptic, sleepless, and anemic" mess into a radiant being full of vim and vigor.[8]

For James, the radiant life of the outdoors trumped the modern industrial urban world which, despite its "pleasures in the ballroom," were accompanied by "languor the next day, ennui, jealousy, heart-burnings, gossiping, cruel slandering, [and] ruination of health."[9] The city was not just full of emotional pitfalls and vulnerability hangovers caused by the overstimulation of the senses, it was inherently unnatural, with the "artificial never equal to the real," as electricity turned night into day and reversed the "natural order of things."[10] Fashionable dress, too, received James's derision as it invited flattery that was "hollow, insincere, and corrupting."[11] To succumb to urban pleasures, many of which were pleasures of the flesh, was to sully the body and weaken the spirit. Though this censoriousness reflects the Christian ideology James expounded upon in his collected writing, his meticulous effort to separate the denigration of the clothed body indoors from the virtues of the naked body out-of-doors also reflected a keen desire to display the very body he shaped. It may have been nature's challenges that whittled away fat, tanned the skin, and hardened muscle but it was in the city where the radiant body had intrinsic value.[12]

For all of James's clear directives for achieving a blissful life, his own was marked by conflict and contradiction. A British Methodist minister, James immigrated to the United States in the 1880s with his wife, first settling in Long Beach, California, only to have her sue him for divorce for adultery and to be defrocked by the church for fraud and sexual misconduct. Smeared in the *Los Angeles Times* for tales of "revolting domestic crimes" and sexual deviance too "filthy" to print, James was all but run out of town.[13] While he would eventually be reinstated, James left his ministry behind and instead pursued a career as a journalist, photographer, editor, booster, and health fanatic, often contributing to *Physical Culture* magazine, pet project of tabloid publisher and body cultist extraordinaire, Bernarr Macfadden. Littered with pseudoscience, radical diet regimens, sex advice, vanity shots of Macfadden in a variety of athletic poses, celebrity exposés, and lots of advertising for beauty-enhancing commodities promising success in the emergent urban industrial world, *Physical Culture*, first published in 1899, represented the height of early twentieth-century body cultism.[14] James's enthusiasm for corporeal and spiritual experiences outside the city, in nature, might seem out of place in *Physical Culture* and yet it was there that the original chapters of *Living the Radiant Life* first appeared and it was to Macfadden that James gave heartfelt thanks in his foreword.[15]

While neither the first nor the only proponent of the modern life lived out-of-doors, James serves as a sublimely articulate advocate of what became the free and natural lifestyle in the United States. In his tastes for nudity, vegetarianism, sexual exploration, primitivism, Southern California leisure culture, mind-body ideology, "God is everywhere" New Thought philosophy, health fads, and physical exercise, James literally embodied the modern impulse to be liberated from the stresses of an urban capitalist life by channeling his energies into one lived "naturally." To be free and natural was not simply to retreat to the wilderness and never to return to civilization. To be free and natural in the modern age was to select carefully from a range of spiritual ideologies, body practices, health philosophies, sexual identities, and commodities to shape a "lifestyle" of free and natural living. The naked body, laden as it has been with conflicted meanings and representations, often served, both in James's time and today, as the key signifier of authentic experience in modern urban environments.

Over a hundred years after James fixated on the body as both the site of toxic moral corruption and the key to robust natural health, Americans continue to pursue a wide range of body practices as a means to achieve optimal well-being and reconnect with the natural world. While some of these *practices* may be subcultural, the *ideas* behind the free and natural lifestyle pervade many aspects of American culture, affecting everything from the interior design of domestic space to the marketing of everyday commodities. *Free and Natural: Nudity and the American Cult of the Body* thus explores the origins, evolution, and cultural practice of a modern lifestyle that privileged nature, nakedness, and a quest for authenticity in tandem with, and in reaction to, the rise of twentieth-century consumer capitalism. By calling it a "lifestyle," *Free and Natural* evokes and retains the complex relationship proponents of natural living had with consumer culture, often absorbing it into their daily lives at the same time that they tried to free themselves of it. The free and natural lifestyle has taken many forms in the United States, ebbing and flowing in popularity while sometimes exhibiting conflicting philosophies, but its practitioners have consistently invested the body, nudity, nature, sex, and their concomitant spatial contexts, with heightened social and cultural significance. These five integrated themes, and their shifting relationship to one another, serve as the foundational framework of this book.

❂   ❂   ❂

James's quest for authenticity and natural living through the body became a prominent feature of the American modern age as other middle-class urbanites also grew fascinated with the upkeep, cleansing, and general fitness of their bodies, producing a new cult of the body when they ascribed attributes of character development and health to physical culture regimens and diets. Purposive exercise, bodybuilding, weight loss, and cosmetic use became both therapeutic and consumer habits of a social class in search of self-identity and status in the midst of urban industrialism and as part of an economy of leisure. Concern with personal physical appearance was intertwined with the anonymity, physical mobility, increased visuality, and consumer practices that characterized daily life in early twentieth-century cities.[16] How one looked and how one was perceived from the outside became critical factors in the successful navigation of urban capitalism. In Macfadden's *Physical Culture* magazine, advertisements for elocution and posture lessons ran alongside the essays on bodybuilding, fitness regimens, and mail-order forms for new health and beauty products like mouthwash and hair cream. For the native-born middle-class aspirant, or the newly arrived immigrant, the message was clear: how you looked, sounded, and smelled on the outside was far more important than anything happening on the inside.[17] In the city, no one knew who you were so the impression you made on the senses, and especially how you looked and carried yourself, mattered. A well-formed body became a highly desired quality in a modern urban culture that increasingly fetishized fitness while the industrial economy, through the use of machines, increasingly relied less upon human strength. Fitness practices and character-building exercises became heralded as antidotes to the male impotence and effeminacy that pre-

sumably followed the corporate restructuring of labor into white-collar classes and gray flannel suits.[18]

Molding the body into an acceptable shape and then using it to assimilate
into American culture as an acceptable middle-class citizen meant that one
was either white or white enough to do so. One of the many crises facing modern urban industrial America was how to reconcile xenophobia and eugenics-
based social science with Progressive-Era goals to absorb the millions of immigrants passing through Ellis Island, across the United States-Mexico border,
or arriving on San Francisco's Angel Island, as well as the internal migration
of African Americans out of the rural South into Northern industrial cities.
One way to navigate the pressures of assimilation and urban racial politics
was to exert white privilege as soon as one could. Constructing a fit white
body while dropping one's accent and ethnic name was a strategy available
to those whose bodies were not racially marked. For women, however, such
strategies were hindered by the sexualization of their presence in public, especially for women of color.[19] White women were never subject to the same type
of surveillance but the combination of late-Victorian gender ideologies about
separate spheres and sexual purity (especially for wealthy women), and a lack
of political power, burdened their public presence at the turn of the twentieth
century with sexual overtones. The objectification of working-class women
was further complicated by new patterns of courtship, especially dating, that
mingled sexual possibility with the treats of the consumer economy. How
these women's bodies looked and were fashioned by clothing and makeup was
closely scrutinized by reformers concerned about working women's safety, but
also about their threat to the social pecking order.[20]

Anxieties also grew among the emerging middle class that their health
was being compromised by exposure to pollution, crowded cities, impover-
ished immigrant populations, and a denatured living experience that shut out
the sun and left them vulnerable to illness. Progressive reformers responded
to these concerns with calls for more parks, regulations to clean up the tene-
ments, and health programs for the urban poor. Some of the wealthiest moved
to suburbs well outside the cities and traveled along the American "health
belt," a route of sanitaria and resorts running through the Southwest, on new
rail lines that promised access to healing climates and a return to preindustrial
calm and physical revitalization. As the twentieth century unfolded, many urban dwellers began to see a tension between their corporeal health and wellness pursuits and the heightened visuality and commercial sexuality of the
body in American popular culture. In other words, what started as a way to

feel good in one's skin was beginning to feel like an odious pressure as the body and its fitness were becoming closely monitored status signifiers of the modern industrial age.

Along with this pressure to reshape their bodies came a new self-consciousness about the environment in which such physical exertion should take place and how much effort ought to go into producing the desired effect. Too much effort, and one could be seen as vain. Too little, and one might be perceived as lazy. Physical culture practiced outside the city, and away from neighbors and colleagues, became a sought-after ideal that included visits to health sanitaria, camping, and out-of-doors adventures permitting exposure to the sun and fresh air.[21] Once rejuvenated, modern Americans could then return to their city life taking some of their free and natural experience back with them. Early twentieth-century celebrities such as Pierre Bernard, the "Mighty Oom," who popularized the physical practice of yoga in the United States, soon capitalized on what they rightly perceived as a market for professionalized body culture, selling wealthy urban dwellers weekend retreats for physical and spiritual nourishment as part of a general regimen of rigorous dieting and exercise.[22] If nature was the place where the body could rejuvenate, it was in the city where the reinvigorated body could be displayed.

○   ○   ○

While quests for perfect health, physical fitness, and youthful beauty were consumer routes to addressing our body's flaws and fundamental impermanence, another strategy was to intentionally leave the body as bare as legally possible. This, too, has a history. Nudism as both a social activity and a means to organize one's daily life and living space emerged in the United States at the same time that modern urban industrialism reshaped American society and the American body. An effort to restore a natural experience to modern life while challenging social pressures to conform to body norms, nudism offered an opportunity to sidestep so much corporeal anxiety. Nudism can also be interpreted as an early alternative health and wellness movement because its proponents have long claimed that sustained sun exposure, outdoor leisure activities, and practiced relaxation naturally strengthen the body and heal the soul.

Nudism, by focusing attention on the entirely exposed body, also promised to authenticate the self. Indeed, white middle-class men were especially susceptible to the concern that they seemed weak and even worse, untrustworthy, in a new marketplace where appearance was everything. Part of the new physical culture regimens to shape the body were suntanning programs to give salesmen and managers the outward appearance of health and vigor. If they could not actually get outside, they could take advantage of the new tanning lamps that hit the market in the 1930s. As an advertisement in *The Nudist* magazine explicitly put it: "Look Successful—Be Successful! A good healthy coat of tan has a surprising effect on your business success. You look healthy and virile and instantly command attention. Your prosperous appearance makes people want to do business with you. Salesmen find their sales actually increase after they acquired a real bronze tan! And you will find yourself more popular, for both men and women are attracted by that healthy outdoor look!"[23] In fact, part of nudism's appeal was the ability to get a year-round allover suntan and show it off to one's nudist friends. But the sunlamp ad also reveals a tension between *being* a nudist and achieving the *look* of a nudist. While the tanning lamp could prove useful for both, one wonders if readers of *The Nudist* in 1937 empathized or snickered at the thought of salesmen desperately trying to buy the "natural" nudist look. To be naked, or at least bear the trappings of a naked life, did not necessarily render one natural or authentic.

The naked body, about as vulnerable and raw a form of self-expression as we possess, thus proved an especially provocative, controversial, and fraught site upon which to hang American hopes for liberation. Though heralded as the key to freedom from modernity's worst excesses, naked living was, throughout the twentieth century, deeply susceptible to capitalism's commodification and objectification of the body. Yet intentional social nudity, whether part of an organized public movement or a private experiment in naked living, has largely been a reaction to consumer capitalism's commodification of the body; a challenge to the capitalization of sexuality in popular culture; a rejection of the corporeal and sexual anxieties of the modern era; and an effort to shape a concept of nature within modern urban life while offering up a cheap health elixir in which sunshine and outdoor living could banish illness, build self-confidence, and make the body strong.

○ ○ ○

Nudity as a strategy for authentic living was welcomed by thousands of Americans largely because modernity provoked deep feelings of vulnerability along with fears of being cut off from nature altogether as old systems of community and identity formation were replaced with urban industrial capitalism and the body subjected to overwork and abuse. Scholars of modernity have long argued that the impulse to be "real," an impulse associated with 1960s rejections of materialism and corporate interventions in daily life, has a history dating back to the nineteenth century and the rise of modern systems of time management, industrial assembly lines, the technological reproduction of goods and images, and the concomitant anxiety of being cheated or defrauded by an economic system intent on extracting one's labor and depleting one's financial resources. By claiming to be "authentic," or at least attempting to live authentically, Americans sought, as cultural theorist Marshall Berman has put it, "a dream of an ideal community in which individuality [would] not be subsumed and sacrificed, but fully developed and expressed."[24] This individuality could certainly bump up against charges of narcissism, and taint an accompanying lifestyle with the exclusivity of class and racial privilege, but it can also be understood as an effort to retain control over one's life, for example, by rejecting processed foods in favor of sustenance grown organically.[25] Authenticity was thus tied to a desire to be more natural, or at least to grasp some semblance of nature beyond the mechanisms of modernity. Naked living offered an opportunity to reclaim one's body, restore it to a state of nature by offering it up to the sun and the elements, and stake a claim to an authentic experience of the self. To be natural was thus to be naked and to be naked was therefore to be real.

The compulsion to be in nature and, in so doing, better the body for the modern age became an organized experiment in the 1930s when social nudists embraced the radical idea that it was the *body* that was natural and the *society* that was unnatural. This impulse was characteristically modern in that it reached back to an idealized Edenic past and gestured forward toward a utopian future in which one's own body, left alone to function outside the pressures of modern capitalism, could be a guide to better health and a more wholesome life. Social nudists took the idea one step further to assert that the naked body was the most natural expression of all and that the ticket to circumventing the worst excesses and illness-producing stress of the industrial age was to relinquish clothing altogether. The rub, as it were, was that by the 1930s more Americans than not lived in towns and cities and, not surprisingly, their neighbors, friends, and colleagues were less than thrilled by public nudity, which was long associated with sexual degeneracy, mental illness, and general troublemaking. To most Americans, it was public nakedness, not socially prescribed norms, that was unnatural. Today, social nudism continues as a subcultural practice but one that still remains difficult to experience outside of private venues, many of which are now part of an international economy of resort tourism and back-to-nature retreats where, for a significant fee, one can buy access to the free and natural lifestyle.

○　　○　　○

While nudism and natural living experiments were organized efforts to reject the material and cultural excesses of the modern age, they were also attempts to reclaim sex and sexuality as natural and wholesome. They were rarely, however, exercises in free love or critiques of heterosexual marriage. Instead, nudist philosophy in the United States reasoned that by not hiding the body, and thereby embedding a sense of corporeal and sexual shame in children from the moment they are told to put on their clothes, Americans could grow up to have a healthy appreciation for their own bodies without projecting all of their emotional needs and anxieties into sexual desire and performance. Living naked would undo the mysteries of gender distinction, certainly emphasized through clothing and fashion, and downplay the importance of sexual difference even if it could not produce complete gender equality. Ridding the body of clothing would also rid one of guilt. As one observer put it in 1926, "by a perverse system of Puritanical reasoning it has made of the body a symbol of sin and shamefulness. . . . Civilization and 'modesty' demand that the body be covered with clothing; the heavier the better—forgetting, of course, that dress is not the secret to but the symptom of modesty and morals."[26]

Concerns about sex shame, as well as capitalism's corruption of healthy sexuality, grew in the early decades of the twentieth century as the new commercial markets for health, fitness, and beauty products promised enhanced sexual vitality while, in the pre–Hays Code era, movies and popular culture grew racier. Morris Fishbein, a doctor and editor of the *Journal of the American Medical Association* throughout the 1920s and 1930s, dedicated his career to fighting quackery and charlatanism, saving special vitriol for Bernarr Macfadden, who Fishbein believed peddled dangerous health advice and salacious body worship. In language that echoed the concerns of American nudists, Fishbein argued "[Macfadden] has taken what should be a beautiful search for health, for vigor, and for strength, and made of it an ugly and discouraging thing to every right-minded individual. . . . The Macfadden gospel is essentially an appeal to a large minority of persons whose eyes are aroused by the flash of nakedness."[27] Like Fishbein, who sought to distinguish between lewd nudity and the pursuit of corporeal health, nudists believed healthy sexuality was supported by social nakedness and were equally eager to put distance between themselves and what they viewed as crass pornographic entertainment. Nudity for physical, emotional, and mental health was distinct from nudity for sexual arousal, and with the flurry of publications meeting consumer demand for all things about the body, the distinction could get a little hazy. *Physical Culture* magazine proved troubling as it celebrated the body and natural health in ways nudists emulated but also commodified and sexualized the body. For nudists—indeed, all naked living practitioners in the United States—the inherent sexuality of the nude body would produce philosophical, cultural, social, and legal contradictions that would prove impossible to resolve, although they would certainly try.

○   ○   ○

Harnessing the new interest in exercise and health to philosophies of naturism taken mostly from German and British nudist practices, proponents of free and natural living in the United States believed they could reclaim the naked body as natural and beautiful, reject deeply held convictions that the body was inherently shameful, make the healthy body a collective goal, and, in the process, reshape society. As the chapters to follow detail, however, naked living in the United States was no easy feat. Practitioners, whether members of nudist groups or not, frequently ran up against anti-obscenity laws, resistance to shifting sexual mores, and intense legal battles over the use of public space. Thus, at the heart of this inquiry are the geographical spaces such as camps, suburbs, and urban beaches where "being natural" was overtly tied to the naked body.[28]

The spaces in which naked bodies are viewed and encountered have everything to do with how nakedness is interpreted. Simply walking around one's own home in the buff with no one seeing you does not qualify as either problematic or radical nakedness. It is private, indoors, and no one knows unless you tell them. Being naked in your house with all the lights on and a clear view in from the outside, however, opens up legal questions about lewd intent. Walking down a residential street alone, while naked, in most parts of the United States will at the very least raise eyebrows and will likely elicit concerns about mental illness and produce calls to local law enforcement. Outdoor nudity in a commercial venue, such as meandering through a shopping mall or promenade, will lead, most certainly, to arrest. The general social and legal consensus is that these are unnatural acts, the acts of the socially marginal and potentially sexually degenerate, and that we are not free to perform them. Indoor nudity is also not perceived as natural, unless in the bedroom or bathroom, but if unseen, does not matter much. Its visibility is what can cause problems. Meanwhile, outdoor nakedness in a place considered more natural than a city street, such as at a beach, has also proven unacceptable to many because being "free" can also be interpreted as not having to see someone else's nudity. Given the problem of spatial context, claiming the naked body as natural in the modern world has proven a difficult paradox and a complex legal challenge for advocates of nudism and the free and natural lifestyle to the present day.

Not only has the meaning of the naked body been tethered to the place in which it is viewed, the interpretative spaces of nudity are often visual, be it film or still photography, and the framing of those images has deeply affected how nudity has been understood. The expansion of the middle class in the mid-twentieth century, and its coupling with consumer capitalism, produced an especially conflicted modernist aesthetic that privileged the idea of the naked body in nature, but often in the most unnatural of settings, such as naked suburbanites serving drinks in an overstuffed living room, preparing dinner in a kitchen full of appliances, or lounging by an intensely chlorinated backyard pool. One of the paradoxes that threads its way through this story is that inasmuch as American nudists sought to reject the judgments of modern body culture and the consumerism that fed it, the private world they built to allow nudism and natural living to thrive was utterly denatured and artificial. Rather than rejecting modernity's artifice, many Americans modified their environment, often their own homes, and just boldly redefined the meaning of nature. Nudist magazines and films therefore had an important role to play in showcasing the free and natural lifestyle as wholesome and fun but also in providing a visual context in which the tensions between indoor/outdoor nudity; public/private space; and natural/unnatural environments, while never resolved, could be neutralized by the sheer delight practitioners found in displaying their own bodies.

Though social nudism and naked living projects took place all over the United States, and this book covers diverse regions including Florida, New York, and Wisconsin, among others, the majority of the case studies come from Southern California, and particularly Los Angeles County. This specific geographical focus is partly a product of the primary sources used, many of which are from Southern California archives including the Pomona Public Library Free Beach Collection, the extensive private collection of the Southern California Naturist Association, and the immense holdings of the Huntington in San Marino. It is also because a disproportionate number of nudist colonies, beleaguered free beaches, and lengthy obscenity fights were found here. Nowhere is the American cult of the body more closely associated with place than Southern California, largely because of 150 years of boosterism tying a lifestyle of leisure displayed through the flesh; the movie industry's globalized celebrity culture; the widespread adoption of cosmetic surgery; the intense fixation on physical fitness; the marketing of beach culture; and the local pornography industry.[29] As artist and writer Eve Babitz, famous for playing chess with Marcel Duchamp in 1963, at the Pasadena Art Museum, while in the nude, once wrote, "It has always seemed to me, ever since I was little, that sex (i.e., inspiring lust) was what L. A. was about."[30] With a climate amenable to naked living and a reputation for beautiful bodies on display, it is not surprising that Southern California would attract the nudist and the bohemian faithful. But reputations are one thing and reality is often something quite different. Southern California, and Los Angeles especially, also have long histories of political conservatism that have devastated public culture in the region and encouraged repressive legislation curtailing the public display of nakedness. Decades of clashes between city and county officials and a range of nudist activists have thus made Southern California an especially rich place to study.

○ ○ ○

While our social and economic circumstances have evolved and changed since the turn of the twentieth century, the anxieties prompted by our competitive social structure, enhanced visual culture, and material desires remain. Peruse any newspaper, social media interface, magazine, television show—indeed, most of American popular culture in the twenty-first century—and one is presented with a startling number of references to sex and sexuality and myriad images of naked, or near-naked, human bodies. In the visual landscape of television, dramatic film, and advertising, the bodies are overwhelmingly young, fit, and highly desirable. Older bodies, and increasingly young ones too, are injected, nipped, tucked, and sculpted in a bid to stave off aging and encourage their sexualization. In contrast, the bodies portrayed in a news brief, documentary, Facebook meme, or widely circulated YouTube video may take on a variety of colors, shapes, and ages not seen in processed entertainment media. In this other visual landscape, we may be privy to stories of the obesity epidemic, plastic surgery gone wrong, murdered black bodies, transsexual bodies, the health hazards of having an old body, abused workers' bodies, or an array of dead children's bodies who, through no fault of their own, became flotsam in an alienating and uncaring world.

In both of these broad, though not exaggerated, examples of how human beings are physically represented in contemporary American culture, the effects are essentially the same. They are exposed in order to elicit a strong reaction. In the case of entertainment media and advertising, we are meant to be aroused by the commodities and commodified bodies displayed and yet it is always an unrequited desire. Neither the BMW nor the model selling it will ever love us back, but we may go to great lengths to own the product that promises to make us as desirable. In the case of the news account of suffering or bravery in the face of terrible odds, the images are meant to arouse us too, either our ire and guilt or our repulsion and shame. The effects of this body obsessiveness have been devastating from both cultural and social perspectives. To take one example, the intense peer and media pressure on teenage girls to conform to unnatural physical standards promoted online has left them alienated from their own bodies, sexually precocious, yet unable to claim their own desire and needs, and vulnerable to rape and assault.[31]

Meanwhile, upper-middle-class adults pursue "wellness," which leads to no end of gym and fitness memberships, yoga, meditation retreats, alternative foods and supplements, a wide range of diets, and therapeutic treatments to keep us in one piece; quite literally, in the sense of mind and body becoming united and healthfully intact. At its best, wellness can bring its practitioners relief from deep and desperate suffering. Given the high rates of stress, and the serious illnesses it causes, these health challenges make wellness a worthwhile goal. But, for the most part, wellness is available only to those with significant disposable income to spend on therapists, life coaches, and exercise classes and excellent insurance to cover the rest.[32] Wellness, and the billion-dollar industry that fuels it, is a symptom of the shift of health from a public concern to a private one. Without the means, wellness is out of reach for most. The wealthy get healthy and everyone else stays sick.

As George Wharton James's story attests, the desire for beauty, sexual prowess, and optimal health is nothing new; in the twenty-first century, the difference lies in the extensive role of social media, personal electronics, and globalization in perpetuating and extensively commodifying the body. Sexual norms, sexuality, gender expression, and beauty standards are more flexible than in previous generations, and accessibility for disabled bodies more readily addressed than ever before; nevertheless, the surveillance of the body has equally intensified, making our personal display and physical achievement of youthful health that much more scrutinized and anxiety-producing. It's no wonder the wellness and beauty industry fares so well.

It is thus revealing, literally, that one of the most popular of cable television's recent reality shows has been the Discovery Channel's *Naked and Afraid*. Introduced in 2013 as an updated variant of the *Survivor* franchise, *Naked and Afraid* puts one male and one female participant together in a challenging natural environment such as a deserted Maldives island, the Florida Everglades, or one of many South American jungles, takes away their clothes and all modern amenities, and leaves them alone with nothing more than fire starter, a machete, and a film crew for twenty-one days. In season after season, practically identical challenges unfold (no water, no food, sunburn, mismatched personalities, dysentery) and the only question is whether they will both make it to the end or will one "tap out" before the other. While about as formulaic as television gets, the show is fascinating for its sidestepping of sexuality and its normalization of nudity. Here, nudity is an expression of physical vulnerability, the bodies, while fit, are so racked by bug bites, wounds, and dehydration as to be rendered asexual, and "nature" is presented as both a brutal, terrorizing force and a healer of modernity's ills. If you can make it through the twenty-one days, your mundane emotional and social hang-ups will seem all the more manageable. In *Naked and Afraid*, nudity is a potent signifier of naturalness and vulnerability even as the participants' breasts and genitalia are blurred out, presumably to protect the stars and the viewers from offense. Nudity, in fact, produces such vulnerability that the contestants need to work together, picking up each other's slack, and benefiting from each other's wilderness skills. While the weight and muscle mass of the competitors is carefully monitored, possibly producing envy in the viewer as each contestant visibly shrinks, the potential sexiness of the experience is elided, making the show unusual for avoiding that obvious narrative hook. Nakedness is not just a device to restore contemporary Americans' essential humanness; it is a form of catharsis that pushes the competitors beyond the shallow needs of sexual desire and material acquisition. Even though it is certainly a commodity—the show sells broadcasting rights and advertising space—and is produced under the inherently unnatural gaze of a camera crew, *Naked and Afraid* highlights how much cultural significance we place on the body in nature, however artificial the experience.

Americans have long sought what they considered a "free and natural" lifestyle manifested through their own bodies; what they encountered instead were some of the longest-running legal fights in United States history and profound resistance to even the concept of public nudity. The body is now more present in contemporary culture than ever before while the notion of "natural" is so tainted by biological determinism, commodification, and the loss of any environment untouched by humans that it has lost much of its early twentieth-century meaning. Harnessing the body to nature was originally an effort by nudists and other proponents of naked living to situate the body outside capitalism; ironically, that same effort ultimately shored up the connection of the body to late capitalism's excesses. It is a complicated story, and my goal is to identify historical moments when the body was not simply a vessel for narcissistic individualism but held the promise of other collective possibilities.

CHAPTER 1

WELCOME TO
THE NUDIST COLONY

During the summer of 1939, the Los Angeles newspapers were full of Hollywood gossip and rumors of scandalous sex. In and of itself, such titillation was nothing new, but circulation skyrocketed in July as the story broke that a young female member of a local nudist colony, Fraternity Elysia, had committed suicide after a boozy night of partying. As the papers told it, nineteen-year-old Dawn Hope Noel shot herself at her home in Van Nuys after a raucous weekend at the nudist camp and an argument, off-site, with her thirty-six-year-old musician husband. The fact that she was the daughter of stage and silent film actress, Adele Blood Hope, who had also died a few years earlier of a self-inflicted gunshot wound, further fueled sensational headlines about the nudist "girl wife" for weeks. Though the Los Angeles homicide bureau ruled the unfortunate event a suicide and closed the case within a day, the local press, together with city and county officials, drummed up scenarios in which Fraternity Elysia camp members, and nudism in general, were really the responsible parties.[1] Against a backdrop of "life in the gay Bohemianism of a nudist colony," the *Los Angeles Times* offered grisly details of the hole blown in Noel's head, while the competing Hearst paper, the *Los Angeles Herald-Express*, printed daily stories of "unspeakable orgies" taking place behind the "impenetrable walls" of Fraternity Elysia.[2]

The tabloid coverage violently brought to light a world of naked living that the city and county of Los Angeles previously had tolerated. Always humming in the background, though, were political concerns that anti-materialist collectives tied to health and the body might threaten the region's social order. The Noel case, with its media-enhanced taint of teen sex, naked debauchery, guns, and drink offered a unique opportunity for local officials to seize on social nudism as a way to earn headlines as warriors against degeneracy and to ban it from the city. As the story unfolded, however, it proved much harder to tamp down Los Angeles's free and natural lifestyle than politicians and legislators ever would have believed, while the smear campaign against nudism would successfully keep it out of the county for almost thirty years. One of the many paradoxes of free and natural living as it took shape in the United States was that as much as its proponents may have wanted to be free of media scrutiny, it would be to both print and film that they would turn to produce a more flattering self-image and to fight the conservative authorities who challenged them.

    ○   ○   ○

American nudism, and the free and natural lifestyle of which it was a part, grew out of *Lebensreform* (or "life reform"), a mid-nineteenth-century German health movement that encouraged urban dwellers to address the ills of industrial society by living more naturally. Nudist philosophy, which was referred to by British practitioners as *naturism*, and by Germans as *Nacktkultur*, included vegetarianism; exposure to fresh air, water, and sunlight; abstinence from tobacco and alcohol; and back-to-nature activities like gardening, hiking, and camping.[3] To explain social nudism to American audiences, and study the therapeutic possibilities of group nudity, Howard C. Warren, a professor of psychology at Princeton, published a widely circulated essay in 1933 in which he described his stay at the German nudist camp, Klingberg, near Hamburg. Klingberg was owned by Paul Zimmerman, who had purchased the property in 1902, in social nudism's very early years, and had raised his family according to the principles and protocols of the emergent body culture. Warren described the features of nudist etiquette, such as wearing clothes when seated for meals and the underpants worn by menstruating women. He joined the rigorous gymnastic regimens, led by physical education teacher, Herr Luhr, who banged a drum to summon camp-goers to morning calisthenics. Warren explained that "in keeping with the ideal of nature living," the floors of the rustic cabins were of "pure sand." He described the diet as strictly vegetarian and the stern camp prohibitions against smoking or drinking alcohol. After eight days at Klingberg, a pleasant visit truncated by an upcoming psychology conference in Copenhagen, Warren concluded that nudists were not "radicals, social rebels, or faddists," nor would he characterize them as "perverts or neurotics." Instead, everyone was relaxed, "natural, and unconstrained." He was especially impressed that by alleviating the anxiety prompted by modern attitudes about the body, what he called the "body taboo," shame and social awkwardness seemed to be swept away. Warren noted the overwhelming fitness of the guests, observing only "two or three men with obtrusive paunches." Most of all, he was impressed how group nudity decreased the significance of bodies themselves or specific body parts producing "less sexual excitement, less tendency to flirt, less temptation to ribaldry in a nudist gathering than in a group or pair of fully clothed young people." As delighted as he was by the experience he wrote up in his essay, "Social Nudism and the Body Taboo," Warren was skeptical if nudism could spread to Western society at large.[4]

Frances and Mason Merrill, a young couple from New York, had visited Klingberg two years earlier and also feared that nudism could never take hold in the United States. In their 1931 work, *Among the Nudists*, the Merrills argued that there would always be strong social, economic, and political pressures opposing progressive body politics, ranging from the Protestant prudery of American social reform movements to the Ku Klux Klan's xenophobia. Not only would nudists appear inherently indecent, but their cultural practice had foreign origins.[5] Trying to take a more optimistic tack, the Merrills also noted that despite American social conservatism, there were "certain factors in American life that might favor the progress of the [nudist] movement. The most obvious is the popularity of sunbathing in recent years. During the past few summers, whether seeking health or merely a fashionable 'sun tan,' countless Americans have been toasting themselves."[6] But the widespread popularity of suntans in the 1920s and 1930s was not symptomatic of a broader social movement; rather, the intentional suntan was tightly connected to a consumer economy directed toward a new youth market with money to spend on outdoor activities and ready-made clothing like the swimsuit and the backless sundress. Suntans signified leisure and wealth, not socialism or social experimentation.

Mulling over the naturist legacies of Whitman and Thoreau, the Merrills concluded in their second work, *Nudism Comes to America*, that the only future a nudist movement really could have in America was one of individual rather than social conviction, practiced in small, atomized groups. The Merrills believe that rather than in the countryside, as in Germany, American nudism would be better suited to cities. In their account of informal naked living in New York City, for example, the Merrills celebrated a set of penthouses where four nudist families arranged with their landlord to have exclusive use of their apartment building's roof for naked suntanning. The Merrills happily reported that "as a result, if one were permitted to go up there now—almost any time, day or night, in comfortable weather—he would find the children of those four families playing, or the adults sun-bathing or lounging about or working, all wholly free of clothes. Here in fact is a group which, though lacking any formal organization, constitution or bylaws, is a nudist 'colony' in a truer sense than any ordinary nudist camp or park could possibly be."[7]

Unfortunately, urban nudism would prove more challenging than the Merrills had thought. In 1931, Kurt Barthel, the German immigrant who transplanted social nudism to the United States when he founded the American League for Physical Culture in 1929 in New York, quickly foundered when he tried to organize urban events for his membership. After renting a gymnasium and swimming pool for a nude social gathering, league members found themselves promptly arrested and hustled into police vans under the watchful eye of the female neighbor who had called it in.[8] Similar incidents ensued and American nudists began to take refuge in the very countryside naturist theorists had suggested they avoid. In case nudists dared to move back to the city, already driven out by police raids on gymnasia and private homes, charges of indecent exposure, and the humiliating news reports that listed their names and addresses, the legislature in Albany, New York, passed the nation's first anti-nudism law in 1935.[9]

American nudism went on the offensive and in 1931, Kurt Barthel, Ilsley Boone, a Baptist minister, and a mutual friend, David Livingston, laid out the proofs for *The Nudist*, a short and rather primitive magazine featuring a nude image on its cover and copies of newspaper clippings covering the league's legal battles with the New York City courts. It clearly made for good reading and *The Nudist* soon had subscribers in the thousands who enjoyed wholesome, often airbrushed, images of naked sports, nude camping, and other back-to-nature exploits along with lengthy treatises about the importance of the sun for optimal health.[10] The original issues of *The Nudist* often featured mixed-gender groups on their covers, avoiding any suggestion that it might be a girlie magazine, with the bodies crouched or turned in such a way as to cover their genitalia. The implication was that nudism was serious business, with potential for fun, but an activity more akin to labor than leisure. On the cover, for example, a group of nudists have hiked to the lakeshore where they are shown resting after shedding their shoes; this is no simple stroll from their hotel to the beach (Figure 1).

Barthel then expanded the opportunities for free and natural living in April 1932 by purchasing property in Liberty Corner, New Jersey, to establish

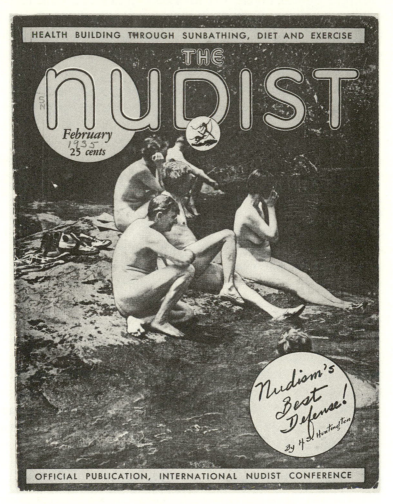

FIGURE I. *The Nudist* 4, no. 2 (February 1935), editor Harry S. Huntington (American, 1882–1981) (New York: Outdoor Publishing). 12 ⅞ × 10 in. (32.7 × 25.4 cm). Wolfsonian-Florida International University, Miami Beach, Florida, Gift of Robert J. Young, XC2000.81.33.4. Photo: Lynton Gardiner.

Sky Farm, the first nudist camp in the country and a member-owned coopera-tive.[11] Shortly thereafter, Boone established his own camp, Sunshine Park, in Mays Landing, New Jersey, which would become the East Coast anchor for organized nudism while his press, the Sunshine Book Company, published *The Nudist*, establishing it as the movement's flagship magazine. Together, the camp and the magazine could communicate Boone's belief "in the essential wholesomeness of the human body and all its functions. We therefore regard the body neither as an object of shame nor as a subject for levity or erotic exploitations."[12] With the creation of the camps, the magazine, and the newly constituted International Nudist Conference (INC), organized nudism took off and inspired the founding of clubs and camps all over country including Ohio, Michigan, California, and New York. By 1933, *The Nudist* listed forty-four clubs and over three hundred card-carrying members of the INC.[13]

Whatever its portrayal in the popular press, nudism held as its most im-portant tenet that the naked body, once accepted as wholesome and natural, would free Americans from unhealthy obsessions with corporeal perfection and sex. While they would never be able to entirely untether nudity from sex-uality, the nudist goal was to live as freely and naturally as modern life would permit believing that the shedding of clothing, with its stark markers of class and gender, would produce a happier, less uptight, and more equitable society. As Boone put it, "The sex significance of nudism lies wholly in the direction of a more wholesome and natural acceptance of men and women on the basis of their total physical, mental, and spiritual selves without making any of these invidious and injurious distinctions which clothes have woven into the fabric of civilization."[14] Though simple in theory, harnessing an overhaul of Amer-ican social norms to the naked body was far more complicated to execute, starting with the fact that public nudity was illegal and subject to the whims of local law enforcement and the reactions of the clothed.

Built into the free and natural lifestyle in the United States was thus a public-private divide that had as much to do with the evolution of nudism as a philosophy and practice as it did with modern American attitudes about sex, which waffled between the personal freedom to express one's sexual de-sires and the impulse to ensure social control through repression and shame. Therefore, American treatises on free and natural living, which often appeared in publications like *The Nudist*, were very clear that the naked body was a beautiful, natural thing but its reception had *everything* to do with context. The warning implicit in these writings is that no matter how normal nudists might find nakedness, American society was a long way from catching up. An example from the early 1940s explained that a nudist "does not conceive of the human body as being in anyway shameful in itself but *carefully* distinguishes between decent and indecent exposure. He accords to every part of the body an equally normal naturalness devoid of any vulgarity or obscenity. In this view an elbow, a pubic arch, or a nose are equally respectable."[15]

Equating the pubic region with the nose could be a tough sell and nudists thereby found themselves in the awkward position of retreating from the highly sexualized world of urban consumerism their cultural movement was trying to combat while using magazines, the newsstands and bookstores that sold them, and the post office that mailed them, to prove their practice was wholesome, healthy, family-oriented and, above all, a natural way to live. Defining nudism and its visual culture as nonerotic while also laying claim to a free and natural experience that, at its very essence, engaged human sexuality, would prove a troubling tension for nudists in the United States. Showcasing their subculture publicly as wholesome and healthy through print was one strategy for addressing that tension while moving social nudity out of the public eye and into private camps and retreats, known colloquially as "nudist colonies" was the other. Early on, American nudists preferred the term "camp" to "colony," feeling that the press and the public used it derisively.

To live the free and natural lifestyle in the early twentieth century was to try to secure a place in nature where one could feel liberated from the excesses of urban life. It was rare that the experience was permanent, as most Americans lived in cities and towns, but the goal was a relaxing, if temporary, retreat. Urban nudism was so frequently threatened by legal action prompted by its popular association with prostitution, pornography, stripping, and sexual degeneracy that it became evident early on that the natural body would have to be taken out of the city. As a result, to be natural, or to live naturally in one's skin, came to mean being outside urban areas despite American nudists' early efforts to create a naked experience within metropolitan borders.[16] Despite the legal challenges, nudist colonies flourished nationwide. In the early years, they were rustic and family-oriented with activities organized around group activities, sports, and, if the members were lucky, the camp swimming pool. Gardening and growing vegetables was also part of nudist camp life, as was participating cooperatively in the cooking, cleaning, and general maintenance of the grounds. The camps operated year-round but rarely had permanent residents. They were communal back-to-nature retreats away from the bustle and stress of modern urban life.

FIGURE 2. "Sunshine Leaguers of Kansas City take a hand in building their own swimming pool," *The Nudist* 4, no. 6–7 (June–July 1935), editor Harry S. Huntington (American, 1882–1981) (New York: Outdoor Publishing). 12 ⅞ × 10 in. (32.7 × 25.4 cm). Wolfsonian–Florida International University, Miami Beach, Florida, Gift of Robert J. Young, XC2000.81.33.7. Photo: Lynton Gardiner.

The association between nature and nakedness has a long history in Western culture, and nudists clung to an idealized, and perhaps naïve, concept of the body in nature as a way to justify their own nudity. In her work on the relationship between environmentalism and nudity, historian Marguerite S. Shaffer argues that photographs highlighting the natural state of nakedness by positioning the body in wilderness environments were essential to American nudist practice.[17] Children were often featured in 1930s pictorials as signifiers of innocence and the potential naturalness of nudity when not tainted by adult sexuality. For nudist urban dwellers, photographs emphasizing the placement of their bodies in natural, outdoor settings served as a tool for the successful straddling of city and rural experiences, confirming the authenticity of their free and natural body practice. Photographs of children with parents also emphasized the pedagogical value of being in nature and implied that a better relationship between the body and the outdoors could produce a stronger familial bond.[18] Given how sexualized the naked "nymph in the forest" trope has

FIGURE 3. "Mother and child gather stores of knowledge," *The Nudist* 2, no. 5 (July 1933). Wolfsonian-Florida International University, Miami Beach, Florida, Gift of Robert J. Young, XC2000.81.33.1. Photo: Silvia Ros.

been in American and European painting for two hundred years, there is a rather sweet irony that nudists believed that nakedness in nature rendered the body less erotic than if the nudity was on display in cities.[19] Indeed, one of the horrors of the Noel case for Fraternity Elysia members was that the camp was founded as a *retreat* from the city, both in the sense that it sheltered members from legal harassment and that it provided an environment free of the excesses of urban life and the social pressures to conform, compete, or consume. The media campaign to discredit them brought the proximity of modern urban life home in the most unpleasant of ways and highlighted the fragility of building a subculture premised on free and natural living.

Further reflecting the legal danger of having nudism and sex associated in the popular imagination, in 1936, at the Fifth Annual Meeting of the INC, held in Valparaiso, Indiana, the membership elected to change the organization's name from the International Nudist Conference to the American Sunbathing

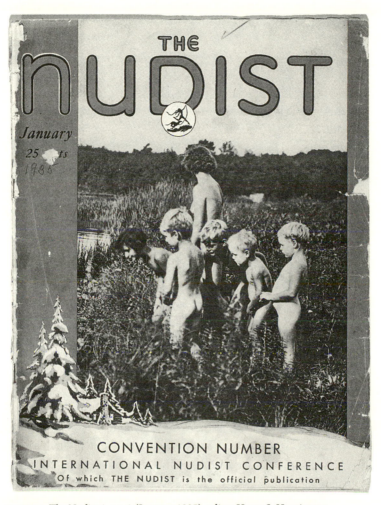

FIGURE 4. *The Nudist* 4, no. 1 (January 1935), editor Harry S. Huntington
(American, 1882–1981) (New York: Outdoor Publishing). Image courtesy
of New York Sunshine League. 12 ⅞ × 10 in. (32.7 × 25.4 cm). Wolfsonian-
Florida International University, Miami Beach, Florida, Gift of Robert J. Young,
XC2000.81.33.3. Photo: Lynton Gardiner.

Association (ASA) and the title of the magazine to *Sunshine and Health* to distance themselves from the word "nudist," which had increasingly taken on eroticized connotations in popular culture. In a published statement, members explained that "no sooner had the nudist movement in this country succeeded in fixing the connotation of the words 'nudist' and 'nudism' than these terms were seized upon by burlesque theater managers, night club troupes, disorderly road houses, and exposition side shows to further their own business enterprise in the field of commercialized pornography. Even the national press services have referred to psychopathic nakedness as 'nudism.' So lamentable has been this abuse of two perfectly good words that in the interest of dissociation of the nudist movement from the morbid and burlesque types of nakedness, these terms shall hereafter be left almost exclusively to the theatrical, the night club, and the pornographic fields."[20]

It seems likely, too, that the political connotations of the words "International Nudist Conference," with possible links to things foreign and leftist, may have inspired the name change. It is certainly plausible that the terms *international* and *conference* evoked too strongly political organizations subject to congressional scrutiny as subversive as well as evoking German *Nacktkultur*, which, by the mid-1930s, was entirely, and inaccurately, associated with the Third Reich. By 1936, the INC had taken great pains to separate itself from German nudism as Hitler had decimated that country's nudist groups because of their leftist working-class egalitarian politics, replacing the physical culture of socialist nudism with the body cultism of fascist Aryanism.[21] *The Nudist* explained that German nudists "were organized along strictly political lines and the strongest groups were among the socialists and the communists, though there were many thoroughly conservative groups also." When Hitler came to power, "he thoroughly suppressed every organization which tended to harbor anti-Nazi sympathizers. In the case of the nudist groups, it would have been far too difficult a task to separate the Nazi from the anti-Nazi elements. The easiest method was to wipe them all out at one blow, which was done."[22] The sharp political distinctions between socialism and fascism were not lost on the INC but its members were too worried about obscenity charges, police harassment, and Comstock laws to take a public stand, seeking instead to fly below the national political radar as much as possible.[23] Thus, names evoking the sun carried the far more neutral connotation of health and fitness than any nudist nomenclature could offer. The German Barthel had been himself dismayed by the naming of the INC, stating "Yes, 'International,' after we had for two and a half years done our durndest to be accepted as American."[24]

To be a nudist was already challenging enough, but to be a foreign nudist on American soil seemed to court disaster.

American nudists may have distanced themselves politically from both fascism and socialism but they could not sidestep racism. American nudist ideology in the 1930s retained disturbing echoes of eugenics, with *The Nudist* publishing essays on selective breeding, describing how nudist mothers raised stronger children (due to early childhood sun exposure), or asking "can we develop a race of super-men?"[25] Maurice Parmelee, a sociologist, political theorist, founder of American criminology, and early adopter of nudism, while committed to fostering an egalitarian society that embraced both feminism and racial equality, had trouble reconciling his intellectual sympathies with the eugenic concepts of biological determinism and social evolution about which he published and taught while a faculty member at the University of Missouri.

In his 1931 treatise, *Nudism in Modern Life*, Parmelee outlined his theory of how the widespread practice of nudism (what he called "gymnosophy") would unite people worldwide and reinforce the democratic, egalitarian, and humanistic ideals he held dear. While ascribing cultural norms to biological race, an understanding of human difference in line with eugenics theory, Parmelee emphasized that what one considered a natural or beautiful body was subjective. For example, he argued that "our standards and ideals of human beauty are determined largely by the fundamental human type, by the racial type to which we belong, and for each sex by the sex type. With respect to the beauty of these types there can be no argument, for they are the types to which we are accustomed, and which are natural and normal for us. Such statues as the Aphrodite of Melos and the Doryphorus of Polycleitus . . . are generally regarded as beautiful because they conform or are supposed to conform to the 'perfect,' that is to say normal human type."[26] Parmelee goes on to argue that as a result of this aesthetic subjectivity, while nudism celebrated the beauty of the natural body, "external racial traits, such as color and shape of the features, are usually regarded as ugly and sometimes as grotesque by other races."[27] While a classicist upholding the physical ideals of white beauty and the supremacy of Western civilization, he also believed that racial prejudice, by keeping people segregated, stood in the way of a nudist social revolution, which was unfortunate because "the racial traits which may at first seem offensive and ugly will soon be ignored under gymnosophic usage."[28] For nudist egalitarianism to work, Parmelee concluded "it is of great importance . . . that race prejudice disappear entirely, or be reduced to the lowest possible minimum."[29] This, of course, was the catch: nudism could undo centuries of racism by exposing the fallacy that there was only one type of beautiful body—the white body. The problem was that centuries of racism fostered deeply held prejudices, prevented people with racially different bodies from growing "accustomed to seeing each other nude as well as clothed," and reinforced the white body as a universal standard of natural beauty.[30] No wonder Parmelee made a point of saying that "race prejudice is, in fact, a serious problem for gymnosophy."[31]

While perceiving that racialized categories of natural beauty were socially produced, Parmelee could not bring himself to accept the beauty of the female body as equally subjective, saving his especially chauvinist vitriol for overweight women:

> While the fat belly is altogether too common among both sexes, it is more characteristic of women, not only because the female body has proportionately more fat, but also because women lead on the whole more sedentary lives than men. This unwieldy mass of flesh, sometimes containing folds and creases, and shaking jelly-like with the motion of the body, is one of the most unpleasant sights in gymnosophic circles. Here its ugliness is not concealed by clothing, so that gymnosophy is the most effective measure for eliminating this monstrous distortion by spreading an ideal of human beauty and shaming those who fall so far short of it.[32]

Nudist colonies did not function, possibly to Parmelee's chagrin, as fat camps, but images of both women and men in nudist magazines overwhelmingly featured trim, young, white bodies, reinforcing a narrow standard of natural beauty however much nudist boosters and philosophers may have claimed to be universally egalitarian in their acceptance of the naked human body. American nudists in the first half of the twentieth century generally celebrated white bodies as more natural and beautiful than bodies of color, a view inconsistent with their romanticism of global indigenous bodies' nakedness, health, and proximity to "uncivilized" nature.[33]

Conflicting racial attitudes produced tensions in American nudist camps between members who accepted racial integration as a central tenet of nudism's progressivism and those who did not, sometimes because they held racist views and sometimes because they thought racial integration to be politically imprudent. These positions, of course, were not mutually exclusive. The International Nudist Conference neither explicitly banned people of color, nor did its mission statement include them, asserting that membership was open to all ages, both sexes, and made no "tests of politics, religion, or opinion, provided that these are so held as not to obscure the purposes of the League."[34] The first decade and a half of the nudist movement made the debate abstract as there were few nonwhite nudists but this would change as soon as World War II ended and African American nudists would organize and challenge the racial segregation in the camps.[35]

The call for integration was sparked in 1944 when E. J. Samuels, an African American nudist from Los Angeles, was invited by *Sunshine and Health* to write a series of columns on the politics and experiences of black nudism. Citing examples of pleasant visits with his wife to otherwise all-white nudist camps, Samuels wrote of experiencing racial equality among his white nudist brethren while also hoping to form his own integrated nudist camp that would feature a substantially more racially diverse membership.[36] The American Sunbathing Association responded by refusing to admit African American members and instead encouraged black nudists to found their own magazines and camps.[37] Samuels swiftly countered with the argument that segregated national nudist organizations were, if nothing else, economically unfeasible: "Less than two percent of the entire white population are nudists. And the Negroes, by themselves, could only support about seven or eight camps in the nation. As to a Negro nudist magazine—it would be out."[38] Samuels went on to suggest that "all nudists belong to the same national organization. Let the local clubs or groups be free to exercise their prerogatives in the matter of members. All support one magazine. In union there is strength."[39] While reminding *Sunshine and Health*'s readers that black soldiers had just fought in Europe to preserve democracy while Southern blacks were struggling to regain voting rights, Samuels envisioned a racially integrated free and natural lifestyle, asking "why not have brown, white, and black bodies drinking in the healthful benefits of our gorgeous sun?"[40]

The American Sunbathing Association continued to oppose integrating the organization and went on the defensive arguing that it was *black* nudists who desired segregation. In a self-congratulatory tone, an editorial in *Sunshine and Health* explained that "throughout the interest recently manifested in the organization of negro nudist groups, the American Sunbathing Association has maintained a thoroughly sympathetic and cooperative attitude and shall gladly continue to do so. We believe that the best interests of nudism and the best interests of the negro groups both lie along the line of cultivating the negro groups until such time as they are sufficiently strong and numerous for

FIGURE 5. Queen Pat of the Central Sunbathing Association, from *American Nudist Leader* 4, no. 29 (1953), editor Mervin Mounce (American, 1909–1995), photographer Ed Lange (American, 1920–1995) (Spokane, WA: A. N. L. Publishing). 11 × 8 ½ in. (27.9 × 21.6 cm). Wolfsonian-Florida International University, Miami Beach, Florida, Gift of Robert J. Young, XC2003.04.1.146. Photo: Lynton Gardiner.

them to have their own national association and possibly their own magazine. Until such time, we are with them and for them one hundred percent."[41]

Some members of the ASA backed the organization's position, arguing that "mixing races in nudist camps at this time might seriously hurt or complicate the cause of nudism" while others, many of whom were ex-GIs, stridently challenged it, explaining that "the white man's denial of equality to his black brother and the white man's reluctance to practice the principles of brotherhood are fascist tendencies."[42] However loud the criticism, the ASA did not change its position until the early 1960s, when it incorporated the assertion that "no test of religion, race, creed, or politics may be made in judging the fitness of any applicant for membership" into its official policy.[43] The damage, however, was done and a 1964 scholarly study from Yale took note of how few bodies of color were to be found at American nudist camps. There were some, but not many. Moreover, the ASA club directory continued to list "black only" groups.[44]

San Diego nudist resort owner and developer, G. Walter Bayne, came to conclusions similar to those of the psychology students leading the Yale study. Concerned about the future of nudism and his investment in Sun-Air Parks, Incorporated, Bayne issued a questionnaire to 240 camp members in 1964 to assess their attitudes, preferences, and complaints. He learned, quickly, that the biggest bone of contention was racial integration. Asked whether African Americans should be admitted, 50 percent of his respondents replied yes, 31 percent said they did not care, and a significant 16 percent said no.[45] President Johnson may have signed the Civil Rights Act that year, yet some white nudists still expressed the racist anti-integration sentiment prevalent in United States society. African Americans did not make a significant appearance in nudist magazines until the late 1960s and, even as late as 1990, academic studies of nudist camps reported that "we know of no resorts or camps that bar African Americans and other minorities, yet their number has not increased appreciably."[46]

FIGURE 6. Photograph from Hal Collins's "Nudism and the Negro" essay in *Sunshine and Health* 33, no. 2 (March–June 1966), editor Ilsley Boone (American, 1879–1968), photographer Bob Edwards (Whitehouse, OH: Church Publications). 11 × 8 ½ in. (27.9 × 21.6 cm). Wolfsonian-Florida International University, Miami Beach, Florida, Gift of Robert J. Young, XC2000.81.33.180. Photo: Lynton Gardiner.

○   ○   ○

While neither the site of the first nudist colony, nor the location of the
first nudist publishing house, Southern California nevertheless looms large as
one of the most storied regions in the United States for naked living and an
important cultural influence for the shaping of the free and natural lifestyle.
Beginning in the 1860s and 1870s, when health seeking became an important pastime for the American middle and upper classes, Southern California
emerged as a national center for tuberculosis sanitaria, health colonies, and
the pursuit of optimal well-being through a wide range of practices including
outdoor sleeping, massage, hydrotherapy, sweat baths, raw foods, and fasting.[47]
As wealthy and newly middle-class Americans sought cures for tuberculosis
and other wasting illnesses, and discovered recreational travel in the process,
the railroads, real estate interests, and other investors sold the East and Midwest hard on the health benefits of the Southland, fostering what journalist
Carey McWilliams dubbed the "folklore of climatology."[48] Boosters sang the
praises of the Southwestern climate far and wide, inviting the sick and weak
to travel West and become well and strong. In his 1946 classic, *Southern California Country: An Island on the Land*, McWilliams explained that the combination of regional boosterism, health seeking, and capitalism also produced
what he coined a "cult of the body" whereby the attributes of place, in this case,
Southern California, became tied to the physical traits of strength, virility, and
beauty.[49] Add to that the climate, which made for especially pleasant outdoor
living, and nudity (or near-nudity) became incorporated into a regional image
already tethered to an expectation of exceptional body display. By the 1920s,
of course, Hollywood celebrity culture and the movies themselves would promote images of the Southern California body, and the commodities to try and
create one, but even by the late nineteenth century, a regional cult of the body
was alive and well, beckoning visitors and well-heeled migrants to indulge in
the sensuality of sun, ocean, and desert breezes.

The abundance of Southern California sunshine was a key selling point,
promoted as it was in the early twentieth century by the American medical
establishment as an important source of Vitamin D and a cure for a host of
ailments. It was also linked to the health tourism of the wealthy and, by the
1920s and 1930s, suntanning, along with physical fitness, was seen as a marker
of leisure time and social status.[50] In 1934, Ernestine H. Middleton, founder
of the El Dorado nudist camp in San Diego, explained: "Everyone who comes
here has the one ambition to develop his or her body into as nearly a perfect

physique as is possible. To replenish health and vitality, to acquire a fine, even tan and to spread the gospel of good living to others by each of us being a good example of what we preach is the ambition of every member."[51]

Not only was the sun perceived as healthy, it was also welcomed as aesthetically enhancing the body. One of the most popular European books on body culture to appear stateside in the 1930s was the German-published *Man and Sunlight*, by Hans Surén. By the time it appeared in English in 1927, it had already gone through sixty-seven editions. The book was full of photographs of incredibly fit, tanned, well-oiled men helping each other into physically challenging postures, so the impetus for the book's blockbuster success is not difficult to grasp. Surén, formerly chief of the German Army School for Physical Exercise, was a diehard sun worshipper. His philosophy on fitness echoed that of British health expert, C. W. Saleeby, who believed that the loftiest goal of humanity, the perfection of the human body, could be achieved by releasing "the body and restor[ing] it to its natural environment of air and light."[52]

In 1933, as nudist camps grew in popularity, a young psychotherapist named Hobart Glassey, his wife Lura, and a friend, Peter Joseph McConville, left their own nudist camp, Olympia, near Peekskill, New York, and moved west to Riverside County, California, and rented a piece of forested land in the Cleveland National Forest overlooking Lake Elsinore. Elysian Fields, which opened in May of that year, was modest, consisting of a few tents, a mountain water well, and two rustic buildings to serve as a dining room and kitchen. Glassey delighted in its privacy. There were no neighbors and the adjacent land was a game preserve unavailable to new buyers. Within days of their official opening, which involved a gathering of about ten, local law enforcement paid a visit, stating: "You can commune with nature all you want as long as you wear some clothes. Otherwise there'll be no colony. Riverside County won't stand for nudism."[53] One of the reasons given for the inappropriateness of the nudist camp was its proximity to a New Deal Civilian Conservation Corps reforestation project employing two hundred young men. The concern was that a sustained view of naked women would "detract from [their] efficiency."[54] While no arrests were made or citations issued that day, Glassey anticipated further unfriendly attention. He was proven right when, later that week, District Attorney Earl Redwine made a surprise visit, with the full intention of making arrests on the charge of public indecency, but found Glassey and the other Elysian Fields members fully clothed. Having missed his opportunity, Redwine huffed to the press that the Glasseys would be "thrown in jail every day of the week if I find anyone here without any clothing."[55]

With the district attorney and county sheriff breathing down their necks, the Glasseys chose not to hide but instead to loudly publicize their camp. They released statements to the local papers and made a slick presentation at the Elsinore Lion's Club explaining the purposes, both healthful and benign, behind the camp. Hobart Glassey explained to a packed house that "clothes are a restraint borne from childhood through life" and that "morality is just as present, and even more so, in a sense, among persons going in the nude than in many other phases of life, for the sham, the parade, the play, and the 'veneer' of civilization are removed."[56] And, in an uncommon strategy, breaking with the usual "good neighbors, if naked" public relations campaign of other nudist camps, the Glasseys invited the Culver City company, Foy Productions, to shoot a commercial film about nudism at Elysian Fields. If the Glasseys were going to be under surveillance, they figured they might as well have a hand in how their colony was depicted.

The result, *Elysia: Valley of the Nudes* (1933), was a forty-five-minute precode exploitation film that allowed the audience entrée into the nudist camp with full views of naked human bodies, but with genitals obscured, either hidden completely or shot from such a distance as to be impossible to see. It would be the first of a "dispatches from a nudist colony" film genre that continued into the mid-1960s. The movie, starring the pretty blonde model and actress Constance Allen and actual members of Elysian Fields, including Glassey himself, is utterly tame, offering lots of shots of eating, sunbathing, baseball-playing, all under the watchful gaze and tutelage of one Dr. King, who leads a shy journalist, James Mack, through the workings and philosophy of the camp. Los Angeles filmgoers were able to see *Elysia* but the movie ran into trouble with censors in other parts of the country. Film historian Eric Schaefer reports that it bumped up against local authorities and morality codes in Detroit, Birmingham, and other cities, while the states of Maryland and New York banned it outright.[57] Nevertheless, the public was intrigued and the screenings continued. In Minneapolis, prompt arrests ensued when a lecture accompanying the film included a live "sun-kissed nudist."[58]

Elysia works in classic exploitation fashion by titillating viewers under the guise of addressing a social ill, in this case, a socially ingrained value system that shamed the body. Indeed, the promotional posters for the film boldly advertised that its sensationalism lay in the fact it was a real place (Southern California, no less), and that its authenticity made it worthy viewing. But while it would be difficult to view *Elysia* as especially progressive, its sustained focus on the lead actress's breasts and sexualization of the nudist camp through Mack's desire for Allen's character, Miss Kent, prevents such an assessment, the film still suggested utopian possibilities lived through the body. If in the mountains above a major city like Los Angeles, hundreds of people lived in cooperative naked harmony, then other subversive experiments might exist on a near horizon. As film historian Robert M. Payne writes: "Although . . . nudist films were never politically 'radical' in the Marxist sense of the word—their raison d'être as commodities and their precarious legal standing precluded any outright political agitation—nudism's unconventional solutions to anxieties stemming from conventional society, especially during the Great Depression, implicitly questioned the very foundations of that society: the drastic, taboo-taking step of removing one's clothes in public intimated that complete correction of social dilemmas might require further measures equally drastic."[59]

In fact, the release of *Elysia* may very well have prompted anxiety in Los Angeles authorities already concerned about a "rising tide" of nudism they associated with a back-to-nature movement that seemed to be sweeping the West Coast. While not necessarily part of the national nudist movement, many Americans during the 1930s took part in a free and natural lifestyle incorporating what we would now consider "alternative health" or "New Age" activities as conduits to a cleaner, less materialistic life that offered a practical, cooperative alternative to the economic system that had just collapsed. Southern California, as the center for health and lifestyle movements, hosted many of them, along with a revival of enthusiasm for earlier collective social movements, such as former Llano del Rio colonists' embrace of Upton Sinclair's socialist End Poverty in California (EPIC) gubernatorial campaign in 1934.[60] The *Los Angeles Times*, which had conspired with the local real estate lobby, and other business interests, to down Sinclair's campaign was also less than thrilled about the energy building behind these new anti-materialist, health-based collectives. The paper often reported on such groups with a derisive, dismissive tone. With a barely contained sneer, one piece covered a gathering in Los Angeles's Griffith Park of four hundred members of the California Academy of Health, who drew winks and sideways glances for dancing around trees in their underwear and drinking "watermelon to 'cleanse' themselves . . . including great quantities of spinach washed down with celery juice and other appetizing preparations."[61] Erroneously called "nudists" by the *Los Angeles Times*, the participants' intense physical fitness nevertheless fascinated the reporter, who reported that the "celery juice must have been hi-octane."[62] News reports of nudist "cults" spreading to Carmel, already a hub of bohemianism, and to Baja California, where a group of two hundred espoused "the theory that a simple, clothesless life lived

FIGURE 7. "Strategically placed peepholes made it easy for expo goers to get a peek at the Zoro Garden nudist colony." California Pacific International Exposition, San Diego, 1935. Credit: *San Diego Union Tribune* Newspaper Collection, San Diego History Center.

as close to Nature as possible and on a vegetable diet will prolong the human life span," dismayed local council members and law enforcement, while greatly entertaining readers.[63] Not only were free and natural lifestyle enthusiasts potentially sexual deviants, they also might be juice-fasting communards whose enthusiasm for exercise and vibrant health might ultimately prove a threat to the established social order. Indeed, national conservative groups like the Society for the Preservation of American Ideals perceived nudism as a potential leftist threat made up of "radicals, aliens, and subversive elements."[64]

Meanwhile, throughout the 1930s and early 1940s, Australian immigrant Marshal South published hundreds of articles in *Desert Magazine* and other American periodicals detailing his life of naked back-to-the-land primitivism experienced with his wife and children in San Diego's Anza-Borrego desert. While eventually exposed as a fraud (South shopped for groceries and did not kill wild prey for dinner, among other published falsehoods), the national popularity of South's reportage revealed a public hungry for tales of alternative living experiments.[65] This public appetite for accounts of naked living was further whetted when, in 1935, the California Pacific International Exposition in San Diego hosted the Zoro Garden nudist colony. The campy exhibit featured twenty women and men lounging in flesh-colored tights and was apparently a big draw for the exposition, which allowed visitors to view the nudists through peepholes.[66] In promotional postcards for the Zoro Garden exhibit, however, the comely young women were entirely naked with their pubic hair removed or airbrushed out. The 1936 call to change the name of *The Nudist* to *Sunshine and Health* was, in part, a response to angry readers who felt that the Zoro Garden exhibit was not just silly but a fraud that appropriated the word "nudist" and turned it into a crass public spectacle. Calling for new American nudist leadership, along with the magazine name change, one Harold Simmons complained of the "unfortunate publicity that resulted from the so-called 'nudist colony' at the San Diego Exposition" because it "served to keep away from us many sincere enquirers and folks of fine character who certainly would not wish to be associated with a movement of which [that] 'nudist colony' was representative."[67]

Landing as it did between growing political concerns about collectivism and popular fascination with social nudity and back-to-the-land experiments, *Elysia*'s release was not in isolation from broader trends in American culture. However sensational its press, *Elysia: Valley of the Nudes* functioned as a visual showcase for the communal, nature-based living experience of Elysian Fields and a handy public relations tool. *Elysia*'s premiere made a splash at Hollywood's Pantages Theater and, not surprisingly, attracted more members to Elysian Fields.[68] Shortly before the film's release, Glassey also allowed Foy to film a nudist wedding. Photographs of the event, with participants shot discreetly from the side, promptly showed up in the Los Angeles papers.[69] Glassey regretted the decision, complaining to *The Nudist* that "the first nudist wedding of fame, or notoriety, however your will, was foisted upon us under pressure and I have no hesitancy in saying that the subsequent publicity was an unfortunate and distasteful occurrence. We have no wish for a repetition of it."[70]

Glassey may have seemed irritated by the publicity but the strategy as a whole was clever and effective. Though they tried, ever-persistent legal authorities continued to fail to catch anyone at Elysian Fields doing anything untoward, and the nudist camp became more of an eccentric local curiosity than anything else—mocked, perhaps, in the papers but ultimately left alone. Membership grew, and the founders of Elysian Fields began looking for larger and more permanent grounds. In 1934, they discovered what they were look-

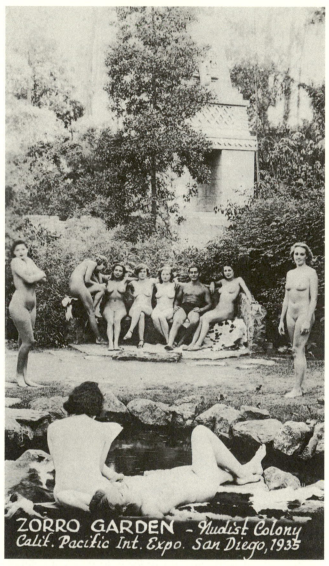

ZORRO GARDEN – Nudist Colony
Calif. Pacific Int. Expo. San Diego, 1935

FIGURE 8. Zoro Gardens postcard. California Pacific International Exposition, San Diego, 1935. Credit: Postcard Collection, San Diego History Center.

ing for a few miles from their original site: a property of over 320 acres, high in the mountains abutting the Cleveland National Forest, which meant that the new property was even more secluded. It also happened to fall on the border of Riverside and Orange Counties. Glassey joked to the press that, by straddling the county line, they'd always be able to avoid local officials: "While the Riverside officers were seeking on their side of the line, we could be hiding on the Orange County side, and vice versa."[71] This time, the Glasseys and Mc-Conville purchased the land outright and incorporated their club, naming it Fraternity Elysia. They had barely been a week on the new property before the three were arrested for stealing tools and portable shacks from their previous landlord. After a weekend in the Riverside County jail, the charges were dropped without even a preliminary hearing as the accused could prove they owned the objects in question.[72]

Other pressures clearly strained the Glassey-McConville relationship because soon after the incorporation and the land purchase, they had a falling out over money and McConville bought out his friends, renaming the property Olympic Fields and joining the INC.[73] The Glasseys took the club name, Fraternity Elysia, with them and set up a new camp in the San Fernando Valley's La Tuna Canyon, which is in Los Angeles County, and within Los Angeles city limits. They promptly spread word throughout the national nudist community that they had expanded their operation to now comfortably sleep dozens of people, that they were publishing their own newsletter, *The Elysian*, and, most importantly, that the new camp was "a sunbathing resort only nineteen miles from City Hall and only ten miles from the heart of Hollywood. [Fraternity Elysia] is . . . closer to three of the major studios than many portions of Hollywood proper. Warner Brothers, First National, and Universal have their studios only six miles [away] and Columbia pictures is even closer." In highlighting their new proximity to the movie industry, as well as modern facilities like hot water, electricity, and telephone service, Lura and Hobart Glassey made it clear that they welcomed the Hollywood crowd, fostered a relationship with filmmakers, and were now offering a free and natural experience that resembled a resort holiday more than a communal nudist retreat. In fact, their advertising assured future guests that they could enjoy the sun and outdoor sports "without sacrificing any of the advantages of hotel life."[74] Their open invitation to the Hollywood scene to join them would ultimately prove to be Fraternity Elysia's death knell as nudism's survival in Los Angeles relied on its discretion; the Dawn Hope Noel case, with its tinges of Hollywood *noir*, literally splattered the local nudist culture across the city's front page.

Following the Glasseys' example to court Hollywood, McConville also allowed a film crew onto his property, resulting in the strange 1938 romantic drama, *The Unashamed*. In this film, the plot revolves around a Los Angeles secretary, Rae Lane, a curvy woman with dark skin and nonwhite features of which much is made although her ethnicity remains unclear. In love with her hypochondriacal boss, Rae lures him to a nudist camp where he perhaps can be healed and hopefully return her affections. When her plan fails, and her love interest falls for a white woman, Rae kills herself by jumping off a cliff and the film abruptly ends. While not especially progressive since Rae's transgressions (aggressive female sexual pursuit, interracial love) are punished by self-inflicted death, it is still notable that it is in the context of 1930s nudism that these themes are even addressed.[75] While *The Unashamed* hardly qualifies as pro-integration activism, it nevertheless absorbs a nonwhite naked body into its narrative along with white ones implying, possibly, that by removing clothing a society might also remove other social markers.

McConville later made history within the American nudist movement when, in 1945, he marshaled the three hundred members of Olympic Fields to fight the state legislature's efforts to completely ban social nudism. Introduced by a liberal Democrat, State Assemblyman Ralph C. Dills, the Dills Bill (AB 344, January 17, 1945) would have added Section 317 to the California Penal Code, prohibiting social nudism anywhere in the state. The bill was left to die in committee after legislators heard ample testimony from nudists convincing them that criminalizing a seemingly harmless activity was pointless. While nudism would face all kinds of restrictions on the local level, this would be the last attempt to restrict social nudism statewide.[76] When Peter died in 1959, members changed the camp's name to McConville and later, in 2000, to Mystic Oaks. The retreat survived under varying owners as California's longest-running nudist camp for almost eighty years, finally closing permanently in 2007.[77] Fraternity Elysia would fare less well. Hobart Glassey died in a fall in 1938 while working on a camp construction project. Lura, widowed with two small children, continued to operate the camp until the smear campaign by the press and the sustained effort by authorities to shut it down forced Elysia to close a few years later.

By the time the Noel case broke in 1939, there were several actual nudist camps, not just groups of nature buffs dubbed health nuts by the press, scattered throughout Southern California including Campo Nudisto, Valley-O-the-Sun, Samagatuma, and El Dorado. While most of these camps were in San Diego and San Bernardino Counties, several hours' drive from Los Angeles, there were a few in Los Angeles County proper, including Fraternity Elysia, Shangri-La, near Calabasas, and Land of Moo, in the Antelope Valley.[78] These were of gravest concern to Los Angeles authorities and the tabloid coverage of Dawn Hope Noel's suicide provided ample opportunity to tarnish social nudism with accusations of degeneracy. In the days following, the *Los Angeles Herald-Express* pushed Noel's death to the back pages and focused instead on nudism as "a return to savagery" and nudists as "barbarians who exposed themselves, their sweethearts, their mothers, daughters, and wives to other naked men."[79] The tone, while clearly sensational, was also indignant that the city and county of Los Angeles would have dared to allow such wantonness to flourish in their midst.[80] The captain of the Los Angeles vice squad was promptly deployed by the county sheriff to survey all the nudist camps in the region to find out if they were adequately secluded or potentially visible to the public.[81]

As there were no laws prohibiting nudist camps, the police had to look for reasons to close them and the Los Angeles City Council and the County Board of Supervisors hopped on board to help the cause. Councilman Roy Hampton introduced a resolution to outlaw nudist camps within city limits, a resolution supported by Mayor Fletcher Bowron, while County Supervisor Gordon L. McDonough made a motion to further investigate the camps for fear that they "are not conducive to the betterment of morals in the community and that under existing conditions county authorities are powerless to regulate them."[82] Yet not everyone in local positions of authority supported anti-nudist measures. County Supervisor John Anson Ford refused to support such regulation without further study in order, he explained, "to avoid any hysteria which might encroach on American freedom along health lines," and he was staunchly supported by his colleague, Supervisor William A. Smith.[83] Chairman of the board, County Supervisor Roger Jessup seemed to speak for the majority, however, when he suggested that the nudist camps, which consenting adults were, in fact, free to participate in if they so chose, had the potential to corrupt Los Angeles youth: "It is not my intention to deprive anyone of his rights, but I feel these nudist camps have a tendency to lower those cultural standards that we are all trying to raise in the home. It is not only what has been done in these camps, but what might happen in the future that must be considered."[84]

It is important, too, to note that the police, like the County Board of Supervisors, were also split on the issue of regulating or banning nudist camps. While the county and city debated what to do about the "nudist menace," Los

Angeles police commissioners Raymond Haight and John R. Buckley heard accounts from both sides at a public meeting and concluded, in consultation with the chief of police, Arthur C. Hohmann, that there was not much of a threat. In between gales of laughter at the prospect of nudists running amok through the streets of Los Angeles, Hohmann pointed out that there was only one colony within city limits, Fraternity Elysia, and that the police were keeping an eye on it to prevent minors from being subject to exhibitions of adult nudity, a prosecutable offense.[85]

Since most of the attention was on Fraternity Elysia, Lura Glassey took a public relations campaign to the papers to explain that social nudism on the whole was rather staid and that the Noel affair was an outlier, with nothing to do with the camp. Her pleas before the County Board of Supervisors in September, 1939, were especially heartfelt: "Nudist camps," Lura Glassey explained, "are refuges where people can get away from the noise, dirt, and bad morals of a city. They take off their clothes and feel like children. They do not feel any different with their clothes removed than you do sitting here with them on." Glassey continued, "I have two children of my own and I certainly would not bring them up in an immoral atmosphere, or to be lewd and lascivious. We are running a nudist camp to make people more decent, not less."[86] Supervisor Ford, a prominent and well-respected county official, again spoke out against legislating nudist camps out of existence arguing that while he personally had never been to a nudist camp, he had never heard of anything immoral taking place there and feared that "in adopting laws like this measure we may be getting back to the witchcraft days."[87]

The efforts of Glassey, her legal team and supporters, and outspoken officials like Ford were in vain, however, and on September 5, 1939, Los Angeles County passed Ordinance #3428 which, by segregating the sexes at nudist camps, and preventing the exposure of one's nude body in the "presence and view of two or more persons of the opposite sex whose persons are similarly exposed," effectively banned social nudism anywhere in the county.[88] When the camps did not immediately close, the police stepped up the number of raids and surprise "visits," hoping to catch people in violation of the new law, which also stated that anyone

> who aids or abets any such act [nude exposure], or who procures
> another so to expose his or her private parts, or as owner, manager,
> lessee, director, promoter or agent, or in any other capacity, hires, leases
> or permits the land, building or premises of which he or she is the

owner, lessee or tenant or over which he or she has control, to be used
for any such purpose, is guilty of a misdemeanor, punishable by a fine
of not more than $500 or by imprisonment in the County Jail for not to
exceed six months, or by both such fine and imprisonment.[89]

The City of Los Angeles soon followed suit with its own ordinance, strongly
supported by Mayor Bowron, that required nudist camps to obtain operating
permits from the police commissioner, pay a not insignificant $150 annual
operation fee, and provide structural barriers between men and women so
that neither sex could see the other naked.[90]

Despite the hostile political climate, the members of Fraternity Elysia carried on in G-strings and bikini tops, but given that the ordinance was essentially a tricky licensing law, it was not long before Lura Glassey was brought
up on charges of operating the camp without the license she could not legally
procure.[91] The Los Angeles Police Department arrested her, and another Elysia member, H. Lyman Broening, on May 26, 1940, for being in violation of
the city anti-nudism ordinance after neighbors complained that they had seen
Glassey's two kids watching the "cavortings of 14 nude adults in the camp."[92]
Broening was promptly acquitted but since Fraternity Elysia fell within city
limits, Glassey was convicted on both county and city charges and sentenced
to six months in jail, which she served.[93] The effects of the arrest and jail time
were, not surprisingly, chilling and brought the era of nudist camps in Los Angeles to an abrupt end. There would not be another one within county limits
for almost thirty years until publisher, photographer, and lifelong nudist, Ed
Lange, established Elysium in Topanga Canyon in 1967.

The fate of Fraternity Elysia is, in some ways, the result of a confluence of
particularly Southern Californian attributes, many of them paradoxical: a notorious and profitable health mecca attracting weirdos and provoking concern
from the civic elite; Hollywood and its reputation for scandal and licentious-
ness; an especially hungry, and nasty, media; intense political concern for Los
Angeles's reputation on the national stage; sharp divisions between progressive, alternative, artsy types and the deeply conservative, often religious, who
found Los Angeles abhorrent, yet called Los Angeles home; a mix of cosmo-
politan urbanity and a huge rural region, which allowed the camps to flourish
in the first place. This list could continue and make the Fraternity Elysia story
another that could "only happen here!" But it is significant that throughout
the Noel scandal, and the press coverage of the repressive legislation to follow,
the stories about nudism in the Los Angeles papers ran alongside reports of

Nazi aggression in Europe; a liberalization of sexual norms permitting girls to shower in groups in Los Angeles schools because, according to the deputy county counsel trying the case "it must be conceded that the human body itself is not unhealthy, obscene, immoral, indecent, or impure";[94] the opening of a nudist school for boys and girls, ages three to twelve, with sex education included, and operated by Boone's camp in Mays Landing, New Jersey;[95] and even news about Bertrand Russell, the British philosopher and progressive social critic who, while teaching temporarily at UCLA, found himself accused of running a nudist camp in England, a charge he firmly denied, as part of a vicious effort to fire him from the City College of New York.[96] In short, the media coverage of, and the legal reaction to, the Fraternity Elysia suicide provoked a social panic that connected a narrow and spurious understanding of nudism to international anxieties about fascism and communism, fear of foreigners, and reticence about changing sexual mores and new, more open, attitudes about the body. Though organized nudism in the United States rarely put forth political treatises or weighed in with any sustained frequency on America's role in international affairs in the 1930s, nudism's cooperative nature, rejection of Victorianism, pursuit of alternative health practices, anti-materialist back-to-the-land ethos, and concern for sexual well-being seemed to many in Los Angeles to be well beyond a mere enthusiasm for nature and generally suspicious to the core.

While free and natural living was previously portrayed by the press as strange but harmless, the Noel affair provided ample opportunity to shape the benign into a moral and cultural threat, a threat that would be evoked again after World War II. In his prescient 1952 science fiction story, "Year of the Jackpot," amid global warfare and nuclear annihilation, Robert A. Heinlein's protagonist finds himself in a Los Angeles where an unknown viral agent makes women catatonically undress in public, transvestitism abounds, and a pastor reinstitutes ceremonial nudity.[97] It is an apocalyptic city where body cults, nudist viruses, inverted gender roles, and libertine sexuality are rampant, representing Cold War anxiety while parodying 1950s American sex panics. Nudism and nudist colonies in real life would continue to be a thorn in the side of Southern California authorities well into the era of the sexual revolution, and Los Angeles, in particular, would continue to court controversy as the center for American experiments in free and natural naked living.

CHAPTER 2

NAKED AT HOME

In December of 1929, crowds of five thousand waited in long lines over two consecutive weekends for the opportunity to tour the Los Feliz home of a Los Angeles celebrity. Neither film star nor movie producer, the homeowner was Philip Lovell, a health guru and natural foods advocate who penned hundreds of advice columns over thirty years in a *Los Angeles Times* feature titled "The Care of the Body." An early adopter and outspoken proponent of the free and natural lifestyle, Lovell took his ideas about health and the body and intentionally built them into a hypermodern house that allowed his practice of sunshine-filled nudity to be lived every day. Unlike Hollywood stars who dodged their fans, Lovell published his address and a helpful map in the *Times* to guide his admirers directly to his home.[1]

Lovell, born Morris Saperstein, was a Jewish socialist and labor advocate from New York City who reinvented himself in 1920s Los Angeles as a "Drugless Practitioner" and proselytized the benefits of a wide variety of alternative healing practices.[2] Alongside vegetarianism, raw foods, fasting, and tanning, Lovell believed that healthful homes were an important strategy for natural living in a modern urban environment and that to reach optimum health, one needed to live nakedly in one's domestic space. Beyond the wildly popular "Care of the Body" essays, his most important legacy were the two homes he and his wife, Leah, commissioned from two Austrian American modernist architects, Rudolph Michael Schindler (Lovell Beach House) and Richard Joseph Neutra (Lovell Health House).[3] For the Health House, Lovell asked Neutra to build a home that fused architectural modernism with the health practices he held dear, including facilities for indoor nude sunbathing, hydrotherapy, sitz baths, and 1920s top-of-the-line kitchen appliances like a vegetable washer, electric dishwasher, coffee grinder, garbage incinerator, and water filter.[4] Neutra responded with a glamorous International Style house built into a tree-covered hillside whose innovative technologies harmonized modernity with nature.[5] Lovell explained that the unusually large quantity of glass used made the residence "really an outdoors home."[6] The house has been subsequently celebrated as a modernist masterpiece, one that architectural critic Esther McCoy suggested "Neutra may have come to resent . . . because it was the scale against which his later work was too often measured—its tensions, its order, and its passionate allegiance to technology."[7]

While Lovell's concept of the free and natural lifestyle was intended for popular practice, these houses were elite projects available only to the wealthiest city dwellers who could afford private architectural commissions. Even so, the Health House was a sensation with the larger Los Angeles public, attracting thousands to tour the innovative home and meet Neutra, who gave lectures on the building's construction and guided visitors to each design innovation.[8] Perhaps only the rich could afford such a place, but clearly others were intrigued by the new living possibilities offered by modern design's incorporation of health, nature, and the body. Later in life, Neutra would appear in *Nude Living* magazine to discuss with editors Ed and June Lange the importance of nudism to healthy sexuality and human expression, while, somewhat perversely, the famous house has served as a symbol of corruption and modernist decadence in Hollywood film, including 1997's *L.A. Confidential.*[9]

Lovell was acutely aware of his audience and he directed his *Los Angeles Times* columns toward the middle-class suburban population that boomed exponentially in the 1920s. Lovell identified the design restrictions of both budget and form, which were circumscribed by modern sanitation and building codes and often formalized by suburban developers. Within the narrow parameters allowed, he encouraged his readers to construct their homes to better their health by balancing natural living with modern convenience. In ways reminiscent of today's green home movement that encourages the use of long-use light bulbs, solar power, and water reclamation, among other contemporary innovations in environmental technology and policy, Lovell too voiced concerns about the chemical makeup of the home. He suggested wood burning over oil, avoiding white walls and fierce artificial light that strained the eyes, and forgoing cheap wallpaper that emitted a sharp chemical odor Lovell considered poisonous. He also advocated for the open air sleeping porch rather than the bedroom arguing that Americans overinsulated their sleeping quarters, trapping germs and preventing the circulation of fresh air.

He considered the shower more hygienic than the bathtub and most emphatically encouraged the construction of outdoor spaces, including flat roofs that permitted naked sunbathing and, as Lovell colorfully put it, allowed sunbathers to "get in touch with the cosmic forces of nature."[10]

Lovell was so keen to spread word of healthful homes that in 1926 he invited Rudolph Schindler, at the peak of his career, to write a series of six articles for "Care of the Body." Subject matter ranged from decoration and furnishing to structural concerns and plumbing. In his final installment as guest writer, Schindler contemplated the obsolescence of dark, overdecorated rooms that plagued historic American homes and were cheaply imitated in contemporary suburban houses as owners sought status-enhancing styles. He suggested that instead of revisiting these flawed decors that rendered one's home both lifeless and tacky, homeowners ought to think more carefully about the direct relationship between the body and its environment. Rather than fearing nature, and building houses that served as protective fortresses to keep nature at bay, healthful homes should let nature in and allow the nude body out: "The house and the dress of the future will give us control of our environment, without interfering with our mental and physical nakedness. Our rooms will descend close to the ground and the garden will become an integral part of the house. The distinction between the indoors and the out-of-doors will disappear. The walls will be few, thin, and removable. All rooms will become part of an organic unit, instead of being small separate boxes with peep-holes."[11]

In short, Lovell, and his modernist architect colleagues, were laying out the blueprints for how the free and natural lifestyle could be built directly into the modern city. While Lovell himself was a nudist advocate, and social nudists would pick up the idea of the health house and run with it, the point of the experiment was to get everyone out from under the commodities and overstuffed sofas of bourgeois materialism so they might live a freer and more natural life. Indeed, as early as 1912, *Physical Culture* magazine insisted that "the most serious defect in the conventionally furnished house is that it is over-furnished. In such a house one feels restricted and confused. . . . One must have space."[12] But highlighting the aesthetics of the naked body by placing it at the center of the home produced a tension between the quest for a natural experience and a desire for a type of glamour in which beauty, youth, and an effortless sense of self became tied to one's living space.[13] Especially within the consumer culture of American suburbia, this tension commodified the naked body as much as it did the home.

○   ○   ○

Since the late nineteenth century, critics had lambasted cities for denaturing the experience of daily living. Some warned that "the absence of sunlight in cities produces a fearful mortality."[14] Others worried about the artifice of indoor spaces. An 1899 *Los Angeles Times* piece scolded readers that "humanity pays the penalty for over-civilization. . . . We have built houses that exclude the cold and have created summer within the walls of our homes while the winter's snow and sleet binds the earth in its fetters, but we have chained disease within the palace, and it waits amid the softest cushions and most luxurious tapestries for its enfeebled victims."[15] It was not simply that cities were poisonous; the artificial environments created by the soft architecture of the overfed classes also posed a health danger.

As concerns grew that the American middle class had fallen victim to flawed architectural designs that failed to allow them to flourish, and not just the poor were subject to dark, crowded, unsafe dwellings, medical doctors, scientists, architects, and health enthusiasts like Philip Lovell became actively involved in designing single-family homes that, by exposing the body to a free source of life-giving light, could spread health to the masses. Sunlight-as-curative entered the international architectural field largely because of the work of Auguste Rollier, a Swiss doctor with a reputation for success in healing tuberculosis. Abandoning traditional nineteenth-century treatments of intense periods of bed rest and patient isolation, Rollier was inspired by the innovators of germ theory and came to believe that strategic medical tactics in the right environment would yield far better results. In 1903, Rollier opened the world's first heliotherapy clinic in Leysin, in the Swiss Alps, where he developed a regimen for patients including exercise, fresh air, and prescribed sun exposure. His remarkable success in treating both tuberculosis and rickets, largely by rolling patients onto roofs and sun porches, influenced the treatment of those illnesses all over the world.[16] Rollier believed his patients fared as well as they did under his care simply because of the analgesic, bactericidal, and bone-strengthening action of the sun. In an address to the International Council of Nurses in 1927, Rollier modestly stated that his treatment was "really no more than a return to the laws of Nature, from which we are divorced more and more by our ultra-civilization and unnatural conditions of life."[17]

By the end of World War I, doctors and nurses in Europe and the United States had gathered alarming evidence that too much sun led to cancerous lesions on the skin while internists and immunologists publicly expressed concern that prolonged, intense sun exposure could devastate the human immune response to a host of bacterial and viral infections.[18] Despite the growing suspicion that the sun might not be the miraculous gift the medical establishment had hoped it would be, there were still enough strong indicators of the sun's benefits to outweigh the early warnings about melanoma and other sun damage to the body. Doctors, including geriatric specialists, encouraged sunbathing so that patients could reap the benefits of Vitamin D for blood health, building the immune system and strengthening the skeletal system.[19] Though researchers in the United States and Europe vigorously debated the effectiveness of heliotherapy, by the early 1930s they had concluded, generally, that regular, moderate, and progressive sun exposure increased metabolism and patient well-being and protected the skin.[20] Suntans were cited as evidence that the body was working properly with the skin renewing, strengthening, and purifying the body.

In promoting Rollier's ideas, American doctors proposed houses built entirely of glass while others recommended the installation of ultraviolet lamps in homes to permit daily light baths, in some cases wholly integrating concepts of the body with the architecture of the home.[21] In 1930, for example, Chicago's commissioner of health, Dr. Arnold Henry Kegel, the gynecologist who innovated "Kegel" exercises for strengthening women's pelvic floor, showcased a "modern house of health" at a local trade show that featured, among other healthful properties, a roll-up diagonal skylight that allowed an indoor sunbather adjustable access to direct sunrays.[22]

That a proponent of women's sexual health also would be a national leader in the push for public sun exposure (Kegel was also an early fan of the urban nude beach) was evidence to conservative critics that there was something prurient behind modernism's embrace of the free and natural lifestyle. In 1937, Leicester B. Holland, one of the country's leading architects and historical preservation specialists, argued in *Architect and Engineer* that "the Nudist costume has much in common with modern architecture; it is functional, it eschews all ornament, it revels in sunlight. . . . All things considered, I am convinced that Nudist and modern architecture do or should go hand in hand." He continued, "Nudism in its philosophy is the negation of ornament, the negation of artificiality, and therefore, I believe, the negation of man's pride in his humanity as distinguished from simple animal nature. It is the negation of civilization."[23] Holland intended his commentary as a critique of bare modernist design, a trend he viewed as a harbinger of Western civilization's decline, and a rejection of the free and natural lifestyle that he clearly saw as degenerate.

However repellent mainstream architects may have found both modernism and nudism, the idea of the home as a seamless interface between human civilization and the outdoors was theorized as a suburban experience by none other than Maurice Parmelee, the sociologist who wrote *Nudism in Modern Life*. Along with his contemplations about natural beauty and biological racial distinctions, Parmelee integrated a concept of biotechnics, Lewis Mumford's theory of the potentially sympathetic relationship of nature and technology, into gymnosophy, the school of thought that argued for a more natural and culturally uplifted human experience channeled through the naked human body. Parmelee's philosophy rejected nudism's anti-urban ethos, feeling strongly that the city and the natural body could organically coexist.[24] For Parmelee, a free and natural lifestyle did not necessitate the rejection of the city; rather, it could "aid materially in bringing mankind closer to nature, in promoting more genuine and sincere relations between the sexes, and in rearing the young. It is symbolic of a life healthier and saner than our present hectic existence."[25]

Concerned about the politically conservative limitations of the American countryside, as idyllic as it might be, Parmelee came to see suburbia as the most viable alternative with its blend of modern convenience and natural space. Suburbia, however, would need to undergo some changes before it would prove appropriate for naked living. The mass consumption undergirding suburban growth was antithetical to the simpler way of life nudism advocated, and thus "unnecessary and unhealthy clothing, useless structures built largely for show, ugly and uncomfortable furniture, much trumpery bric-a-brac intended for decoration, and many superfluous and injurious kinds of food and drink," much of it part of middle-class domestic life in the 1930s, would have to go.[26] Meanwhile, architects and designers would have to accommodate nude suburban living with furniture that was comfortable against bare skin.[27]

In Parmelee's estimation, by reshaping the American relationship with the body, nudism could reshape modern American life. Suburban nudism could encourage people to forge a free and natural lifestyle that coupled sprawl and nature, individual fulfillment and collective living, technology and the body, all while cutting back on consumer durables. Suburban naked living would heal society's malaise and build a stronger society by building better, more beautiful bodies and, concomitantly, better and more beautiful homes. While the emphasis on beautiful bodies to build a better society might queasily remind one of fascist body cultism, Parmelee pointedly warned of the troubling "potential for the aesthetic discourse within nudism to be co-opted into militaristic nationalism" and envisioned instead a utopian suburbia where flesh met sun and adults shared property and experience, accepting the imperfect body as part of the experiment.[28]

Parmelee's designs for suburban nudism adapted elements of turn-of-the-century British planner Ebenezer Howard's Garden City, which integrated nature, industry, agriculture, and affordable housing. Much like German *Lebensreform*, which in fact adopted Garden City plans in the early twentieth century, the Garden City movement in England strove to produce a healthier and more equitable living environment amid the overcrowded and unsanitary conditions of urban industrialized Europe.[29] Parmelee appropriated Howard's famous "wheel and spokes" design, replacing Howard's plan for industrial sites and health sanitaria with nudist amenities such as fields for sun exposure and exercise: "In the first stage enclosed recreation centers can be established in vacant spaces in cities or on their outskirts. The next stage will be in the development of garden cities on the outskirts or just outside of cities. Here each gymnosophist can have a small plot of ground to till, and can build a shelter, cabin, cottage or house for temporary use or permanent occupancy. In the middle of the garden city should be a large open space for the use of the inhabitants where they can play games and enjoy the sunlight."[30]

By the 1930s, whatever Parmelee's protests to the contrary, the movement of nudism from a collective outdoor rural pursuit into an indoor suburban activity was actively tied to consumerism. As early as 1937, advertisements for home sunlamps appeared in nudist magazines promising Palm Beach color in the privacy of one's own room.[31] In 1938, *The Nudist* featured a review of the Florida-invented "sun tub," a prefabricated, enclosed mobile unit that allowed nudists to follow the sun's rays around their private backyard. In a perfect homage to Mumford and Parmelee's merging of modern technology with the organic, as well as an integration of Richard Neutra's and Arnold Kegel's philosophies of home and the body, the sun tub allowed a nudist to fully enjoy the natural rays of the sun and all she "has to do to keep her body fully exposed to sunshine during her bath is to reach out with one hand and turn the steering wheel, much like that of a modern motor car."[32]

o   o   o

The outbreak of World War II, subsequent social surveillance, and the rationing of consumer goods made naked living and the free and natural lifestyle more difficult to practice. Not only was national attention focused

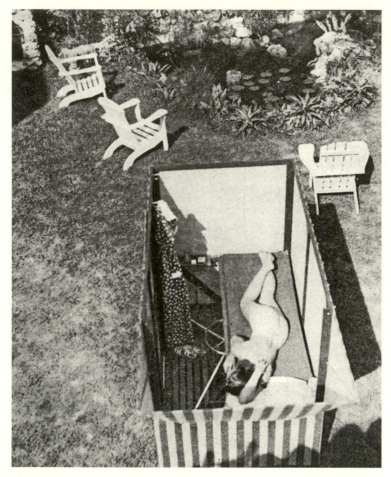

FIGURE 9. Woman in a suburban backyard "Sun Tub," from *The Nudist: Sunshine and Health* 7, no. 6 (June 1938). Wolfsonian-Florida International University, Miami Beach, Florida, Gift of Robert J. Young, XC2000.81.33.34. Photo: Silvia Ros.

on the war, and its effects domestically and abroad, but nudism's historical connections to German body culture could make it highly suspect. One of the founding fathers of American nudism, Alois Knapp, immediately went on the offensive, writing in a May 1942 issue of *Sunshine and Health* that nudists made good patriots as they rationed textiles as a way of life and were inherently frugal: "As a rule they carry their lunches with them and have no time for elaborate layouts. Liquor restrictions do not bother them because the stuff is taboo at camp anyhow. Sugar rationing is hardly a problem for most of them do not use sugar. Many of them do not smoke. Many do not eat meat. Nudists are intensely patriotic because they love liberty. Freedom is the first principle next to health in our way of life."[33] Fearing the loss of a community that had taken years to build, Knapp and others recommended that members of local clubs and colonies take their practice home with them. Though much of the ideology behind naked living was linked to a natural outdoor life, American nudists began to experiment with a private indoor practice they called domestic nudism.

Domestic nudism meant converting what was essentially a communal outdoor social display into a hidden indoor private activity. It also meant either rethinking the health ideologies behind nudist practice, as sun and open air would be less accessible, or redesigning one's home to accommodate the nudist family's desire for healthful, natural living while in the city. Domestic nudism was not meant to supplant the organized social life of summer nudist camps or yearlong communes but, instead, was a way to allow continuity

FIGURE 10. Entertaining at home while a domestic nudist, *Sunshine and Health* 25, no. 6 (June 1956). Wolfsonian-Florida International University, Miami Beach, Florida, Gift of Robert J. Young, XC2000.81.33.115. Photo: Silvia Ros.

in one's life and to promote natural living and self-acceptance among one's family.[34] While efforts had been made to construct housing in cities that permitted nude exposure to sun and air, it was in suburbia, with its readily available building materials, cheap land, and plentiful household goods, that do-it-yourself free and natural living could take hold. Not everyone who wanted indoor-outdoor living or a suntan was a nudist; but American suburbia, especially when it grew exponentially after the Second World War, proved fertile ground in which new ideas about health, fitness, sexuality, and the body could be played out in a built environment shaped by commodities, leisure culture, and single-family housing. By creating a type of vernacular modernism whereby structural aspects of high-end designer houses were applied to modest suburban houses, free and natural lifestyle enthusiasts adopted "small houses for the sunshine," sculpting a sun-friendly, health-oriented corporeal experience out of their domestic space by building nakedness directly into the private family home. [35]

Though Americans returned to the camps in the 1950s as part of a resurgence nostalgically remembered as the "golden age" of nudism in which hundreds of new privately owned camps and affiliates opened, some with thousands of members, *Sunshine and Health* continued to publish articles addressing the benefits of domestic nudism.[36] Popular "how-to" guides to redesigning one's backyard, fence, deck, and pool, along with helpful suggestions such as installing an intercom system to warn nude family members of non-nudist visitors, made domestic nudism that much more accessible.[37] As the magazine reported in 1954, "the simple fact is that except in downtown metropolitan areas and in multi-story areas, practically every home and backyard lends itself to the addition of [a] modest-cost . . . outdoor area for a family to enjoy seasonal, if not year round, nude sun and air bathing."[38] Even the Sunshine Park national nudist headquarters building in New Jersey, for example, appears on the cover of *Sunshine and Health* as a middle-class suburban nudist fantasy.[39]

Clearly, domestic nudism had merged with the postwar suburban landscape. Most striking is how evocative the published images are of standard 1950s suburban fare, with attractive, white nuclear families engaged in gender-normative activities in their commodity-filled homes.[40] On the surface it appears that nudism, for all its original anti-materialist and communal appeal, fit seamlessly into postwar consumer culture and its concomitant social conservatism grounded in traditional gender roles and private home ownership. In some ways suburban nudism did not contradict or challenge the broadest

The simple, modern treatment of the exterior would fit well in any setting.

A Small House For The Sunshine

HERE is the first of SUNSHINE & HEALTH'S new series of homes for nudist living. This one—a simple cabin primarily for weekend use—is worth careful study for the manner in which it has been planned to provide all the equipment and facilities needed for human comfort and convenience within the confines of a very compact and economical plan. Note how the space has been apportioned to include all needed mechanical equipment, an ample space for dining or game-playing and an ingenious adaptation of the double-decker bed.

The exterior design is, of course, subject to a variety of treatments. As suggested here, construction would be of stud and joist framing with exterior sheathing of large-sized wall board or plywood. Built thus it would prove a sturdy and practical week-end home—simple enough in most details so that any person who had a reasonable skill with tools could build it almost entirely alone.

Those who like to imagine developments beyond the drawings can see a great many attractive possibilities in the little house suggested here. It is adaptable to a variety of decorative treatments, both inside and out; and nudists with the green thumbs can see it properly set and blooming with flowers and shrubs, vines and trees.

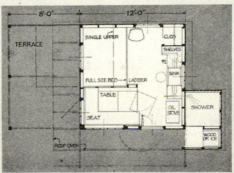

The plan, amazingly compact, provides for a lot of convenience with full equipment for comfortable week-end living.

FIGURE II. "A Small House for the Sunshine" from *Sunshine and Health* 18, no. 1 (January 1949), editor Ilsley Boone (American, 1879–1968) (Mays Landing, NJ: Sunshine Publishing). 11 ½ × 8 in. (29.2 × 20.3 cm). Wolfsonian-Florida International University, Miami Beach, Florida, Gift of Robert J. Young, XC2000.81.33.80. Photo: Lynton Gardiner.

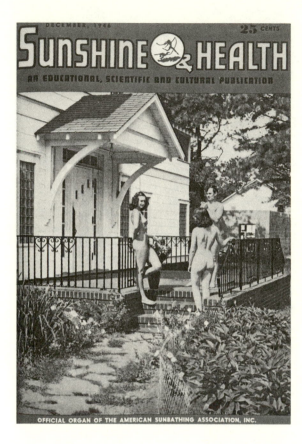

FIGURE 12. American Sunbathing Association Headquarters at Sunshine Park near Mays Landing, New Jersey, *Sunshine and Health* 15, no. 12 (December 1946). Wolfsonian-Florida International University, Miami Beach, Florida, Gift of Robert J. Young, XC2000.81.33.72. Photo: Silvia Ros.

parameters of American Cold War culture. Instead, it could be nestled quite nicely next to advertisements for barbeques, automobiles, clothing, and suburban homes.

The phenomenon of DIY suburban nudism caught Ilsley Boone's eye and, in 1960, *Sunshine and Health* magazine published a series of articles describing the architectural challenges of designing homes for the free and natural lifestyle. For the previous twenty years, featured architect Kenn Trumble had built a career designing modest suburban houses that accommodated "the recent trend toward outdoor living."[41] Traditional clients generally requested that some sort of patio, lanai, or other backyard living space be added to their home with the expressed concern that it still resemble other houses in their subdivision. The desire of the suburban dweller for both outdoor living *and* a nudist practice, however, created additional architectural problems. Common

FIGURE 13. "Stay at Home and Like It," a nudist suburbia pictorial, *Sunshine and Health* 29, no. 9 (September 1960). Wolfsonian-Florida International University, Miami Beach, Florida, Gift of Robert J. Young, XC2000.81.33.164. Photo: Silvia Ros.

zoning restrictions against high fences made it impossible to add an open yet private patio to the outside of standard suburban homes and the glass doors that made the outside visible to the inside exposed naked residents to their neighbors' gaze, potentially an unpleasant source of personal humiliation or legal action.

When a dissatisfied client sold his Trumble-designed home, the architect learned that suntanning was a crucial element of the free and natural lifestyle and that for this particular demographic, the benefit of suburban living meant the ability to lie naked in the sun as much as it meant a seamless flow of movement from indoors out. This inspired Trumble to incorporate small, fully enclosed screened patios into the homes' basic design: "By keeping the privacy problem of the nudist in mind I . . . incorporated the outdoor living aspects of a home right into the basic concept of the house rather than trying to attach a chunk of outdoor living to the rear wall of a conventional house."[42] The drawings for Trumble's standard 1950s one-story ranch house show enclosed patio rooms with open roofs above to allow for private nude sunbathing. Because

Alternate #1—Concrete block—flat and shed roof.

Alternate #2—Frame—flat and shed roof.

FIGURE 14. Kenn Trumble's designs for the "Sun-Fan House, Alternates #1 and #2," *Sunshine and Health* 29, no. 4 (April 1960). Wolfsonian-Florida International University, Miami Beach, Florida, Gift of Robert J. Young, XC2000.81.33.159. Photo: Silvia Ros.

there were no extensions attached to the house, from the outside at least, the nudist home looked like any other postwar suburban dwelling.

Privacy from nosey neighbors and easily accessible sun exposure were not the only problems, however, that a savvy architect would need to address in order to satisfy the midrange suburban nudist customer. It was also important to allow visitors entry to the home without forcing everyone inside to frantically pull on their clothes every time the doorbell rang. To this end, Trumble designed a floor plan that included a reception room off the main entry and a conveniently placed planter-and-screen combination that blocked views of the rest of the house without obviously hiding the other rooms. As with the patio additions, clients worried that their house not look too radically different from others on the block and that their nudism remain unknown to the neighborhood. Even if this was the era of backyard bomb shelters, no one wanted their home to look like a bunker. Trumble addressed this aesthetic concern by setting a large picture window into the front street-facing wall, thus emulating an archetypal 1950s suburban architectural feature while still camouflaging the house's nudist function.[43] Picture windows were ubiquitous in postwar suburban housing developments and served to frame the neighborhood for those looking out but also permitted a great deal of looking *in*, making the house a kind of "quasi-public space" that showcased the commodities found inside.[44] For suburban nudists who wanted to participate in the competitive exercise of home ownership *and* make their interior space private, those desires meant that creative architectural adaptations had to produce, at least on the surface, a visual continuum between indoors and out.

Trumble's entrepreneurial goal was to sell his "Sun-Fan" house to a broad United States public, but the market was in the new Sunbelt suburbs that sprang up in the late 1950s and 1960s and ran from Florida through the Southwest and into Southern California. Sunbelt suburbs typically housed white middle-class families and retired couples seeking a leisurely lifestyle at a cut-rate price.[45] With an easily exploitable immigrant labor force, expanded service-sector economy, powerful anti-union lobbies, and minimal taxation that intertwined with federally subsidized business and real estate development, the Sunbelt offered cheap housing and a convenient suburban life to a mostly white, and conservative, middle-class clientele.

Specifically, Trumble focused on Land O' Lakes, a suburban region of Pasco County, Florida, whose nudist history began in 1949 when Dorothy and Avery Weaver Brubaker founded the Florida Athletic and Health Association and opened a nudist camp, the Lake Como Club, on their 210-acre property.[46] Subsequently, other nudists set up shop in the area, taking advantage of west central Florida's cheap land, warm climate, and natural environment conducive to nudists' outdoor activities. By the 1970s, suburban Tampa began to surround the quiet, semirural area. Rather than move, the nudist community of Pasco County grew, with a surge of new membership in the 1980s and 1990s. The camps, which generally offered mobile home rentals, trailer lots, and tent sites, became more sophisticated and competitive; some, like Caliente, have developed into clothing-optional tourist resorts with pools, spas, luxury hotel accommodations, and condos for sale at both the midrange and high end of the market.[47] Paradise Lakes became a nudist subdivision with seven hundred homes ranging in size from tiny four-hundred-square-foot studios priced under $100,000 to million-dollar homes. Realtors estimate that 60 percent of Paradise Lakes is occupied by full-time residents. Others, like Oasis, The

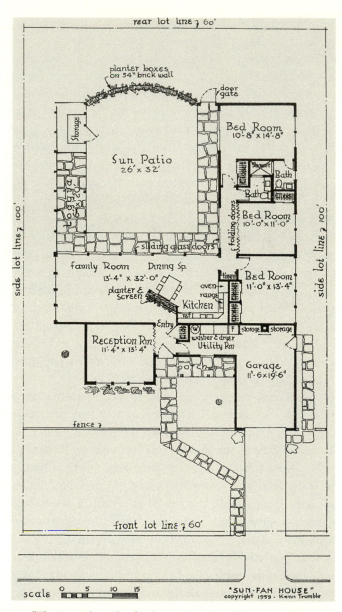

FIGURE 15. "The Basic Floor Plan for the Sun-Fan House," from *Sunshine and Health* 29, no. 4 (April 1960). Wolfsonian-Florida International University, Miami Beach, Florida, Gift of Robert J. Young, XC2000.81.33.159. Photo: Silvia Ros.

FIGURE 16. Paradise Lakes, Florida, 1986. Photograph by Gerald Davis. © Gerald Davis Estate.

Woods, Riverboat Club, and Lake Linda Circle, feature mixed developments with anywhere from twenty-five mobile homes to subdivisions featuring hundreds of moderately priced small houses with pools and backyard sunbathing decks, most of which were built in the past twenty-five years.[48] These communities are marketed as clothing-optional nudist environments, but realtors describe residents as living a "hybrid" experience: clothed in the front yard but nude in the fenced backyard. In an effort to branch out to new customers, in 2004, Quaker Bill Martin opened a 240-acre Christian nudist resort in Hudson, in the far northwestern corner of Pasco County with another five hundred homes for sale.[49] Concentrated along a six-mile stretch of US Highway 41 in suburban Pasco County, Land O' Lakes remains the epicenter of American nudism, hosting six nudist resorts and hundreds of acres of gated, privately held land with several thousand residences.[50]

When Trumble met with nudist families in the midst of constructing homes in a Land O' Lakes subdivision in 1960, it was already an area known for its nudist camps, but it is unlikely that the subdivision itself was built with nudists in mind; hence the market for a nudist-friendly architect who could shield them from potentially unfriendly surveillance. While socializing na-

FIGURE 17. Kenn Trumble and clients by the pool, *Sunshine and Health* 29, no. 4 (April 1960), editor Margaret A. B. Pulis (American, 1905–1985) (Mays Landing, NJ: Sunshine Publishing). 11 ½ × 8 ½ in. (29.2 × 11 cm). Wolfsonian-Florida International University, Miami Beach, Florida, Gift of Robert J. Young, XC2000.81.33.159. Photo: Lynton Gardiner.

ked by the pool, architect and clients discussed floor plans for prefab designs like the Sun-Fan "Islander," which featured "South Sea flavor that is compatible with casual living and yet is sufficiently 'conventional' to be built in any area," while the Sun-Fan "Tropical" offered a more modern exterior for the client with a taste for the avant-garde.[51] For twenty-five dollars, individual families could buy blueprints to build their own Sun-Fan house, but Trumble hoped to attract developers of moderately priced subdivisions.[52]

While it is unclear if Trumble himself designed more than a few houses in the Land O' Lakes area, his plan for midrange naked houses was not unprecedented in the history of Sunbelt architecture. In much the same way as

Southern California ranch house designer Cliff May reconfigured blueprints for resort hotels into prefab suburban homes, Trumble's designs adapted high-end naked homes for a mass market.[53] As Lawrence Culver notes in his study of the postwar appetite for Southern California leisure culture, Sunbelt suburban developments often appropriated the indoor-outdoor modernist Southwestern designs of elite private commissions and repackaged them as affordable middle-class homes.[54] Part of the appeal of these cheaper homes was their embrace of a glamorous body-centered lifestyle made popular in exotic tourist locales like Palm Springs, St. Barthes, and Monaco. Even if ritualized nudist practice was not intentionally part of the design (although many of the early twentieth-century modernist homes built for the Hollywood jet set incorporated screened patios and sun porches for nude sunbathing),[55] desert homes built by E. Stewart Williams, Albert Frey, and Richard Neutra were awash in natural light, featured a seamless indoor-outdoor living experience, employed sensual materials that drew the eye, and innovated heating and cooling systems to ensure the body, clothed or unclothed, the utmost comfort.[56]

Aware that many could not afford professional architects, midrange or not, *Sunshine and Health* suggested DIY alternatives such as fiberglass paneling, which could vertically extend a backyard fence, at least as far as building codes allowed. Ideally, however, one's backyard retreat would also include a covered patio and a carefully groomed recreation area, which would require the hiring of contractors. But, as millions of suburbanites were encouraged by banks and the federal government in the 1950s and 1960s, credit and installment plans would make the American dream of private home ownership possible for the nude as well as the clothed: "The backyard retreat for nudist use does represent a substantial amount of money, however, in essence it is an investment which will pay rich dividends in health and happiness for the whole family. When and if the home with the backyard retreat such as is shown here is sold, the investment will pay off handsomely in hard cash. Spreading the payments over a several year period make it possible for people of modest income to enjoy these modern luxuries."[57]

The postwar enthusiasm for the free and natural lifestyle fueled the trend for indoor-outdoor living and the suburban architectural innovations that allowed for it. The irony, of course, was the desire for natural living could usually be met with only the most unnatural of amenities. One of these was the backyard swimming pool. Before the Second World War, pools had existed only in public spaces, like city parks, or as a private amenity of the rich. Yet, by 1959, there were more than 250,000 private swimming pools in the Unit-

The patio shaded with aluminum awnings is a setting for a family barbecue.

FIGURE 18. "The Patio Shaded with Aluminum Awnings," from *Sunshine and Health* 29, no. 12 (December 1960), editor Margaret A. B. Pulis (American, 1905–1985), photographer Lee Edmunds (Mays Landing, NJ: Sunshine Publishing). 11 ½ × 8 ½ in. (29.2 × 11 cm). Wolfsonian-Florida International University, Miami Beach, Florida, Gift of Robert J. Young, XC2000.81.33.167. Photo: Lynton Gardiner.

ed States with over a third of them in Los Angeles alone.[58] Swimming pools helped produce a glamorous aesthetic that enhanced the beauty of the body and the home in such a way that naturalized the relationship between bare skin and suburban life.[59] For the suburban nudist family, the backyard pool was less an indulgence than a necessary commodity that enhanced their domestic life with a free and natural experience that felt good and highlighted the comfortable ease of naked living. The backyard swimming pool brought the free and natural lifestyle to the private home allowing families, as *Sunshine and Health* reported, "to enjoy nudism, [and] *not* behind pulled curtains."[60]

While nudists may have preferred outdoor pools as part of their natural embodied experience, other suburbanites celebrated their social status by bringing the outdoors in. In 1959, the significance of the swimming pool to the suburban home was elaborately illustrated in the widely read *House Beautiful* annual "Pace Setter" feature celebrating the dramatic indoor-outdoor liv-

FIGURE 19. Building a
backyard retreat, *Sunshine
and Health* 29, no.
12 (December 1960).
Wolfsonian-Florida
International University,
Miami Beach, Florida,
Gift of Robert J. Young,
XC2000.81.33.167. Photo:
Silvia Ros.

ing space designed by architect Alfred Browning Parker. Claiming to offer its
Coconut Grove, Florida, residents "more control over their environment than
has ever been known in America," the house took a pool and its surrounding
sundeck and placed it in the middle of an open-plan suburban living room.[61]
The house, owned by Mr. and Mrs. Graham Miller, had all the features of an
ideal suburban home, including the latest appliances, open-plan kitchen, and
multiple bathrooms, but its key innovation was a pyramid-shaped sunroof
that not only drew sunlight into the swimming pool below, but also dispersed
it to all corners of the house. Virtually every room had a direct sightline to the
pool deck but even rooms that did not, such as the master bath, had their own
sunbathing space. *House Beautiful* waxed adoring over its choice for most for-
ward-thinking architectural design of the year; especially the "tiny enclosed
patio gives the bathing area a new meaning—it becomes a seclusion for the
healing balm of sun and water."[62]

The popularity of swimming pools in 1950s suburbia created the need for
new backyard features and home adaptations. Obviously, building a spectacu-

lar indoor pool was one extreme but American suburbanites usually made
more modest changes to their homes. Tasteful cabanas and diving decks were
some of the innovations, especially those that led guests around, rather than
through, the main house, while freestanding sun shelters with overhead laths
and plate glass window panels were another because "there comes a time
when every sun-worshiper, no matter how dedicated, wants to cool off in the
shade or read a book out of the sun's blinding glare."[63]

The demand for translucent materials that filtered direct sunlight led to a
consumer market for new, artificial materials like plastics and corrugated fiberglass that promised to lend sunny elegance to homeowners' patios and to permit the construction of backyard solaria. In the early twentieth century, glass
technologists in Britain developed "Vita" Glass, a type of window that, as John
Stanislav Sadar notes, was meant to "enable ultraviolet-rich light to penetrate
interiors and thereby transform buildings into therapeutic instruments."[64]

FIGURE 20. The Mason family's backyard from "The Private Life of a Nudist
Family" in *Nude Living* 1, no. 2 (August 1961). Courtesy of Stéphane Deschênes,
Bare Oaks Family Naturist Park, Sharon, Ontario.

FIGURE 21. Ezra Stoller, photographer. Mr. and Mrs. Graham Miller's House, designed by Alfred Browning Parker, Coconut Grove, Florida, in *House Beautiful*, February 1959, 113. Canadian Centre for Architecture.

Though the innovators of "Vita" Glass actively had to seek and create a market for their product in the 1920s, post–World War II suburban America was more than ready for cheap ways to get the promise of health-giving sunshine into their homes. As the Alsynite Fiberglass Panel Company asked in a tantalizing advertisement, "is the sunlight more beautiful at your house?"

Alsynite, of course, provided the answer, promising that with their fiberglass coverings, "the sun's rays are diffused to a soft, restful glow, shaded with Alsynite's own lovely built-in color."[65] Another new product was acrylic fiber that replaced traditional canvas in the making of patio awnings and other

THE MASTER SUITE *continued*

*A sun-bathing patio gives
the master suite its own outdoors*

A tiny enclosed patio gives the bathing area
a new meaning—it becomes a seclusion for
the healing balm of sun and water.

Just a few feet of fenced-in space add the refresh-
ment of a garden to the bedroom retreat. The marriage of indoors and outdoors, seen everywhere in

FIGURE 22. Ezra Stoller, photographer. Sunbathing patio of Miller House, designed
by Alfred Browning Parker, Coconut Grove, Florida, in *House Beautiful*, February
1959, 91. Canadian Centre for Architecture.

backyard shades. The Sunbrella Company used the material, trademarked Ac-
rilan by Monsanto, to create freestanding backyard sun cabanas. The advertisements promised that the Sunbrella fabric "won't shrink or crack or peel or
harden and it won't be affected by mildew or rot."[66] Meanwhile, the American
Sisalkraft Corporation manufactured Sisal-Glaze, which was advertised as a
"magic new plastic semirigid film-like material . . . [that] comes in rolls, 36 and
42 inches wide, is adaptable not only for sunbath houses but for portable cabanas, cold frames, green houses, swimming pool enclosures, breezeways and
carports." No matter what the intended use of one's plastic backyard structure,
anyone could renew a fading tan because "one of the amazing features of this
Sisal-Glaze is that it will transmit almost 100 percent of ultraviolet tanning rays
and infrared heat waves."[67] According to the manufacturer, the advantage of
Sisal-Glaze over other materials was the promise that it retained heat, meaning
that suburbanites in colder climates could access the sun year-round in their
outdoor solaria.

FIGURE 23. Edward Topham's residence, designed by Wurster, Bernardi, and Emmons Architects, with Thomas Church, landscape architect, in *House Beautiful*, April 1959, 136. Canadian Centre for Architecture.

Sunbelt sun worship was balanced by an equally strong desire to control how much sun exposure one received despite the suggestions in DIY in-ground pool handbooks for placing the deck where it would receive as much sunlight as possible.[68] While all-glass walls and patio doors were designed to allow the homeowner much-coveted sunlight, these same all-glass features could also create terrible glare and overheat the interior of one's home. To address this concern, suburban homes in Florida often featured large overhangs, or "eyebrows," protruding side ribs, white roofs, baffles, and screens to block light.[69] Meanwhile, suburban homes in Arizona were built with windows placed high on a wall, lengthwise, and parallel to the ground to ensure the roof overhang blocked direct sunlight. Patios to allow sun exposure were frequently built into the home design but tucked under a shady canvas roof.[70] Awnings, of course, were obvious ways to block the sun and landscape architects and designers worked to produce elaborately designed coverings made of steel strand webbing, small reinforcing rods, and woven canvas bands, creating huge backyard sunshades.[71] Architects also built screened rooftop sleeping huts to allow for comfortable outdoor slumber at night and sunbathing by day.[72] In postwar Miami-Dade County, owners of modest new suburban homes turned their roofs into an additional floor for free and natural living simply by adding lawn furniture and umbrellas. Letting the outdoors in may have been the goal, but Cold War fears of vulnerability were ever present. While celebrating the outdoor exposure their structures allowed, homebuilders of the Leisure City community in Homestead, Florida, also promised to protect residents from atomic blasts.

With the success of the nudist-designed suburban tract homes in Land O' Lakes, Trumble envisioned applying his techniques for sun-drenched outdoor privacy to multiple-unit garden apartments that suggested that the free and natural lifestyle could encourage neighborly nudism and move beyond the single-family home. In 1977, this concept was picked up by Southern California developer Jim Williams, a practicing nudist and free beach activist, who formed the Fullerton-based company, Living in the Buff Recreation Association (LIBRA). With plans to construct a series of clothing-optional apartment buildings (with twenty to sixty units), LIBRA's promotional materials celebrated the relaxation and "personal freedoms" offered by their living arrangements and sold prospective residents on the "special privacy and security" of the community, promising that "residents are able to enjoy the unique benefits of this total lifestyle."[73]

In 1978, Williams purchased an apartment building in Arcadia, a middle-class suburb at the base of the San Gabriel Mountains, an especially dry and hot part of Los Angeles County, and solicited applications for the forty-unit complex, charging hefty rents and membership fees to join the community. As with Trumble's designs for private nudist homes, Williams designed a screen to block views of the building from the street. The Regional Planning Department considered the complex illegal but was unable to prevent Wil-

FIGURE 24. An "indestructible" home in Homestead, Florida, built by Florida Sun Deck Homes, Hialeah, Florida. Post–World War II postcard. Collection of Larry Wiggins.

FIGURE 25. "Cool, ultra-modern design for tropical living—moderately priced. U.S Department of Defense recommends solid concrete homes for the protection of the public against the Atom Bomb." Description of a Homestead house built by Florida Sun Deck Homes, Hialeah, Florida. Post–World War II postcard. Collection of Larry Wiggins.

liams from moving ahead with the private residential project because, according to the Los Angeles City Building and Safety Department, the municipal
"zoning code doesn't regulate that aspect of human behavior and [doesn't find
it] proper for a zoning code to do so."[74] Freed by the absence of applicable
zoning laws, Williams built yet another clothing-optional apartment complex
called Sundaze, in the Mount Washington neighborhood of Los Angeles, just
two miles north of downtown overlooking the city. In the promotional write-
up in a popular nudist newsletter, *Bare in Mind*, Sundaze was celebrated for its
deluxe clothing-optional amenities including a pool, sunbathing area, and a
giant Jacuzzi. Opened in 1980, Sundaze functioned as more than just an apartment building for nudists, but as a club, organizing excursions to other nudist hangouts in other parts of the Southwest. Together with the Arcadia and
Sundaze buildings, Williams pulled together enough capital to open a third
clothing-optional apartment complex in Venice Beach, fetching large rents
because of its proximity to the water and its high-end facilities.[75]

In contrast with Trumble's designs, Williams's apartment complexes appealed mainly to unmarried single people and couples without children. The
naked living of apartment life may have included corporeal display, sunshine,
and modern amenities, but it dispelled the notion of wholesome family living,
any claim to authentic nature, and the secrecy cultivated by domestic nudism.
By the late 1970s and early 1980s, Jim Williams was selling a nude adult social
experience as an all-inclusive free and natural lifestyle package.

○   ○   ○

Ultimately, the cultivation of the free and natural lifestyle in the inherently unnatural environment of postwar suburbia produced unresolvable
contradictions. As much as suntanning meant exposing and conspicuously
displaying the body, much like the picture window displayed the accumulated
commodities found inside, it ultimately meant an inward-facing domestic life
away from the street, the sidewalk, the open yard and the front porch in favor of enclosed solaria, high backyard fences, and rear-facing rooms.[76] Just
as television and electric air conditioning drew the family indoors, backyard
sunbathing indicated a preference for individual privacy over public environments such as beaches, parks, and hiking trails. Reflecting the atomized nature of the Cold War American family, as well as the atomic fears of the nation,
home design magazines sympathized with concerns for security and privacy,
"particularly in a society and an age that is allowing less time—and space—for

[privacy]. There is a need to be alone to re-orient oneself, to have a few moments for undisturbed thought, to have a quiet moment in which to restore one's atomized self."[77] The 1959 *House Beautiful* Miller house was, in fact, credited with creating a "domestic environment in which, without shutting *in* its inhabitants, does turn inward as a means to secure privacy and to shield its inhabitants from the encroachment of near neighbors and the onslaught of the omnipresent automobile civilization."[78]

Along with the paradoxical quest for privacy while cultivating a body suitable for public display, the adaptation of suburban architecture to the free and natural lifestyle dispensed with the natural landscape altogether. Maximizing sun exposure created the irony of making the inside of one's home seem more natural (flooded with light, full of plants, large plate glass windows offering outdoor views) while utterly denaturing the outside. A common feature of many postwar suburban homes was the paved outdoor terrace, which frequently coated most of the yard. If a homeowner could afford it, a basic cement pavement would be layered with tile, completely covering any organic material that might grow there. Overhead, patio roofs replaced shady trees, ripped out by their roots, as the roofs' wooden lath structure allowed for more sunshine.[79] Other features of indoor-outdoor living that tamed any organic matter that happened to be in the way included aluminum venetian blinds, hung outside one's house from the roof, creating an outdoor living room complete with tile and fireplace.[80] A less pricey option was to use a roof overhang for shade and install outdoor carpeting.[81] Sun-oriented suburban homes frequently featured raised wooden decks above paved yards and "sun galleries," rooms walled entirely with glass, that opened up onto the terrace, usually covered in deck furniture, including the ubiquitous chaise longue. The more an indoor suburban home resembled the outdoor environment, and the outdoor environment the indoors, the more radical the modifications to nature.

It is important to note that there was also a racial politics to all this sun seeking in segregated suburbs. There is an unpleasant irony that those desiring suntans for aesthetic and health reasons were benefiting from the white privilege of private home ownership produced when postwar federal urban policy intentionally segregated the new suburbs through redlining and race-based mortgage lending.[82] Whatever the well-meaning impulses of free and natural living, there remained pronounced socioeconomic inequality in accessing the suburbs and a racialized performance, however unintentional, in adopting a tan that could later be shed to reveal the whiteness of the skin beneath it.[83]

PHOTOGRAPHS BY MAYNARD PARKER

Sun and Shade (continued)

The best way to keep the house comfortable in summer is to keep the walls from warming up. The obvious way to do that is to keep the sun off the walls. (Even after you've exhausted all the possibilities of doing this, you still insulate your walls.)

In winter the story is the same—only the other way 'round. How you feel depends a lot on the temperature of your walls! If the walls are cool, they *shine* coolness at you, and you feel cool. Now, it's easier to make up for wall-chill than to make up for those oppressive warm walls. All you have to do is heat harder. But still, it's hard to get quite comfortable in a room with a cool wall. If you heat hard enough to make up for wall-chill, then the air in the room gets overheated and stuffy.

In other words, there are many ways to keep warm. You can have warm air and cool walls, or cool air and warm walls, or middling air and middling walls. You may feel warm enough in any of these three ways, but there's a different *flavor* to the warmness. It has to do with the feel of the air in your lungs, in your nose, on your skin, with the humidity of the air (over-heated air gets very dry). It also has to do with such things as the ozone content of the air. The doctors do not yet understand ozone—but it's a big Factor X. The flavor of the warmness of a house has a strong effect on body and nerves and mind. Generally, you'll feel more cheerful, less cooped-up if the air is not too warm and the walls not too cool.

Cure for west porch

A west-facing porch isn't very use-ful unless it is shaded from low sun. This cure does two things: makes porch more habitable, and stops sun heat before it hits walls of house itself. Pair of aluminum Venetian blinds turn back sun rays, store away in protective boxes up on ceiling when sun is gone. A perfect control measure for keeping west wall of house cool. Home of Dana Lathams.

The "eyebrow" for south walls and windows

When you don't have a roof overhang (as in two-story houses) to cast shade on south walls and windows, all is not lost. Use an eyebrow. It can be made of canvas, vines, wood louvers—anything the sun won't shine through. An eyebrow can be added to old houses that were built before we understood about such things. A trellis to support deciduous vines looks well anywhere.

EMIL SCHMIDLIN, ARCHITECT

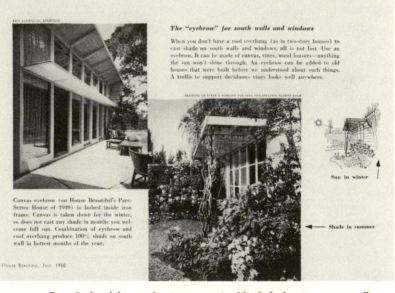

DESIGNED BY STYER'S NURSERY FOR 1950 PHILADELPHIA FLOWER SHOW

Canvas eyebrow (on House Beautiful's Pace-Setter House of 1949) is lashed inside iron frame. Canvas is taken down for the winter, so does not cast any shade in months you wel-come full sun. Combination of eyebrow and roof overhang produce 100% shade on south wall in hottest months of the year.

Sun in winter

Shade in summer

FIGURE 26. Dana Latham's home, aluminum venetian blinds for keeping a west wall cool, in *House Beautiful*, July 1950, 44. Photographs by Maynard Parker. Canadian Centre for Architecture.

In the context of postwar suburbia, these awkward tensions between exposing the body and seeking privacy; pursuing a free and natural lifestyle that involved denaturing everything in sight; and wanting a glamorous indoor-outdoor life while striving for authentic experience in the most artificial of environments, spoke less to hypocrisy than a complicated effort to address cultural confusion about health and the body, display and privacy; and technology and nature in the setting of the family home. The prevalence and popularity of suburban adaptations like backyard pools, fiberglass fence extensions, and suntanning spoke to an overlap between the conspicuous consumption of suburban domestic life, key tenets of nudist philosophy, and the liberationist fantasies of the free and natural lifestyle. The movement of naked body culture from nudist colonies into the private home reflected the national trend toward atomized domestic life but it also signaled the beginnings of inner-seeking pursuits that would merge the corporeality of naked living with the mind-body integration quests of the 1960s.

CHAPTER 3

THERAPEUTIC NUDIST RETREATS

Twelve men and twelve women, some couples and others single, gathered by a large outdoor Jacuzzi. Greeted by their guides, several undressed and descended into the pool where they floated, laughed, and enjoyed the water's 102-degree temperature. Others slowly joined the fun while a few tentative members of the group remained clothed and watched from the sidelines. As darkness finally fell on the summer night, a light show projected patterns of dots, stripes, and warm swaths of color onto the nude bodies, which were now swaying, dancing, and sensually moving. After a discussion of what it felt like to be naked with what was, for the most part, a group of strangers experiencing their first nude social encounter, everyone crawled into sleeping bags for a night of out-of-doors slumber.

In the morning, after a lengthy guided naked hike, the group gathered inside for their first session of nude psychotherapy led by psychologist Paul Bindrim. Coached to discuss their insecurities, traumas, and relationship troubles, participants in the encounter session experienced angry outbursts, hysterical crying, contained violence (one man beat his "wife," actually a bench, with a roll of magazines), and exhausted emotional depletion. On the third day, the Sunday that would close the weekend seminar, the two dozen participants gathered favorite objects they had been asked to bring with them, objects that provoked "peak stimuli" including candles, fruit, flowers, records, stuffed animals, and, in one case, a salami. First, each participant sat across from a partner into whose eyes one stared with as little blinking as possible, a technique called "eyeballing." Next, participants closed their eyes, smelled and touched their selected objects, and tried to access their life's peak experience of happiness. Some described witnessing their children being born, others described sublime experiences in nature, while others had more abstract moments of joy in which states of pure beauty or calm were achieved. Without the help of psychotropic drugs, participants left their conscious minds behind, experienced heightened emotional connections with each other and the universe, and were "swept clean of all personality 'hang-ups.'"[1]

What Aileen Goodson, a practicing nudist and participant in Paul Bindrim's weekend group encounter session, described above in her short, published pamphlet, was an experimental nude psychotherapy marathon, which took place in June 1967 at the Deer Park Nudist Resort near Escondido, in San Diego County. It would be the first of a series of such sessions that Bindrim would host over the next fifteen years and, by his own estimate, Bindrim guessed that by the 1980s over six thousand people had participated.[2] The idea of naked group therapy, which tapped into popular interest in psychoanalysis, nudism, health fads, and countercultural experimentation, captured the American imagination, ending up in *Time* magazine's "Medicine" section as an example of the new psychological frontier and in a July 1968 feature in *Life* describing Bindrim's twenty-four-hour marathon nude therapy sessions he was then leading in a heated pool in Palm Springs.[3] The photographs show nude adults standing shoulder-deep in water, arms wrapped around each other, gazing into each other's eyes, and surrounding a fellow participant as he floats on his back.[4]

While nude psychotherapy's proponents claimed its healing properties came from peeling back layers of inauthentic modern life, a clear echo of American nudism's 1930s credo that a return to a state of nature was the surest route to happiness, Bindrim's naked therapy smacked of the suburban conveniences of postwar domestic nudism with its carpets, appliances, and backyard swimming pools. Participants in the marathons, which could last twenty-four to thirty-six hours, paid $100 each for the weekend or $45 for the session alone. Meanwhile, the marathons were often held in the exquisitely artificial environments of desert resort hotels with pumped-in water, potted palms, and room service. As Ian Nicholson writes in his history of nude psychotherapy, "Ironically, although a self-declared enemy of the inauthentic, Bindrim sought psychological deliverance from the very artifice he decried. Far from being spontaneous returns to 'nature,' his marathons were carefully orchestrated performances of psychological ingenuity and financial opportunism."[5]

Paul Bindrim's techniques, philosophy, and strategies bore more than a passing resemblance to those of earlier body cultists and spiritual seekers. Ordained as a minister in the Church of Religious Science in 1958, Bindrim's

spiritual pursuits drew on the same New Thought principles of limitless human potential that inspired George Wharton James.[6] Meanwhile, his academic interest in the paranormal led him to study extrasensory perception
(ESP) in the 1940s under J. P. Rhine at Duke University, a pursuit that placed
him within the zeitgeist of Church of Scientology founder, L. Ron Hubbard,
and Jack Parsons, the Cal Tech rocket scientist and occultist, both of whom
were intrigued by the marriage of science and spirituality. Indeed, Southern
California with its potent regional mix of body culture and self-realization
pursuits drew Bindrim to Hollywood from New York and, much like Philip
Lovell, he set himself up in a hypermodern home and established a private
practice as a licensed psychologist to enable the realization of his psychotherapeutic dreams.[7]

Bindrim's theories about accessing the spirituality of the human mind by
liberating the body from emotional and sexual repression were influenced
by the pioneering work of Abraham Maslow, a towering figure in humanistic
psychology. Maslow believed that human beings held the potential for growth
and transcendence well beyond the limitations of environmental or sexual
stimuli. Key to Maslow's work was the concept of the "peak experience" in
which a person could feel fully integrated with the world, with oneself, and
at peace. Achieving this state of bliss was compatible with the 1960s counterculture's experiments with LSD, and Maslow was impressed with the drug's
research potential.[8] Bindrim, however, felt that peak experiences could be
achieved without the lysergic acid diethylamide but with provocative therapeutic techniques including the group setting, introduction of objects and activities to induce the peak state and, of course, nudity. [9]

While perhaps a bit of a publicity gimmick, the integration of nudity
into psychotherapeutic treatment was suggested in Maslow's early work and
the controversial sex theories of early twentieth-century social psychology
pioneer, Wilhelm Reich.[10] A student of Freud, Reich gained notoriety in the
United States after fleeing Europe in 1939 and settling in New York to teach
at the New School. There, Reich announced his discovery of "orgonomy," the
study of the cosmic energy of orgasm. If this energy could be gathered at great
enough strength (in sex boxes called orgone accumulators), Reich believed it
could destroy cancerous tumors. Orgonomy was an extension of Reich's earlier theories that anxiety and sexual repression caused illness, which he treated
with touch therapy and psychoanalysis as patients sat in their underwear or
in the nude. Needless to say, these practices were all highly irregular, and ultimately Reich's radical medical treatments channeling the cosmic forces of

orgasm undertaken at his Orgonon research center in Maine would run afoul of the Food and Drug Administration. He would die of heart failure in Lewisburg Federal Penitentiary in 1957.[11]

Bindrim's genius was his ability to take controversial treatments that had attracted public attention decades earlier and package them with credible psychotherapeutic methods, contemporary self-realization pursuits, popular psychology, and the shock of social nudity. It might not have taken hold at another moment in history, but in Southern California, the land of free and natural living, fitness enthusiasm, body cultism, and spiritual seeking, the late 1960s proved the perfect time to introduce Americans to the marathon nude therapy encounter session. Getting people to take off their clothes to rid themselves of psychological inhibitions, integrate their mind and body, and find their authentic selves made Bindrim a famous man. His notoriety also led to litigation when novelist Gwen Davis Mitchell attended one of his nude therapy marathons and then wrote the fictional work, *Touching*, based on the experience. Bindrim was insulted by the unflattering portrait Mitchell drew of him and his techniques so he sued both Mitchell and Doubleday Press for libel. Bindrim won the case in 1979, received $75,000 in damages, and a sympathetic ruling from Appellate Justice Robert Kingsley, who found that the defendants entertained actual malice in producing the book.[12]

While Bindrim was the most famous nude psychotherapist in the United States, if not the world, he was part of a larger academic scene intrigued by nudity's potential as a therapeutic tool.[13] One of the major sites for this research was in Long Beach, California, where William E. Hartman, a sociology professor at California State University, Long Beach, and Marilyn A. Fithian, a sexologist, founded the Center for Marital and Sexual Studies in 1968.[14] They became best known for their work on sexual dysfunction, particularly in women, and for adopting the dual-sex team approach of famed sexologists William Masters and Virginia Johnson.[15] Their sex therapy text, *Treatment of Sexual Dysfunction*, published in 1972, was considered, by experts in the field, to be as innovative as the studies conducted by Alfred Kinsey and Masters and Johnson.[16] Hartman and Fithian met in their late forties while already married to others, each with a brood of grown children. They divorced their spouses and lived together until Hartman's death in 1997, never marrying.[17] Their sex research is remarkable for its scope as well as subject matter, interviewing over 750 male and female subjects as they gathered data on sexual performance, which they often watched, compiling over 10,000 observation hours over twenty years.[18] They gathered more information on female orgasm than any other researchers and were highly vested in women experiencing sexual pleasure.[19] In fact, Hartman spent a year in the mid-1960s working under Dr. Arnold H. Kegel at a clinic at the Los Angeles County General Hospital. Hartman and Fithian trained their female patients in the Kegel method of vaginal strengthening and stimulation as well as coming up with several new vaginal exercises of their own.[20]

While it was the sexology studies that brought them the most academic acclaim, Hartman and Fithian's first major research project was on nudism, published in 1970. It originated with Fithian's master's thesis, which she had worked on with Hartman, one of her professors at Long Beach, but grew into a massive study involving over two thousand nudist interviews at over one hundred nudist camps and clubs.[21] With Donald Johnson, author of the best-seller *The Nudists* (1959), Hartman and Fithian put together what remains the most comprehensive study of organized social nudism in the United States. The study was based largely on their own observations at nudist camps and the data gathered from questionnaires with hundreds of questions ranging from reasons for and benefits of being a nudist to why people dropped out of the scene. The data uncovered that the reasons for being a nudist were a sense of freedom, the health benefits of relaxation, and acquiring an "all-over-tan."[22] The reported causes of leaving organized nudism were remarkably similar to abandoning any regular social or recreational activity including lack of time, financial cost, traveling distance, unpleasant social cliques, and clashes with camp management.[23] While a relatively small percentage of the nudists reported dropping out, of this group, almost half remained "private" nudists who continued their practice at home, either alone or with their family. In fact, Hartman and Fithian concluded that 90 percent of all nudists, whether in clubs or not, were also domestic nudists.[24] In answering the question about areas of the home where one was most often nude, the overwhelming majority reported while sleeping, followed by when having sex. Gardening was the least commonly reported domestic nudist activity.[25]

Sweeping in its breadth, *Nudist Society* confirmed what nudists had been saying about their body practice for forty years: it was a free and natural lifestyle that encouraged physical, mental, and social health. It strengthened the body through sun exposure and physical activity, supported easy friendships by breaking down social barriers, and helped build strong family bonds through wholesome outdoor togetherness. Hartman and Fithian's study also made it clear that the majority of participants were white, heterosexual, middle-class professionals, small business owners, or skilled manual laborers, with at least a high school education, if not a college degree. The 1970 study showed, too, at least at the nudist clubs and retreats Hartman and Fithian investigated in the four Western states of California, Arizona, Washington, and Oregon, that there were still few nudists of color and there remained a discomfort among some white members about racial integration. Many encouraged it, but the study also reflected "the presence of anti-negro bias" among a small percentage of respondents.[26]

In their chapter "Nudism as a Therapeutic Community," Hartman and Fithian's study merged with Bindrim's ideas about naked psychotherapy."[27] Here, they evoked Maslow's theory that "nudism, simply going naked before a lot of other people, is itself a kind of therapy, especially if we can be conscious of it, that is, if there's a skilled person around to direct what's going on."[28] They also cite Reich's student, Alexander Lowen, whose study, *The Betrayal of the Body*, suggested that positive body image could encourage mental health, a theory Hartman and Fithian felt played out nicely in the nudist environment.[29] But, most importantly, Hartman and Fithian joined Bindrim at the Deer Park Nudist Resort in June 1967 to help guide the first nude marathon session, followed weeks later by two other marathons held in private homes with smaller numbers of participants and, in one case, only couples. At the third marathon, Hartman and Fithian, always the diligent data gatherers, circulated a specifically designed questionnaire to the ten participants. While Hartman and Fithian stated expressly that they could "attach no great significance to the statistical results of these questionnaires," they were impressed that the majority reported feeling that the experience improved their sense of self, their marital relations, their body image, and resolved "conflicts between sexual and sensual feelings," allowing them to express affection more easily.[30]

Hartman and Fithian shared and contributed to Bindrim's findings that social nudity created a productive therapeutic environment that helped people literally and figuratively be more comfortable in their own skin by pushing past the "overly repressive puritanical influence of our clothed society."[31] In fact, their participation lent much-needed academic credibility to Bindrim's experiment. But their fundamental conclusion after all the data collection, analysis, historical contextualization, and on-the-ground participant-observation was that nudism was not an overtly sexual experience, but one that could encourage sexual health as part of a free and natural lifestyle that supported a positive self-image. In drawing this conclusion, Hartman himself relied upon the statement of an anonymous sex researcher whose observations fit comfortably with his own, that "far from being significantly sexual [nudism] tends toward being relatively non-sexual, and in some instances significantly antisexual or at least antierotic. . . . Moreover, it is not unlikely that the minority who move through social nudism to extensive involvement in nonconventional sexual practices (e.g., wife-swapping and the orgy scene) are not furthered in this development significantly by the nudist contact. It is more likely that for one reason or other these are persons already alienated from conventional norms and their transitional attachment to nudism may only be an experiment."[32] In case readers were still unconvinced that nudism did not cultivate sexual degeneracy or provide the environment for untoward sexual exploration, Hartman and Fithian included in their first appendix the complete text of Princeton psychology professor Howard C. Warren's 1933 essay, "Social Nudism and the Body Taboo," in which he clearly stated that "social nudism does not in any way foster eroticism—that it tends if anything to promote a saner sex outlook and more natural relations between men and women, even during the years of early sexual maturity."[33]

While never explicit in *Nudist Society*, the conclusions Hartman and Fithian drew about the unerotic, yet sexually healthy, nature of social nudism were rejoinders to late 1960s popular sexology, such as that by Manfred F. DeMartino, a former ad man and script writer for CBS, which was critical of traditional nudism for being conservative, ascetic, faddish, and not just asexual, but anti-sex. DeMartino's 1969 bestseller, *The New Female Sexuality: The Sexual Practices and Experiences of Social Nudists, "Potential" Nudists, and Lesbians*, published in a light pink dust jacket to appeal to female readers, insinuated that as social nudism shed its conservatism, its practitioners became more sexually experimental. Citing the newly sexy nudist magazines available on the market as evidence that social nudism was catching up with the sexual revolution, DeMartino ultimately concluded that nudism fostered strong senses of selfesteem and thereby encouraged a healthy sex drive and exploratory impulse, particularly in women. In DeMartino's estimation, social nakedness, if shorn of the restrictive rules of traditional nudism, could be very sexy indeed.[34]

In the 1991 revised edition of *Nudist Society*, Hartman and Fithian admit to being bewildered by the heightened interest in public nudity in the 1970s and 1980s and were completely caught off guard that the call to "free beaches" became an organized political movement with ties to other social movements of the time.[35] For the authors of *Nudist Society*, in 1970, these soon-to-be-radical activists were just a bunch of unorganized skinny-dippers it did not occur to them to interview. Much like the writers of early treatises on nudism from the 1930s, Hartman and Fithian treated nudism in isolation from mainstream society and accepted its rituals and rules on face value, as one often does when closely studying a subculture. In fact, their first forays into the study of nudism involved discussions with the old guard of Alois Knapp and Kurt Barthel.[36] This is not to suggest that Hartman and Fithian ignored the sexuality of their nudist subjects—in fact, *Nudist Society* has a sensitive section on "swinging" as a more feminist expression of "wife-swapping," among other observations— rather, nudism meant something distinct, organized, with an agreed-upon ideology that the body was inherently beautiful and natural and any sexual awakening or joy that took place was a healthy response to feeling really, really good. This was entirely different from looking to nudism as a place to express and act out one's sexual desires. Indeed, this is precisely what Hartman and Fithian meant when they reported that Bindrim's nude psychotherapy marathons resolved the tension between sensual and sexual feelings. One could feel sensual when socially naked without entertaining overt sexual acts.

While Hartman and Fithian's important study would try to be definitive on the subject of nudism and sexuality, the cultural question of where nudity ended and sexuality began was difficult to resolve, especially as nudism, even protected by its rites, treatises, and protocols, ran up against the sexual revolution's calls for liberation and a complete overhaul of all American sexual norms.[37] For nudism to stay in the game, it would have to encourage the publicity of nude therapy, which tapped perfectly into the spiritual inner quests of the 1960s counterculture, and it would have to be more overt about sexual experimentation. The irony, of course, was that after years of court battles at local and federal levels to permit nudist camps and nudist publications, suddenly it seemed *everyone* was getting naked. Yet the new permissiveness was not only unwelcome to social conservatives, who one would expect to be offended, it was also viewed with a degree of suspicion by social nudists who rightly felt that the sexual revolution, and public fascination with it, might not ultimately help their cause. At the center of the collision between social nudism and the sexual revolution was Ed Lange and his publishing house, Elysium Growth Press.

A lifelong nudist, activist, retreat founder, photographer, and publisher of nudist magazines, pamphlets, and books, Lange looms large in the history of American nudist culture. He joined the movement in the early days when nudism was still a pretty rustic, isolated enterprise but understood quickly that he could capitalize upon nudism's visual and countercultural appeal and serve as an active organizational link between its claims to the body natural and the sexual revolution's potential for jazzing up nudism. Lange joined

FIGURE 27. Human mandala at Elysium, 1968. Photograph by Ed Lange. © Elysium Growth Press. Courtesy of the Southern California Naturist Association.

Fraternity Elysia as a young man, shortly before its close, and was deeply affected by what he thought was the unjust and discriminatory behavior of the Los Angeles judicial system in arresting Lura Glassey and effectively outlawing social nudism in Southern California. He became actively involved in the American Sunbathing Association (ASA) and, while dedicated to organized nudism's quest to spread the gospel of wholesome naked living, Lange envisioned a nudist culture that represented the body in more realistic ways and embraced the sexuality inherent to the human experience.[38]

Lange was born in Chicago in 1920 to a practicing Baptist family, but it was in college in Illinois that he first consciously confronted contradictory and repressive ideas about sex. He rebelled against the ideas that the body was unclean and sex dirty because he "didn't see the results of that kind of thinking bringing about meaningful relationships. . . . There had to be something more than that."[39] He joined the Marine Corps in 1940 and was stationed in San Diego where he worked in aircraft, after which he moved to Hollywood.[40] There, Lange became a freelance photojournalist throughout his twenties and thirties, designing art, furniture, and fashion layouts for major magazines like *Vogue, Glamour, Bazaar, Architectural Forum*, and *Arts and Architecture*.[41] While working as a stock boy at Paramount Pictures, Lange had his big break when he met George Hoyningen-Huene, one of the world's top fashion photographers. Lange left Paramount and became Hoyningen-Huene's assistant, clearing the way for his own career in fashion photography. At the same time, Lange discovered Southern California's nudist retreats and was intrigued by the interplay of one world, where clothing and bodily ornamentation meant everything, and another, where the unclothed body was a badge of health, personal freedom, and a rejection of materialism. Later in life, in an interview with Art Kunkin, founder of the *Los Angeles Free Press*, Lange stated that "it was the going from the one—the sophisticated fashion world—to the barefeet-in-the-dirt world that gave me a sense of balance."[42]

Photography and the personal pursuit of a free and natural lifestyle dovetailed nicely, and Lange supplemented his income in the early 1950s by selling photographs he had taken at nudist camps to Ilsley Boone's *Sunshine and Health* magazine. Lange was careful to get signed releases from his subjects to allow

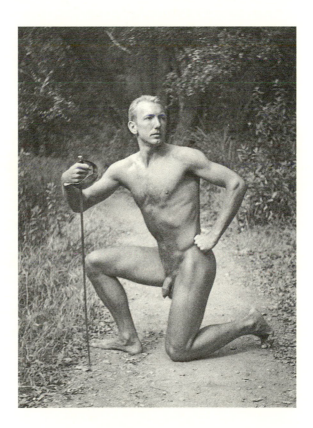

FIGURE 28. Ed Lange, age 32 (1952). Photographer unknown. Courtesy of the Southern California Naturist Association.

for sale and distribution of the images and was thus dismayed when Boone airbrushed out the genitals and nipples in order to send *Sunshine and Health* legally through the mail. Since 1947, the United States post office had been seizing issues of Ilsley Boone's *Sunshine and Health* magazine not just because of the nudity, but because they contained images of white women's breasts (although those of black women were acceptable) and pubic hair, which the post office considered obscene.[43] In 1953, after years of such seizures, the post office directly stopped a shipment of *Sunshine and Health* from Boone's Sunshine Book Company office in Mays Landing, New Jersey, provoking Boone to seek an injunction and subsequently to file what would become a precedent-setting federal lawsuit against the postmaster general, *Sunshine Book Company v. Summerfield*. Defended by the ACLU, Boone won the suit as the judges of the DC Circuit Court found *Sunshine and Health* not only *not* obscene but singularly unsexy and unlikely to arouse anyone. Boone won a permanent injunction against the post office preventing any future seizure of the magazine.[44] The case, however, did not end there because the post office again stopped the mailing of the magazine. This time, when Boone and the ACLU filed a civil suit, the presiding judge, Justice James Kirkland, was far less sympathetic and found the images in *Sunshine and Health* to be, indeed, obscene.[45]

Kirkland's reasoning reflected remarkable candor and showcased the swirl of complex, paradoxical ideas about sex, race, and the body that characterized the 1950s. Kirkland explained that pictures of naked children promoted healthy sexuality, according to Dr. Spock; photographs of bodies of color were acceptable because they were not considered erotic; and nude images of attractive women were absolutely fine; but that any photographs depicting penises were "foul" and "filthy" as were those showing fat women who did not conform to the white middle-class American beauty standard of slim, fit, and young. Indeed, Judge Kirkland's decision in the Boone case spoke to the rabid homophobia of the era and an underlying presumption that what was sexually arousing to straight American men was all the same. Thus, since he did not find men or overweight women attractive, he assumed no one other than a moral degenerate could either. *Sunshine and Health*, in its entirety, was not obscene but as Brian Hoffman has explained, "the fact that nudists offered *S&H* 'freely for sale to the general public who were not members of the nudist organization' while also exhibiting photographs 'clearly revealing genitals, breasts and other portions of the body normally covered in public' revealed the profit motive of the magazine and according to Judge Kirkland, made it obscene and non-mailable."[46]

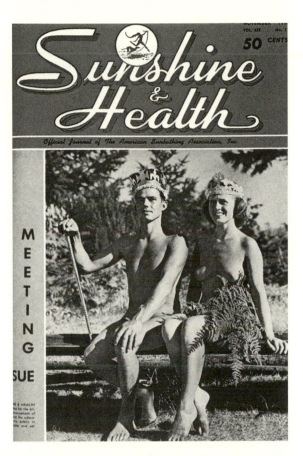

FIGURE 29. Periodical, *Sunshine and Health* 19, no. 11 (November 1950), editor Donald Johnson, photographer Ed Lange (American, 1920–1995), publisher Ilsley Boone (American, 1879–1968). 11 ⅛ × 8 ¼ in. (28.3 × 21 cm). Wolfsonian-Florida International University, Miami Beach, Florida, Gift of Robert J. Young, XC2000.81.33.81. Photo: Lynton Gardiner.

Boone challenged the court's decisions again and this time, in a favorable twist of legal fate, had the help of the 1957 US Supreme Court decision in *Roth v. United States*, which, while upholding the conviction of bookseller Samuel Roth for selling pornography and sending him to jail for five years, produced a split decision that distinguished visual and textual representations of sex from the commercial distribution of smut. The distinction the court tried to draw was between material that had social merit (scientific representations of the body, artful nudes, literature) and lewd works solely meant to provoke sexual arousal.[47] Intended as a liberal reading of the First Amendment, the court narrowed "the standard for judging obscenity . . . [to] whether, to the average person, applying contemporary community standards, the dominant theme of the material, taken as a whole, appeals to prurient interest."[48] While a flawed decision that failed to put to rest the issue of protecting sexually explicit texts and images under the First Amendment, *Roth* expanded the freedom to publish more graphic depictions of sex and nudity.[49] When Boone's case went before the US Supreme Court, the justices overturned Kirkland's decision on the basis that *Sunshine and Health* had therapeutic and recreational merit and its images were not pornographic.[50] After five expensive years, Boone won *Sunshine Book Company* v. *Summerfield* on January 13, 1958, and could freely send *Sunshine and Health* through the mail to subscribers without fear of reprisals, and presumably, without airbrushing its photographs.[51]

However innocuous *Sunshine and Health* ultimately seemed to the courts, it had attracted a large audience, both nudist and not. In his excellent history of nudist magazines and obscenity law, Hoffman reports that sales of the magazines varied from 40,000 to 100,000 a month with 6,000 to 8,000 mailed to subscribers and newsstand sales accounting for the remaining issues.[52] With numbers cited in court transcripts, in February 1955, 40,000 issues of *Sunshine and Health* were printed, 10,000 of which were mailed to subscribers.[53] Hoffman suggests that part of *Sunshine and Health*'s impressive postwar appeal was the homoerotic male imagery that disturbed Judge Kirkland. When sandwiched between photographs of naked women, images of remarkably fit, young nude men slipped right by the censors.[54] The fact that newsstand sales far outnumbered subscriber sales implies a pornographic appeal, but one may also reasonably assume that several thousand monthly readers were, in fact, practicing nudists: indeed, by 1958, the American Sunbathing Association alone claimed almost 7,800 members.[55]

The troubles in nudist publishing were strongly felt in Los Angeles, where Lange was based. Despite all its connections to Hollywood and its free and natural lifestyle, Los Angeles was a surprisingly tough town to navigate. While the national tide had moved toward a liberalization of pornography laws, Los Angeles was still politically conservative and had a long history of controlling its visual representation, whether it was public sculpture or abstract art hung in museum galleries. The 1950s was an era of strict artistic censorship with a brief, but notorious, ban on modernist abstract art in public spaces.[56] The repressive atmosphere continued into the 1960s and was well-documented by Ken Price, a longtime ASA member and camp photographer who spent two years covering Los Angeles's censure of nudist magazines. For the better part of the 1950s, Price had served as a staff photographer for *Sunshine and Health*, hosting amateur photography contests for the readership, as well as teaching technique so nudists could put aesthetically pleasing pictures in their family photo albums. Some of his suggestions were basic, such as not shooting into the sun, while others were more specific to nudist culture, like waiting for someone's tan to fill in because "'cottontails' (new nudists whose skin is yet untanned) often look as though the subject had just risen from a snowbank, being merely blobs of black here and there on a white frame."[57] While making the point that taking flattering pictures of naked people was an art form better left to the professionals, Price underscored that nudist photography was meant to promote a specific lifestyle in a manner understandable and palatable to a bigger public.

Price was concerned that readers understand that the publishing of nudist images was not about seeing each other in magazines, although that had a certain thrill. It was really about visually showcasing the free and natural lifestyle in the best possible light in order to attract new members and protect nudism from legal action. This concern was well founded. In a 1961 exposé, Price reported that *Sunshine and Health*, along with other nudist magazines, was widely available on Los Angeles newsstands, but with stickers where women's breasts should have been. Despite federal court rulings that nudist magazines were not obscene, Los Angeles continued to uphold an old section of the municipal code that made it unlawful to display images of female breasts. Fearful of fines, newsstand owners simply stuck pasties on the magazine covers.[58]

Frustrated with the local censorship of *Sunshine and Health*, Lange began selling what he called "packages" to other publishers, including Chicago's *Modern Sunbathing*, and to Mervin Mounce of Spokane, Washington, who had cornered the West Coast nudist market with *Eden, National Nudist Leader*, and several other magazines. Like Boone, Mounce, a former president of the American Sunbathing Association, also found himself charged with peddling smut when United States customs officials seized nine thousand European nudist magazines he had imported for resale. Convicted in 1957, Mounce, with the support of the Justice Department, successfully appealed to the US Supreme Court to overturn the lower court's conviction using the *Roth* "community standards" test for obscenity.[59]

Rather than selling individual pictures, Lange sold whole collections of images to nudist publishers, often with stories included, which proved lucrative as the presses could print the material more quickly.[60] Together with his wife, June, Lange hoped their images and reportage would break down organized nudism's entrenched conservatism. In a 1959 piece for *Sunbathing Review*, for example, June reported on a hubbub at a gathering of the ASA caused by "the [apparently] disgraceful way California women tamper with their bodies."[61] A group of adult female California nudists had shocked their Midwestern brethren by appearing in the buff with bleached, trimmed, or entirely bare pubic areas, a practice forbidden at some nudist colonies because it sexualized the mons pubis. June's response was given that men shave their faces and it was acceptable for women to remove hair from the rest of their bodies, why did it matter if they took if off their genitalia? Since it had been airbrushed off nudist photographs for years in order to render the nether region suitably nonsexual for the post office, it seemed a peculiar fixation to insist that pubic hair stay intact. To argue that pubic hair was natural and removing it was unnatural— and perhaps a breach of free and natural lifestyle protocol—was one thing, but to argue that dressing it up or taking it off made it more *sexual* seemed a stretch. For the Langes, the problem with nudism was its pretense that sex organs were not sexual in the first place. Hair really wasn't the issue.[62]

One of the immediate effects of Boone's win in *Sunshine Book Company v. Summerfield* was an uptick in the number of nudist magazines on the market, many of which were more sexually exploitative than practicing nudists were comfortable promoting. As the full repercussions of the 1958 decision were felt in the publishing industry, legitimate nudist magazines were squeezed out of the market by sexier titles that used nudism as the cover for soft-core erotica. The most prolific of these publishers was Milton Luros, an artist who built his career in the 1930s and 1940s creating beautiful, highly elaborate covers for science fiction magazines and pulp novels. In the wake of the *Roth* and *Sunshine Book Company* decisions, Luros teamed up with Stan Sohler, a photographer, former president of the ASA, and friend of Ed Lange, to publish a new line of nudist magazines that would be more titillating than *Sunshine and Health*'s staid images of family togetherness and camp life. The result was Sun Era, which published titles like *Urban Nudist*, *Nudist Idea*, and *Backyard Nudist*. These were highly popular with subscribers but "disappointing to the nudism faithful who view[ed] Luros as strictly an opportunist and Sohler as a traitor," according to rare book dealer Stephen J. Gertz.[63] The effects of these new publications on nudist culture were swift and unpleasant as the long-fought-for public self-representation as healthful, family-oriented, and wholesomely free was pushed aside in favor of young male and female models showcasing an eroticized world of greasy sunbaked skin and group sex shenanigans. Not surprisingly, these new magazines drew audiences away from the traditional nudist visual format, and *Sunshine and*

Health could not compete; Boone declared bankruptcy in 1963 and his Sunshine Book Company went out of business. His friend and caretaker, Edith Church, bought the title to *Sunshine and Health,* but was unable to keep it afloat. She, in turn, sold the magazine to another publisher, but after a few issues, that venture also failed and the venerable flagship publication of the American nudist movement was no more.[64]

An examination of the covers alone explains why traditional nudists might have resented the intrusion of pornography into nudist publishing and found Luros and Sohler's enterprise offensive. With indoor naked bodies depicted in the ecstatic throes of an adults-only gathering or actively seeking one out (*Urban Nudist* declared that "happiness is a bare-skin party"), nudism of the mid-1960s seemed a far cry from the serious and collective nudist movement of the 1930s or the family togetherness of the 1950s. Now nude adults were engaged in activities that seemed a whole lot sexier than spending a weekend digging a hole for the colony pool. In Luros and Soher's version, the traditional aesthetics of nudist family life were replaced with sexy bodies far more evocative of *Playboy* magazine's soft-core imagery of playful adults-only sexuality. Moreover, the long-established significance of the body-in-nature trope that highlighted the wholesome family experience of the free and natural lifestyle was pushed aside as the private suburban home hinted at a new kind of sexual potential. *Jaybird,* another of Luros and Sohler's magazines, explicitly celebrated the sexuality of the suburbs with a bohemian mix of pornography and hippie performance art. With professional models, film sets, a Technicolor layout, and lots of "clam" shots, *Jaybird's* glossy pages gleefully undid the clean-cut world fostered in *Sunshine and Health. Jaybird* hit a public nerve and became one of Luros and Sohler's most popular publications, selling about twenty thousand copies per issue in 1968.[65] Ed Lange briefly tried to compete with *Jaybird,* retitling his *Sundial* magazine, *Sundisk,* and giving it "a groovy psychedelic makeover. Clearly competing with the hippified *Jaybird,* his models not only bared their charms; they shoved them in the reader's face."[66] Nudists were horrified, wanting nothing to do with pornography, and Lange, whose inroads into the genre could not outshine *Jaybird* anyway, had to let his new enterprise go.

Navigating censorship laws while trying to shake up traditional nudism had proven disheartening, so in 1961, Lange decided to found his own firm in Los Angeles where he could publish whatever he wanted. Calling it Elysium Growth Press, a homage to Fraternity Elysia, his first nudist camp, and a gesture toward classical concepts of paradise, Lange would publish titles related

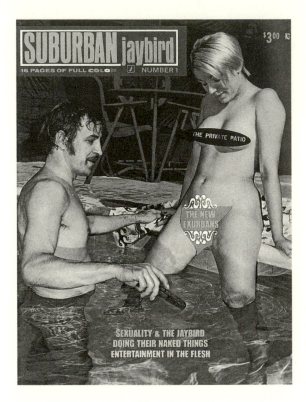

FIGURE 30. Nudism meets
erotic suburb in *Jaybird*,
Milton Luros and Stan
Sohler's late-1960s hippie
nudist magazine. Collection
of the author.

to nudism and sexual freedom for the next thirty years.[67] He started with the
magazines *Nude Living*, *Sundial*, and *Nude Look*, all of which varied in approach, some focusing more on the free and natural lifestyle in general while
others showcased specific nudist clubs and retreats.[68] Lange's *Ankh* magazine
differed from the others by having more of a research emphasis exploring,
for example, the counterculture's approach to nudity and sex, how to have a
three-way, new therapeutic discoveries, and the history of body culture, from
circumcision to fertility goddesses.[69] Then, starting with *The Shameless Nude*
in 1963, Lange began publishing books that went well beyond the pictorials
and proselytizing of the magazine genre to get deeper into the meanings of
nudity, body acceptance, and human sexuality. From his little office on Fern-
wood Avenue in West Los Angeles, Lange launched a veritable nudist and
sexuality publishing empire. One could order from the Elysium Growth Press
any number of nudist magazines, serious analyses of obscenity cases, collections of erotic art, and, by the late 1960s, whole series of booklets and texts on

FIGURE 31. A selection of Ed Lange's 1950s and 1960s nudist magazines. ©1968 Elysium Growth Press. Courtesy of the Southern California Naturist Association.

nudity and the behavioral sciences, including Aileen Goodson's *Experiment in Nude Psychotherapy* and Hartman, Fithian, and Johnson's *Nudist Society*.[70]

Lange explicitly stated that the "purpose of Elysium is to disseminate information to the behavioral science community relating to nudity and the body taboo neuroses so prevalent in our culture."[71] Some titles were specifically about nudist culture, such as *Nudism Explained in Words and Photographs* while others were about exploring sex, such as Justine Hill's *Women Talking*.[72] For significant financial outlay, $95.00 in the 1960s, one could order sets including a lengthy pamphlet, one hundred projection slides, and an audio tape on topics like "Body Self Image" and "Body Self Appreciation." Produced by Lange's media division, Sensate Media Service, these sets were intended for educational and therapeutic settings where students and patients could allay any concerns or curiosities about human sexuality and the body.[73]

With all the shake-ups in the increasingly competitive nudist magazine business, Lange made another shrewd financial move when, shortly after *Sunshine and Health* went under, he offered to produce a forty-eight-page pictorial magazine for the ASA, called *Nudism Today*, which would essentially replace Boone's signature publication as the official magazine of American nudism.[74] By marketing a range of nudist books, magazines, and educational products, Lange would be able to bankroll future nudist projects and pay the legal fees incurred as the line between pornography and non-lewd nudity would continue to waver and shift. As savvy a countercultural capitalist as Lange was, he would overestimate Southern California's progressivism and Elysium Growth Press was raided more than once by the Los Angeles Police Department for distributing obscene material. The charges never stuck, but they would come back later to haunt him.

Directly confronting these legal and cultural challenges while branching out to explore psychotherapy, yoga, self-love, and especially the outer limits of human potential, became Lange's lifelong métier. Lange was deeply influenced by the intellectual marriage of personal growth and the humanities, arts, and sciences that Michael Murphy and Dick Price spearheaded when they founded the famous retreat center, Esalen, in 1962, in Big Sur, California. Based on Aldous Huxley's concept of human potentialities and Maslow's theories of self-actualization and humanistic psychology, Esalen's teachings were also infused with elements of Eastern philosophy and yogic principles. Alan Watts was Esalen's first speaker and Huxley himself would pay the retreat center a visit shortly before his death in 1963.[75] Murphy and Price's project evolved into the Human Potential Movement after George Leonard, a writer for *Look* magazine researching new methodologies in American psychology, met Murphy and together they hatched ideas for merging the exciting range of ideas and methods for achieving truth and happiness that were floating around the 1960s zeitgeist.[76] Neither cult nor organized religion, the Human Potential Movement was more of a configuration of philosophical and behavioral science concepts that merged beautifully with the psychedelic consciousness-raising of the era. As the American religious studies scholar, Jeffrey Kripal, puts it, "Esalen is better seen as a flowing together of two separate but connected lineages: the psychoanalytic stream, which focused on various mystical, occult, and erotic understandings of *energy*; and the gestalt stream, which focused on the nature, creative constructions, and awakening of *consciousness*."[77]

Lange quickly understood that the Human Potential Movement, with its tethering of psychotherapeutic techniques of self-exploration to body practices like yoga and meditation, had strong resonance with nudism's pursuit of physical fitness, self-love, and overall well-being. Tying new developments in psychotherapy to his press, in 1964, Lange founded the Elysium Institute as the nonprofit educational wing of his nudist publishing enterprise. Its beginnings were modest, with an office in Los Angeles where Lange could also invite speakers and host small gatherings, but he set his sights on something much bigger that would allow a community of like-minded seekers and nudist practitioners to grow, hopefully unhindered by law enforcement, neighbors, or the courts.[78] Most importantly, Elysium would acknowledge the sexuality inherent in nudist practice and, by 1965, Lange had started putting announcements in the magazines introducing the radical idea that people were sexual beings. He explained that, "we wanted people to be more free and open about that which had been suppressed and repressed, to help people be less frightened by the sexual interests they might have.[79]

In 1967, the funding and the opportunity came together and Lange bought eight acres of land in Los Angeles County's Topanga Canyon, an especially beautiful part of the Santa Monica Mountains and famous home to artists, writers, bohemians, and refugees from Hollywood. Three miles outside the Los Angeles city limits and ten miles from Malibu, it was accessible and yet remote, surrounded by hills too steep to build on and adjacent to a state park and thus not threatened by future development.[80] In tying the Human Potential Movement to nudist philosophy, Lange explained "the Elysium Institute promotes self-acceptance and acceptance of others through a wholesome attitude towards the human body and its functions, both physical and emotional, which includes candid recognition of man's sexuality."[81] Elysium would be a back-to-nature retreat but also an experimental space. This was not going to be an old-school socialist-cooperative camp nor a white, middle-class nudist resort with shuffleboard, volleyball, and cocktail hour. It would be a genuine therapeutic center at which hard work on mind, body, and soul could take place.

Elysium opened to a dues-paying public on Memorial Day, 1968, and was immediately a big hit with the therapeutic community and sixties seekers of truth in the broader Los Angeles area.[82] There was a large, beautiful swimming pool that formed the center of the retreat. Nearby were buildings for eating, meetings, yoga classes, and for leading the myriad seminars available on self-esteem, body image, and stress reduction. There were tennis courts, a heated hydropool, and a sauna.[83] The rolling grounds encouraged walking and many of the activities took place outdoors. Trained professionals provided meditation sessions. Clinical psychologist and sculptor, Jean-Paul Mauran, led "guided fantasies" in the Ankh Room and created outdoor sculpture to further beautify Elysium. Psychologists sometimes brought their whole encounter groups to Elysium, while in 1978, forty-five European psychiatrists, psychotherapists, and behavioral psychologists gathered at Elysium for three days expressly to experience Southern California's therapeutic specialties of human growth potential, relaxation, and sexual health.[84] Lange explained that Elysium offered the perfect sanctuary for the uninitiated into social nakedness or group therapy by creating a transition whereby "they don't *have* to remove their clothes, but they come into a scene where [nudity] seems so natural and logical and comfortable that they can do it if they so choose without traumatic consequences in an environment which is supportive and not threatening."[85]

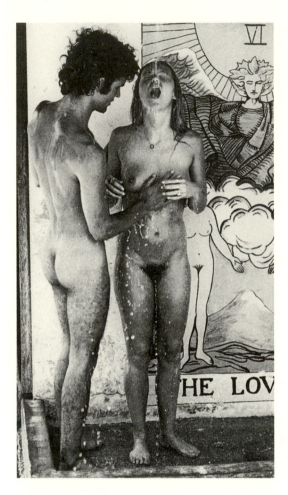

FIGURE 32. Outdoor shower, Elysium. Photograph by Ed Lange. ©1968 Elysium Growth Press. Courtesy of the Southern California Naturist Association.

Lange refused to call the place a nudist camp or resort, preferring Human Growth Center, which refocused public attention on the educational seminars and self-help workshops and away from the stodgy associations of traditional nudism. As he put it, "the nudist connotation in those days was 'funky,'" and not in a good way.[86] Dispensing with the nudist camp formulation altogether, Lange believed shaping Elysium into a "growth center" gave the whole place a more academically reputable stature and more contemporary vibe that would attract a different type of membership that was down with getting naked but also seriously interested in the seminars, workshops, healing therapies, and consciousness-raising curriculum Elysium offered. At the same time, his

FIGURE 33. Elysium Fields, Topanga Canyon, California, ca. 1980. Photograph by Ed Lange. Courtesy of the Southern California Naturist Association.

FIGURE 34. Elysium, 1970. Photograph by Ed Lange. Courtesy of the Southern California Naturist Association.

philosophy for Elysium still upheld American nudism's ethos that "exposure to sun, water, air, and to nature is a helpful and basic factor in building and maintaining a healthy attitude . . . and a strong body," adding that "the depiction of Man in his entirety and completeness in photographs and text requires no apology nor defense."[87] For Lange, social nudism practiced in a therapeutic environment and the visual representation of nudity as free and natural remained an integrated credo.

In a move that traditional nudists found troubling, however, Lange made Elysium "clothing optional" rather than "nudity required," long a protocol standard at nudist camps intended to discourage voyeurism. Instead of being required to remove your clothes, at Elysium, Lange explained, "you're required only to be a reasonable peaceful human being."[88] There were rules dictating basic safety and behavior. Nudity was required in the pool and sauna, cameras were forbidden, minors were allowed only with guardian consent, and smoking was permitted in safe areas not prone to fire. There were no published rules about sexual behavior other than not intruding on others—uninvited sexual display was forbidden.

While the combination of a clothing-optional code and freewheeling attitude toward sexuality already distressed traditional nudists, Lange incorporated other discomforting features into Elysium. According to Gary Mussell, an Elysium member, free beach activist, and former president of the Southern California Naturist Association, one of these was the "Meditation Room," which was used for sexual activity. Operating for fourteen years, from 1970 to 1984, the room had rules (couples could only have thirty minutes and had to clean up their own sheets and towels), but it was notorious within the broader nudist community for transgressing all previous prohibitions against open sex at nudist camps. Another offense, which would seem benign by today's spa standards, was the outdoor massage table where masseurs could do body work. Lange figured if members saw others getting a massage, they would want one too and thus generate more business for Lange and the massage therapist, who split the proceeds. Massage, however, had been long associated with the sex trade, so traditional nudists not only found it appalling to offer it at all, but to do so publicly.[89]

Lange's innovations may have offended the old guard but they were big with a younger generation. So Elysium flourished. It had hundreds of members who paid annual dues and anywhere from five hundred to eight hundred visitors on a summer weekend.[90] But big trouble was brewing because, under

FIGURE 35. Group nude therapy, Elysium, ca. 1970. Photograph by Ed Lange. Courtesy of the Southern California Naturist Association.

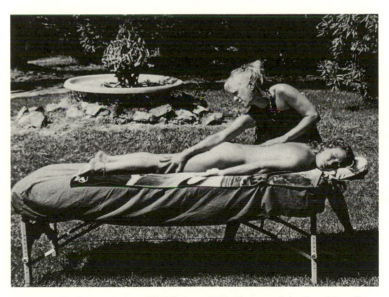

FIGURE 36. Outdoor massage table, Elysium, 1999. Photograph by Gary Mussell. Courtesy of the Southern California Naturist Association.

the 1939 county ordinance that banned social nudism in Los Angeles in the wake of the Dawn Hope Noel case, Elysium was in direct violation of local law. On June 23 and June 29, 1968, the sheriff's vice squad led two raids on Elysium, arresting or citing twenty-six people for committing the crime of appearing nude in the presence of two nude members of the opposite sex. The arrested parties promptly filed for a restraining order and temporary injunction against Sheriff Peter Pitchess and District Attorney Evelle Younger.

Meanwhile, Lange, well-seasoned by the legal struggles that had brought about the end of Fraternity Elysia, as well as his own troubles in the nudist publishing business, filed a federal petition to have the county's anti-nudism ordinance declared unconstitutional. The claim was that the ordinance "violates constitutional guarantees of privacy, free expression, free association, due process and equal protection under the law." In response, Assistant County Counsel Edward Gaylord, who had drawn up the original 1939 ordinance, told reporters that "free speech guarantees the discussion of anarchy but not the actual practice of it."[91] Lange challenged him directly, arguing that the old law was out of date, was in violation of constitutional liberties, and made Los Angeles look old-fashioned and silly given that San Diego, San Bernardino, and Riverside Counties had long tolerated nudist camps with little trouble. Lange also pointed out in the papers that the wording of the 1939 ordinance could ban families from being naked in front of each other, which, if a legal violation, was surely not one that could hold up to challenge in a federal court. Gaylord admitted that the ordinance could ban family nudity but that was "not the spirit in which it was drawn and it was never enforced in that manner." He continued to warn that if "the nudists' interpretation of the rights of free expression and free association were carried to a logical extreme, they could lead to nudism in public."[92] As outrageous a possibility as this may have seemed to Gaylord, public nudism was already brewing as an important political and cultural issue in California as the free beach movement had begun, with Lange a longtime activist proponent. However reactionary it might have been, the old Los Angeles city anti-nudism ordinance had been upheld in 1947, and the US Supreme Court had refused to hear challenges to it.[93] Things were shaping up to be quite a fight.

On July 12, Federal Judge Pierson Hall upheld the county ban on social nudism and rejected the petitions for an injunction and a restraining order. Lange was represented by the famous civil rights attorney, Stanley Fleishman, who specialized in obscenity law and had argued free speech cases eleven times before the United States Supreme Court. He would be a formidable foe, and his first move was to again challenge the constitutionality of the ordinance, this time in the local Malibu courts.[94]

True to form, Fleishman knocked it out of the park. The presiding judge, Justice John J. Merrick, declared the nudism ban unconstitutional and void on the basis that it violated the rights of free association and expression, privacy, due process and equal protection under the laws guaranteed by the Constitution and its amendments. Part of Merrick's ruling was on his argument that the ordinance was void because it was preempted by State Penal Code Section 314 prohibiting indecent exposure and lewd or obscene conduct.[95] This would have important legal ramifications in the free beach struggles of the 1970s because the California courts, starting in 1972, began ruling that for nude exposure to be lewd or obscene, the intent had to be as well. Thus, an indecent act like flashing one's genitals at an unsuspecting viewer was a violation of the State Penal Code, and could result in serious sex offense charges, but just lying naked on a beach was not an intentionally lewd act. It was important for Elysium's survival that Merrick struck down the 1939 county anti-nudity ban, but it would be ever more critical on the state level as the nudist movement expanded into public areas.

As significant as the Merrick decision was, and it was celebrated by nudists nationwide, it was also supported by Los Angeles county supervisor Kenneth Hahn. Arguing that since the Merrick decision confirmed that the state preempted the issue of obscenity, Hahn rather coyly proposed to abolish the County Commission on Obscenity and Pornography, since Los Angeles County no longer had jurisdiction over porn. The commission, long a thorn in the side of Los Angeles progressives, had banned nude images on Los Angeles newsstands and created the "pastie" issue.[96] Other county supervisors, however, including the notably conservative Warren Dorn, rejected Hahn's proposal, while the Los Angeles district attorney fought Merrick's ruling, even after three appellate judges upheld the dismissal of nudity charges against the Elysium members. Los Angeles's conservative establishment was rattled by the progressive changes afoot, and it was soon rumored in the papers that the county would try to circumvent the Merrick decision with new licensing regulations.[97]

Indeed, the rumors proved to be true, and in July 1970, County Counsel John Maharg wrote an amendment to existing legislation to require a license specifically for regulating nudist camps and to instruct the Regional Planning Commission to conduct hearings to determine whether or not nudist camps could be prohibited in Zone A-1, a zone relegated to light agriculture.[98]

As written by Maharg and Assistant County Counsel Gaylord, the new ordinance, No. 10,600, was obviously an effort to shutter Elysium. Its main focus was "Growth Centers," which were defined as "any place where three or more persons not all members of the same family congregate, assemble, or associate for the purpose of exposing their bodies in the nude in the presences of others or of each other."[99]

As soon as the new ordinance went into effect, the Los Angeles County sheriff's license detail ordered that Elysium immediately apply to operate legally.[100] Under Fleishman's counsel, Lange refused to file for a license, facing citation, fines, arrest, and six months in jail.[101] Instead, Lange sought another injunction and restraining order to keep the county sheriff off his property. Lange's main argument was the egregiously prejudicial nature of the ordinance, which included "growth" and "behavioral science" centers, an obvious reference to Elysium. Lange commented to the papers that "there are some people who object to our lifestyle and educational program and because they don't approve, they want to deprive us of our rights as property owners."[102]

At the heart of the controversy were rumors that Elysium was a deviant sex club masquerading as a group therapy center. As American sexual norms loosened up and the experiments of the sexual revolution spread into mainstream practice, nudism appeared deeply suspect to outsiders resistant to the changes afoot. At the same time, nudists found the rapidly shifting cultural ground unnerving as it was no longer clear where nudism ended and licentious sexual permissiveness began. At a large community meeting, with over 350 in attendance, the Chamber of Commerce voted to support the ordinance requiring operation licenses for growth centers. There were also loud conversations among Topanga residents about how to stem the tide of "hippies" into the canyon and control "pornography and morally objectionable activities."[103] The concern seemed to be less nudism than a "growth center invasion" that could bring with it sexual depravity.[104] In fact, much of the anti-Elysium discourse smacked of conservative backlash against the counterculture and its ethos of free love, as well as a more generalized social panic about youth and sexuality. More than one outraged canyon dweller evoked the 1969 Manson family killings, while others feared the sexual exploitation of their rustic canyon lifestyle. As one Topanga resident, Barney Berkey, colorfully put it, "[Elysium members] insist that pornography is a matter of geography; i.e. the lap of Nature's fields of verdure splendor. They're welcome to their opinion that it may be splendid in the grass but please, not at the expense of the comfort and peace of mind of neighbors."[105] In the thick of the licensing fracas, nude and topless bars, a mainstay of Los Angeles's legal sexual economy, also faced newly restrictive city and county ordinances which threatened to revoke liquor licenses if women performers didn't cover up.[106]

Unintentionally, Berkey had stumbled on a brilliant way to think about the relationship of place to nudism. In fact, pornography *is* a matter of geography. For decades, nudists had been trying to explain that, by being naked in camp settings and by displaying their naked selves in tasteful nudist pictorials, their carefully tuned geographical sensibilities asserted that nudism was *not* pornography: it was a free and natural lifestyle! Lange, who knew perfectly well where the line lay between nudist photography and pornography, both legally and philosophically, had pushed the envelope at Elysium by overtly embracing sexuality as part of his human potential project, which put nudism in a new and uncomfortable light.

Despite Lange's breaches of traditional nudist protocol, the American Sunbathing Association stalwartly took his side and appealed to the Los Angeles County Board of Supervisors to drop the requirements for the licensing of nudist activities. A letter by ASA vice president, Robert Johnston, explained that "to license the wearing of apparel or lack thereof on private property is as absurd as the establishment by the County of rules pertaining to the clothing one must wear in a church or office. It would be only a short step to the 'licensing' of food which may be eaten or subjects which may be discussed in the privacy of one's home. [In] Ordinance No. 10,600 Los Angeles has taken a step backward into the historical days of oppression and witch hunting."[107]

Not surprisingly, vocal support came from the psychoanalytic and behavioral therapy community. The Committee of the Los Angeles Psychologists for Social Action wrote a strongly worded letter to the County Board of Supervisors arguing that shuttering growth centers like Elysium could interfere with the important mental health work being done at the center in the form of group therapy and couples counseling. Not only was the new licensing ordinance repressive, the Psychologists for Social Action felt "that any effort to curtail such services can only add to the already too heavy burden currently borne by our County Mental Health Department."[108] Since the public health system was woefully undersupported, it was important that those who could afford private therapy have access to it. To close Elysium would unnecessarily disrupt a method of mental and emotional health treatment that, by all professional accounts, seemed to be working.

Many local residents were also upset by the proposed legislation, fearing it would strip Topanga Canyon of the very countercultural features that made

FIGURE 37. Anger therapy workshop, Elysium, ca. 1970. Photograph by Ed Lange. Courtesy of the Southern California Naturist Association.

it so appealing. One Mrs. J. E. Dryer, a Topanga resident and Elysium member, wrote to the local paper that the movement to ban growth centers seemed "to be indicative of the conspiracy, backed by big land developers, to eliminate the 'different' people, reducing Topanga to another middle-class suburb. This, to many Topanga residents, including myself, would be a tragedy."[109] Others, like Elizabeth Putnam, felt that "as long as the people at the growth center practice nudity on their own property they are not interfering with anyone else's freedom."[110] One especially irate Topanga Canyon resident, Stanley Russell, wrote an impassioned four-page letter to the County Board of Supervisors, sending copies to each supervisor individually, pointing out that not only was Elyisum *not* a nuisance but was, in fact, the *victim* of vandalism and the pettiness of just one family, that of a retired fire chief, and the Topanga Chamber of Commerce, who had taken it upon themselves to stir up trouble for Lange and his colleagues.[111]

Despite garnering such vocal support, Lange and the Elysium membership were disappointed when Judge Merrick, the hero of 1968, upheld the legality of the new licensing ordinance. Merrick argued that the issue was not "people vs. nudism" but licensing regulation which, in this case, he saw as appropriate as the regulation of any lawful business.[112] Of course the problem, as Robert Johnston pointed out in his letter on behalf of the ASA, was the arbitrary nature by which the police could grant the licenses.

For the next year and a half, Lange and his attorneys fought the licensing ordinance tooth and nail while the issue raged in the local papers. Just when things could not get more litigious or expensive, a grand jury in Kansas indicted Lange on thirty-three counts of obscenity for mailing Elysium publications like *Nude Living* and *Ankh*.[113] Lange was ultimately acquitted but the anti-growth-center crowd seized on the news to tar him as a pornographer and possible pedophile, which, while morally unsavory, was especially bad for housing values, their key concern.[114]

Much to the horror of Los Angeles county supervisor Warren Dorn and county counsel Edward Gaylord, Ed Lange won the case in the spring of 1972.[115] In a 2 to 1 decision, the California State Court of Appeals found the Los Angeles County ordinance requiring licenses of nudist camps unconstitutional. Judge James A. Cobey wrote that "the right of the county to license commercial nudity centers may not be questioned"; however, the extent of the licensing cannot interfere with the constitutional protections of the First Amendment, which included the right of nudists to assemble. Cobey added that nudity was "a form of personal, non-verbal expression" and could be considered protected under the First Amendment as well.[116] It was a decision that found social nudity on private property to be constitutionally protected. "This was an important decision," Stanley Fleishman explained. "It held the First Amendment protection of the right of association includes people who choose to associate nude just as it protects some people who choose to associate dressed in religious costume."[117] Lange, of course, was delighted, stating in a press release that "the Court's ruling has reaffirmed our basic premise that nudity is not lewdity [sic] and recognizes the inherent decency of the nude body."[118]

The legal battle would not end here, however. Lange would spend the next twenty years fighting the county on the issue of zoning. Humming in the background of the licensing ordinance fracas was a county strategy to zone Elysium out of Topanga Canyon if the licensing ordinance failed. Indeed, the strategic shift from licensing nudist activity to zoning the geographical site in which the nudist activity took place reflected similar tactics used by anti-pornography and, often, also antigay, interest groups to enforce social control. In cities like Los Angeles and Boston, when the courts could not legally prevent the showing of pornographic films, either by charging proprietors with breaches of obscenity law or by withholding commercial licenses, municipal authorities would target the physical site of the movie theater through zoning ordinances and police raids.[119] Once the Gaylord ordinance was thrown out, Supervisor Dorn enlisted the Regional Planning Commission to help shutter Elysium by zoning it out of existence, but the county could never do it.[120] The effect of incurring endless zoning violations, though, was to keep Elysium in a chronic state of legal limbo, with Lange sometimes holding operational permits, and sometimes not. He often spoke to the newspapers, frustrated by the intrusion of legal authorities into his therapeutic retreat: "It takes a dirty mind to infer that a massage workshop involved public coitus or that skinny-dipping promotes criminal behavior and loose morals. Elysium is a very nice environment to relax in but it is also far duller than minds filled with pornographic images would imagine."[121] When the case finally ended in 1992, it had cost Lange over a million dollars and was the longest-running zoning fight in Los Angeles history.[122]

Elysium might seem to have been a contradictory place—it invited nudists but was clothing-optional; it encouraged sensual exploration yet had strict rules against public sexual display. Clarifying his motives in shaping the Elysium experience, Lange explained "for 38 years I've been involved in the 'nudist idea.' That is what we called it at first, but it's far more than that. It's the idea of self-esteem for the body and its functions that I'm really the champion for."[123] To be sure, Lange invited the contradictions by merging idealism about nudity for social health with the sexual discovery he encouraged in his publications and instructional films. Elysium was, ultimately, the final battleground in the war over the legality of social nudity on private land. Whether or not nudity could go public would be the critical issue taken up by the free beach movement, but Lange's legal victories would ensure that nudist camps and nudist literature would endure, at least under the law. Cultural upheavals, however, would change the free and natural lifestyle.

Lange may have won the zoning fight, and pretty much any fight that came his way, but these victories came at a cost. Though the 1980s marked the heyday of Elysium, with over a thousand members, by the mid-1990s, membership had begun to drop by 30 to 40 percent, maintenance expenses were high, especially since one of the conditions of the operating permit was a costly road expansion, and, most importantly, times had changed.[124] The sixties and seventies were long over, previously esoteric practices like yoga, meditation, massage, and other therapies had moved into the mainstream, and AIDS literally killed off the Aquarian dream of free love. Nudism continued to flourish in the United States but in private retreats that were more like vacation resorts. In the 1990s, Elysium might have seemed a little hokey. Then, on May 7, 1995, Ed Lange died of prostate cancer. With their fearless leader gone, Elysium fell victim to the all-too-common infighting over the estate. After five unpleasant years of legal wrangling, Lange's daughters sold the land and the Topanga era was over. The membership was devastated and tried to reestablish Elysium at a site in Malibu, but it was too expensive and closed in 2001. With Elysium went Los Angeles County's only nudist camp and the end of the United States' singular publisher of nudist and sex therapy literature.

As much as nudism tried to be a social movement tied to the wholesome pursuit of bodily health, academic studies of human psychology, a channel for building self-esteem, and a means to marry the spiritual quests of the 1960s to a lengthy American history of body perfectionism, the sticky wickets were sex and capitalism. Neither one doomed the nudist enterprise, but they certainly changed the landscape of possibility in unanticipated ways. Hartman and Fithian's surprise at how political public nudism became as feminism, gay rights, and environmentalism gathered momentum around the issue of free beaches was one indication that the free and natural lifestyle had grown outward and more radical. The encounter between nudist retreats and the sexual experimentation of the 1970s, however, suggested that the free and natural lifestyle had also turned inward, producing a more hedonistic side of American body culture that flourished in the privacy of suburban homes.

CHAPTER 4

SWINGING SUBURBS

Journalist Gay Talese spent most of the 1970s researching the effects of the sexual revolution on the American cultural landscape.[1] He was less interested in the most sensational aspects of the sex industry, or the deviance revealed by the Kinsey reports, than how mostly white, professional, middle-class Americans spent the postwar era exploring and consuming sex. The result, published in 1980, was his hit five-hundred-page exposé, *Thy Neighbor's Wife*. In it, Talese explained how the sexuality simmering under the surface of the repressive 1950s resulted in legal challenges to the Comstock Laws, including the 1959 overturning of the US ban on publishing *Lady Chatterley's Lover*, *Fanny Hill*, and *Tropic of Cancer*; the success of Hugh Heffner's *Playboy* empire; the mainstreaming of erotic art films like *Last Tango in Paris*; and a whole swath of new sexual attitudes and behaviors.[2] What made Talese's book a bestseller, though, were his "on the beat" investigative reports and his "new journalism" technique of literary embellishment that immersed his readers in the narrative. *Thy Neighbor's Wife* opens with a boy masturbating to photographs of nudist model, Diane Webber, in *Sunshine and Health* magazine, and ends, appropriately enough, with Talese receiving a "happy ending" from a New York City masseuse who "sprinkled his groin with puffs of powder and adroitly proceeded to stroke him to orgasm."[3]

The critics pretty much hated the book, finding it to be an already outdated, even naïve, view of American sexual liberation, with Talese "like a Rip Van Winkle waking wide-eyed in the arms of a sex-therapy group" and sexist to boot.[4] Susan Jacoby, traumatized by Brian De Palma's *Dressed to Kill*, argued that the fact that the movie had come out on the heels of *Thy Neighbor's Wife* and Nancy Friday's best-selling *Men in Love*, a compendium of male sexual fantasies, was a foreboding indicator of the state of American sexual politics. Jacoby wrote in the *New York Times* that "the male fantasies [Friday] has catalogued in graphic detail are the raw material, uninterrupted by digressions on the Comstock laws or the *Playboy* empire, of Mr. Talese's attempt to ingest, digest, and regurgitate the whole history of sex in America." While colorfully evoking vomit in describing *Thy Neighbor's Wife*, Jacoby reminded readers that the sexual revolution mostly liberated men, not women, as "the consequences of living out certain sexual fantasies—specifically, fantasies of impersonal sex—weigh more heavily on women than on men. In Mr. Talese's ode to the sexual revolution, there is no mention of venereal disease or pregnancy."[5]

However much critics may have disliked the book, the public loved it and Doubleday knew they would, having given Talese an advance of over a million dollars. Six months before it came out, *Thy Neighbor's Wife*'s film rights were bought by United Artists for $2.5 million while a combination of paperback and excerpt rights added up to another million in split profits for Talese and Doubleday.[6] All totaled, *Thy Neighbor's Wife* fetched one of the largest selling prices of any book optioned in the American publishing industry, a record that would be tied only in the early 1990s by John Grisham's *The Client* and Michael Crichton's *Disclosure*.[7] Whatever Talese's shortcomings, according to the East Coast literati, his book hit a public nerve and its popularity signified deep fascination with the sexual behavior of everyday people. Ultimately, that was what made *Thy Neighbor's Wife* different from other books about sex—it wasn't dealing with the sensational, deviant, or far-out, and it wasn't itself pornographic, although plenty of pornography was referenced. In fact, one of the major criticisms was that it was simply dull—today, it reads well although it is startlingly straight and gender normative. There are few references to homosexuality and not a trans person to be found.

What the critics failed to explain was how one gets from the adolescent masturbatory potential of nudist magazines to the casual sexuality of an urban massage parlor and that was, by far, the most interesting part. The bridge between nudism and the sexual revolution's fallout was what the *New York Times* dismissed as a "free-sex colony."[8] Indeed, the longest section of *Thy Neighbor's Wife*'s was dedicated to the marriage of John and Barbara Williamson who, like many couples in the 1970s, explored the sexually liberated possibilities of "open" marriages. Unlike other couples, the Williamsons achieved international notoriety for establishing the Sandstone Foundation for Community Systems Research in 1969, better known as the Sandstone Retreat.

A clothing-optional, sexually permissive, members-only swingers club nestled in Los Angeles's Topanga Canyon, near Elysium, Sandstone married nudism to the sexual revolution, producing the ultimate eroticism of free and natural living. At Sandstone, social nudity was beside the point as members paid dues to explore group sex, public sex, and the exchanging of marital partners. Being naked was no big deal. A 1975 documentary about Sandstone is remarkable for many reasons explained below but it is especially useful for its unintentional contrast between 1970s natural body aesthetics (casual nudity, long hair, untrimmed pubic hair, no makeup or tattoos, scant jewelry, long outdoor shots of Sandstone's well-manicured grounds) and the depictions of Sandstone's sex parties, which were indoors, awkward, and cradled in Naugahyde, floor-to-ceiling drapery, mirrors, wood paneling, and lots and lots of carpeting. At Sandstone, the free and natural lifestyle and the sexual revolution found a home together in what was essentially a suburban rumpus room. Complete with dinner parties, lawn mowing, and lots of hosing down of its immaculate driveway, Sandstone, tucked away in Topanga Canyon, away from the hustle and bustle of the city, was the suburban nudist fantasy imagined on the cover of *Sunshine and Health* in 1946, but with a lot more sex.

○   ○   ○

Not only did Sandstone signal that the free and natural lifestyle had been eroticized, it also indicated that domesticity had been, too. Family life was presented at Sandstone as compatible with sexual exploration, and the pastoral setting, a suburban canyon, lent the whole exercise a communal ambiance. For social nudity to become sexualized was unsurprising given the pervasiveness of pornography in American culture. The eroticism of nudism in Milton Luros and Stan Sohler's pornographic magazines had already made that shift evident. Sandstone's suburban context, however, also revealed that the sexualizing of domestic life had made inroads into the free and natural lifestyle. This was an outcome of sexual exploration, certainly, but it also exposed a fetishism of suburban domesticity already prevalent in postwar pulp fiction and B movies.[9]

Suburbia in the 1950s, like many features of the Cold War cultural landscape, was racked with anxiety as it was presumed by social observers and medical experts to harbor social ills such as emasculated sexual inadequacy and female nymphomania while it simultaneously cradled good, healthy, patriotic American families.[10] While critics of the suburbs over the past thirty years have rightly focused on the racial segregation that accompanied suburbanization, as well as the alienating experience it created for women, popular and academic criticism in the 1950s and 1960s smacked of an ugly misogyny that reflected a deep fear of the feminization of suburban living space. In September 1955, for example, the National Institute of Mental Health presented a report to the American Society of Planning Officials and the Community Planning Association of Canada that was harshly critical of the "matriarchal society" that suburbia had birthed.[11] According to one Dr. Leonard J. Duhl, "the suburbs are dominated by mothers, and children know fathers only as night-time residents and week-end guests. This is responsible for maladjusted children . . . as youngsters have become oriented toward their mothers only, rather than toward both sexes, which they need for normal development."[12]

Meanwhile, *Playboy* magazine, playing to every insecurity a suburban adult male might have had, suggested that the domesticity of the postwar tract home infantilized and feminized their readers with its family rooms and open-plan layouts that minimized male privacy (and the ability to enjoy *Playboy* in peace, one might gather). As historian Elizabeth Fraterrigo notes, *Playboy* offered an alternative whereby "the magazine mapped out space in the penthouse and the city to counter both the apparent encroachment of women into the public sphere and the 'feminized' spaces of suburbia."[13] Whatever Hugh Heffner's contributions to the sexual revolution, his magazine's anti-suburban marketing strategy fell neatly in line with the unapologetically sexist view that male desires for entertainment and sexual fulfillment were to be found *only* in urban venues rather than suburban homes. In *Playboy*, suburbia, by virtue of its married female inhabitants, was a frigid, emasculating force. This created a troubling cultural paradox because suburbia, with its family-making role in American society, was upheld in the postwar era as a sexualized key to national economic prosperity, political and social stability, and a consumerism-based domestic ideology that could fend off the Cold War's communist threat.[14] The problem seemed to be that suburbia should promote sex, but only the procreative kind that bred little American consumers. Fun, commitment-free sex was to be found elsewhere.

The free and natural lifestyle, with its focus on sexual health and wholesome family togetherness, would seem well-placed to absorb some of these contradictions and offer a drug-free antidote to so much cultural angst. To be sure, the free and natural lifestyle already had been nicely absorbed into suburban life with its emphases on indoor-outdoor living and the integrated display of bodies and commodities by the backyard pool. If not overtly sexual, suburban domesticity certainly could be *sexy*. Indeed, it was in the suburbs that swinging took hold as the middle-class married variant of the sexual revolution and it was in suburban settings that the dalliances of nymphomaniac housewives played out in seedy pulp fiction and B movies.[15] The suburban promise of safe, supervised, family life was often portrayed in cheap novels as under threat, or a fallacy to begin with, but the city was no salvation, either. Unlike *Playboy*'s celebration of urban settings as male sexual playgrounds, fictional narratives did not hold up the city as a salve for frustrated libidos so much as yet another troubled landscape, this one corrupted by corporate greed and state bureaucracies that undermined whatever good American values one might hold. Buried in pulp's baroque plotlines and erotic films' settings were tensions between suburban and urban life that were neither resolved by repressing sexuality nor alleviated by encouraging sexual freedom.

Pulpy novels with racy plots pervaded 1950s and 1960s American popular culture. Sold largely to white, middle-class men through mail-order catalogues, adult bookstores, and newsstands, cheap erotica was widely available, mass produced, and very popular.[16] There were many subgenres of pulp erotica, ranging from white-collar sexcapades like *Expense Account Sinners* (1961) and *Erotic Executives* (1964) to freaky circus sex, such as *Sex Carnival* (1965), *Psycho Circus* (1966), and *Caged Lust* (1967). One of the largest of the subgenres, however, was sexy suburbia, which may have revealed as much about the demographics of its readers as it reflected popular fantasies about white, middle-class sexuality. Titles like *Suburban Wife* (1958), *Suburban Sin Club* (1959), *The Big Bedroom* (1959), *Bachelor in Suburbia* (1962), *Suburban Sex* (1963), and *Shopping Center Sex* (1964) promised readers an inside peek at wife-swapping, orgies, key parties, lesbianism, and booze-fueled infidelity. An insatiable public appetite for popular sexual academics meant that pulp erotica could also masquerade as scientific study and American suburbia provided a rich research lab. Irving Wallace's *The Chapman Report* (1960), a fictional account of Kinsey's *Sexual Behavior in the Human Female*, explored the sensual exploits and sexual pathologies of women in wealthy Los Angeles suburbs.[17] Uncovering the people behind a sexologist's dry statistics may have been the stated goal of *The Chapman Report* but the science was lost, according to a scathing *New York Times* review, "in a swamp of hectic erotica."[18]

There are too many suburbia-themed erotic pulp novels to survey here but an examination of a few highlights the subgenre's major themes, all of which speak to a general fear that American domesticity was not all that it was cracked up to be. For starters, the novels frequently feature a difficult marital tension, often related to women's labor. Popular culture may have celebrated the 1950s happy housewife but the fact is most women, including married ones, worked for wages. In Oren A. Lang's *Shopping Center Sex* (1964), all the

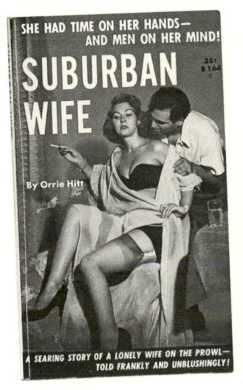

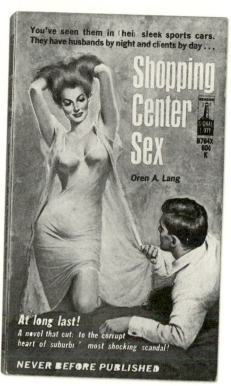

FIGURE 38. Pulp fiction eroticizes suburbia in the late 1950s and early 1960s. Collection of the author.

women work—as doctors, models, and prostitutes—and the men function mainly as props. Sex is often a figment of overactive imaginations, rather than an actual act, and seems less important than acquiring clothes, household goods, and status. Sandra, who pimps out her neighbors to pay for a busted sewer line, finds that "money and glamor even bought friends."[19] In *Suburban Sex* (1963), Harry and Sonia Felton experience marital strife stemming from Sonia's boredom in the fictional suburb, Belle Valley. Before their move from the city, Sonia had happily worked in a department store where she had made a good salary, so good, in fact, that Harry "had been hurt, bewildered, confused that his wife earned more than he did."[20] Not especially interested in motherhood, and left alone for much of the day, Sonia enjoys sex regularly with two different boyfriends and Winnie, the housewife next door. When Harry finally catches her in flagrante at the novel's end, Sonia packs up and returns joyfully to the city, reuniting with her lover, Luke, who proposes. Sonia agrees, but only on the condition that they will "never, never, never live in the suburbs!"[21]

If Sonia Felton found suburban domestic life oppressive, Korean War veteran, Daniel Sprague, the protagonist of Edward Ronns's *The Big Bedroom* (1959), finds his beautiful suburban housewife to be, well, *too* suburban. He sees Joan's constant personal upkeep as troubling, "this abject slavery to fashion was unnatural and disturbing," and her attention to housekeeping pathological: "One of the changes was this compulsive neatness she exhibited, her efforts to keep the house always just so, as if it awaited at any moment a swarm of neurotic photographers from one of the national housekeeping magazines."[22] Tempted into an affair with his ex-wife, Faith, Sprague finds himself ensnared in a blackmail scheme too convoluted to follow and learns, ultimately, that he loves his family despite his reservations about his life as a "commuter, moving back and forth in a daily routine, the perfect image of the twentieth-century robot. Cookouts on the lawn in summer, a do-it-yourself carpenter's bench to work at in the winter, fuel bills to worry about, car repairs, irritations over the failing railroad service."[23] Suburbia might be boring but its predictable, if relentless, cycle of work and consumerism seemed preferable to messing around with the manipulative floozies connected to his diabolically corrupt boss.

Most authors of pulp erotica wrote under pseudonyms because they had to navigate the same treacherous legal waters as the nudist magazine industry but one true master of the genre, Orrie Hitt, proudly published under his own name. Born in 1917, Hitt raised a family in Port Jervis, New York, and made a living as an insurance salesman, radio announcer, hunting and fishing club manager, and writer of erotic fiction.[24] His novels are notable for their snappy dialogue and sympathetic characters troubled by bad decisions, difficult situations, and forces well beyond their control. The novels also have a strong sense of place. Pulp fiction enthusiast, Brian Greene, writes that "the towns (usually rural New York) depicted in Hitt's novels are often clearly split between 'good' and 'bad' sections, and it's the latter that generally get covered in the books. Often, there is one particular, shameful street in the burg, where all the prostitution, drug dealing, and such occur, and this is where many of Hitt's characters work and live."[25]

Hitt's *Suburban Wife* (1958) is a case in point. Millicent Ford, and her husband, Andy, live in a working-class suburb of New York. She spends her evenings drinking at the Central Bar, hoping that gum and perfume will cover the smell of booze when Andy returns home from his city job at an advertising agency. Bored, broke, anxious to have a child, neglected by her husband, and rapidly descending into a state of desperate alcoholism, Millicent seeks reprieve in her sexual encounters with the equally unhappy married men who float around her town. Millicent is racked by fears of aging, getting impregnated by one of her flings, and having her deviant behavior discovered by her husband, who she resents, but whose attention she craves. Her body is her currency and Millicent is frustrated that her body has not shaped the life she wants: "There was nothing else to do, nothing else to think about, so she looked at her legs. They were nice legs, tapered and smooth. Free of all hair. The kind of legs that most men thought were exciting. But Andy didn't care. He didn't care worth a damn."[26] Millicent's body attracts plenty of men but, unlike the protagonist of *The Big Bedroom*, Millicent finds neither solace nor escape. One of her lovers turns out to be a psychopathic insurance salesman and Millicent is implicated in his crimes. In the end, Millicent and Andy patch up their marriage and recommit to their suburban life. Free and natural living does not have much of a place here; Hitt's world is not one of health seeking and wholesome nakedness. In fact, Millicent's relaxed attitude toward nudity seems to be a source of her husband's angst: "She always slept in the raw, and though Andy hadn't said so she knew he thought there was something indecent about the habit."[27]

     ○   ○   ○

If fictionalized suburbia was subject to the erotic fantasies of a mass readership, the wholesome domesticity presented in nudist films was also affected by the ease of access to pornography. The initial effect was on where the films could be seen more so than what the films showed, although that would change, too. The sharp contrast between the safe, familial space of nudist films' projected visual haven, and the seedy urban space of the cheap theaters where the movies were shown, disturbed the nudist faithful and posed a challenge to advocates of free and natural living: if both suburbia and the city were eroticized zones, where does one go? In 1959, Ken Price, a nudist and ASA staff photographer, tried to find out, first by visiting the reputable Paramount Theater in downtown Los Angeles to see a movie marketed as a visit to "an American nudist colony," *The Naked Venus*. It was, Price reported, like many nudist films, a snooze and, like many features proclaiming to showcase actual nudist camps, ridiculous. As Price put it, "no one camp I've ever heard of offers mountain scenery, a splendid beach, California shrubbery and Florida palms, members supplied by Central Casting (only 36" busts, please) and social companions whose figures terminate abruptly at the belt line."[28] Price also sought out a theater on Los Angeles's seedier Main Street showing *Back to Nature*, which actually did take place at a real nudist camp in California, but it too was an embarrassing exercise for Price who, while sticking unpleasantly to the cheap plastic theater seats, cringed as he recognized friends in the background footage.[29]

Price's point in contrasting the two theaters was to highlight a problem with publicizing nudism through movies, especially during an era racked by conflicting ideas and laws about what constituted obscenity and a surge in newly explicit film. Nudism was either showcased as "art," and subsequently cheesy, unrealistic, and a tacky way to show breasts, or it was documentarian in style, reasonably realistic in depicting the day-to-day activities of the camps, but shown in midnight movie theaters and other sketchy venues. As Price put it, "even after thirty years of nudist progress, nudism on film is still forced to keep miserable company." [30] Nudist films, queer film, and pornography often made strange bedfellows as their purveyors were subject to the same obscenity codes as they frequently shared the same spaces. In the wake of a progressive 1957 court decision involving a gay movie theater, the Coronet, for example, Los Angeles theaters could feature nudist films like *Garden of Eden* but often alongside sexier homoerotic titles, a fact that distressed readers of *Sunshine and Health*.[31] Ironically, given the legal struggles actual nudists continued to have, slapping "nudism" on a soft-core B-movie title seemed to get it by censors more easily than not. But as Price pointed out, by putting "the true story of the origin of nudist cults" in the tagline or having a title that smacked of illicit sex, as in *Forbidden Paradise*, the producers alerted card-carrying nudists that this was yet another lame "nudie-cutie" antic.[32] Nudists may have created the genre themselves but they were losing control of it and nudism was in danger of being forever a popular joke or tethered to the sex industries.

While the spaces in which nudist films could be seen might have become seedier, film producers held on to their signature formula of wholesome fun-in-the-sun family togetherness, no male frontal nudity, and plotlines, while often featuring a romantic subnarrative, focused on nudism as a glorious social experiment. *Garden of Eden* (1954), produced by Walter Bibo and shot by cameraman Boris Kauffman, winner of an Academy Award for *On the Waterfront*, featured high production values and the usual tame narrative in which a visit to a nudist camp restores personal freedom and strength of character through natural living. Moreover, *Garden of Eden*, by bringing together a family broken by widowed motherhood and a cold and domineering father-in-law, also reinforced the trope of 1950s suburban domestic ideology that was standard in the nudist magazines and reflected in American popular culture at large. Nevertheless, the release of *Garden of Eden* provoked the wrath of censors when it attracted packed houses from Boston to Los Angeles, and led to another major obscenity case, *Excelsior Pictures Corporation v. Regents of the University* when, in 1956, the Board of Regents of the University of the State of New York refused to grant the film a license.[33] Bibo fought back and, on July 3, 1957, won. The New York State Court of Appeals, led by Judge Charles S. Desmond, found that the State Education Department's motion picture division had overstepped its authority. In penning the court's majority opinion, Desmond wrote that "this picture cannot lawfully be banned since it is not obscene. . . . Nothing sexually impure or filthy is shown or suggested in *Garden of Eden* and so there is no legal basis for censorship."[34] The case was an important one in that it essentially ended the ban on nudity in movies and led to a lot more nudist films.[35] Following on the heels of *Roth*, the decision by the New York Court of Appeals further supported the claim, long made by nudists, that human nakedness was not inherently obscene.

The growing numbers of successful anti-censorship cases also led to a flood of new kinds of cheap, racy films, including the "roughies" of the mid-1960s (campy movies featuring bondage, drugs, "good girls gone bad," and rough sex, hence the nickname), and the soft-core pornography of the early 1970s. The more court cases nudist publishers and filmmakers won, the more the public representations of nudist culture as wholesome and healthy were undercut by the graphic nudity and explicit sexuality that those same cases now legally permitted. Producers of nudist films stayed in the game as long as they could but the intrusion of sexual liberalism and pornography would ultimately doom the genre.

Doris Wishman, a Jewish middle-class woman from New York, made a name for herself as a prolific director, writer, and producer of dozens of exploitation films when, in 1959, she found herself suddenly widowed and needing a way to support herself. With industry connections honed while working as a film booker for a relative, Wishman borrowed $20,000 from her parents and shot the nudist camp feature, *Hideout in the Sun*, in 1960.[36] Other nudist features soon followed, including *Nude on the Moon* (1961), which the New

York State censorship board banned on the basis that it only permitted movies about nudist colonies on Earth, not interstellar nudity.[37]

Perhaps the best-known of her work in the genre, *Diary of a Nudist*, hit theaters in 1961. Delightfully campy in its stilted acting and awkward screen shots, *Diary of a Nudist* tells the tale of Stacy Taylor, girl reporter, deployed to a nudist retreat by her "anti-nudist" boss to write a series of damning undercover exposés. Finding out, of course, that she loves the nudist experience because of its "honesty" and "sincerity," Stacy instead writes a favorable story and gets herself fired. With her feelings deeply hurt, plucky Stacy stays on at the nudist retreat with her new friends only to be horrified when her boss, Arthur, shows up to complete the original exposé. He, too, finds that the place is wonderful, runs a positive front-page story, and the two newly converted nudists realize they are in love with each other. *Diary of a Nudist* is a standout, not just because it almost seems a parody of the genre (although it most certainly is not), but because there is actually very little nudity at all. With the exception of few shots of nudists by the pool, viewers mostly see the actors from the chest up.

As the public taste for nudist films waned in the face of more pornographic options, Wishman began to make racier movies like *Bad Girls Go to Hell* (1965), *Another Day, Another Man* (1966), and *Indecent Desires* (1968). While these films showed neither explicit sex, nor full frontal nudity, they featured breasts, panty shots, and plenty of rape. Breaking with any of the conventions of professional filmmaking, erotic or otherwise, Wishman's roughies had "a quirky personal style: bizarre cutaways to ashtrays, lamps, and squirrels; suggestive lesbian subplots; and gratuitous nudity and violence."[38] If you are watching a black and white film that suddenly zooms in on discarded underpants on the floor, then a boudoir wastepaper basket, and then, suddenly, a skyscraper, you know you are in Wishman territory.

Unlike her nudist films, Wishman's roughies were definitely *urban*. They were filmed in New York, and Wishman luxuriated in long shots of Central Park, the Port Authority bus terminal, and the flow of pedestrians on the street. The sexy stuff happened in apartments and there are no kids to be found. Female protagonists lounge around in lacey bodysuits, often reading, and undressing together. The city is a place where one can find the most exciting, sexy people but it is rife with dangerous predators. Urban life is also expensive; female protagonists frequently find themselves hustling for money, desperately seeking cheap rooms to rent, and ending up selling themselves

FIGURE 39. Nudist offerings, including Doris Wishman's *Diary of a Nudist*, on the marquee of the gritty Town Theater at 444 South Hill Street, Los Angeles, 1965. Photograph by William Reagh. William Reagh Collection, Los Angeles Public Library.

as escorts or prostitutes. Elements of suburban domestic life are sexually fetishized in Wishman's films—housework, hosting, home decoration, high-heeled house slippers, sofas—but it is the city that is eroticized.

With directors like Wishman leaving the nudist genre behind, one stayed in the game just a little longer. In *The Raw Ones* (1965), John Lamb featured a real nudist camp, the Swallows Nudist Resort in El Cajon, a suburb of San Diego. Resisting the traditional nudist narrative of lots of free and natural family togetherness, *The Raw Ones* was presented as *cinéma-vérité* showcasing the nudist activities of fit, young, and, presumably single, adults. Shot silently with a droning voiceover narration that drew connections between nudism and the sex theories of Sigmund Freud and Havelock Ellis, the film relished in lengthy scenes of naked people on trampolines, in swimming pools, and running in the desert. Not only did the lack of family togetherness or any plotline at all signal that *The Raw Ones* was a different kind of nudist film, the multitudinous penis closeups indicated that the era of the traditional nudist film was over. Framing the film as educational documentary did not help with censors, however, and *The Raw Ones* ran into trouble in Los Angeles's Silver Lake district in 1966, when the manager of the Vista Theater was convicted on obscenity charges for screening it.[39]

Lamb, like Wishman, let the nudist genre slide and instead had a more lucrative career producing kinky sexploitation flicks like *Mondo Keyhole* (1966), *Big Beaver Splits the Scene* (1971), and *Sex Freaks* (1974). *Mondo Keyhole*, directed by Jack Hill, which features a drug-addicted, nymphomaniac, suburban housewife whose disinterested husband can only achieve sexual satisfaction by raping the unsuspecting female victims he preys on in the city, marries the sexualized space of American suburbia, as depicted in pulp fiction, to the gritty urban scenarios of mid-1960s pornography. In *Mondo Keyhole*, suburbia is no domestic heaven; it is a disastrous moral void endangering the city where suburban degenerates go to play. In this cultural landscape, there is *nowhere* for free and natural naked living to find a home.

The Sandstone Retreat, and its filmic portrayal, is thus especially useful for thinking about where the free and natural lifestyle landed as the sexual revolution continued to roll through American society. Sandstone founder, John D. Williamson, a charismatic thirty-eight-year-old Alabaman, Korean War veteran, former communications specialist for the US Department of the Interior, and designer of complex missile support systems for Lockheed, believed that a free and natural life could be engineered through behavioral therapy, nude psychotherapy, and sexual exploration. Together with his wife, Barbara, and about two hundred dues-paying members, Williamson practiced sexual intercourse as part of a therapeutic experience he described as human communication exercises. As the promotional brochure distributed to prospective applicants explained, "the concepts underlying Sandstone include the idea that the human body is good, that open expressions of affection and sexuality are good. Members at Sandstone may do anything they like as long as they are not offensive or force their desires on other people."[40]

Like Elysium, Sandstone also offered therapeutic workshops but these were on explicitly sexual topics like "The Cosmic Orgasm" and "Dealing with Sexual Inadequacies in the Singles World." Members were encouraged to bring lotion, incense, a notebook, and a pen.[41] Whereas Elysium was famous in the American nudist community, and achieved notoriety in Los Angeles because of the headlines prompted by its legal controversies, Sandstone received more attention largely because of its coverage in *Rolling Stone* and *Penthouse* and the wild popularity of *Thy Neighbor's Wife*.[42] By the time the book hit the best-sellers lists, and Talese had taken to the airwaves, even discussing Sandstone on *The Tonight Show*, Sandstone had already been closed for four years.

The main reason Sandstone would live on as a cultural touchstone is Jonathan and Bunny Dana's remarkable 1975 documentary.[43] Shot on standard 35 mm film, but with amateur angles and the occasional glimpse of the naked sound guy, *Sandstone* is an incredible artifact for its portrayal of the Williamsons' utopian dream of a new way to live, the casual nature of the sexual encounters depicted, and simply the communal nature of the place. Young children flit about on the outskirts of the film shots. In one scene, two young, and possibly stoned, Sandstone members go shopping for supplies at a wholesale warehouse and spend a fair length of time trying to find the perfect box of individually wrapped chocolates to make the most members happy. In another, Marty, Sandstone's head of promotion, is visited by his middle-aged aunt and her friend. Fully clothed, and giggling nonstop, Marty's aunt cannot get over how nice the place is. She is downright thrilled to be there.

The film's opening scene, however, is another story. The font of *Sandstone*'s opening credits and its gritty electronic musical score evoke typical 1970s pornographic movies and set the stage for the first shot, a tight close-up of a middle-aged white man who looks to be a hard-partying fifty. In the background, one hears Jonathan Dana ask "have you been involved in other sexual situations?" to which the man responds that he had been swinging for six or seven years but explains that the usual scene at private homes produced too short an association to really get to know someone. In contrast, Sandstone, and other "places where they think this way" was the perfect culmination of privacy, individual freedom, and "the great people" that generated real relationships. The camera then pans back and the viewer sees that the man is naked, at a bar, and sitting next to a very young, very pretty, blonde topless woman who is smoking a cigarette. It seems abundantly clear, suddenly, why swinging might have such appeal for the male subject. As the viewer processes the couple's significant age difference, the woman is prompted to explain how she was convinced to join Sandstone and she says, "by my Dad." That's right—she is his daughter. Dana then asks the father if he had watched her having sex and he replies "no," but it "wouldn't bother me" because "what's wrong with making love?"[44]

The scene is intentionally transgressive—the idea of a barely twenty-year-old girl joining her father at a suburban sex club remains shocking and a permissive extreme of sexually liberated living. It is certainly an uncomfortable reformulation of domestic family life. It is also unusual within the logic of the documentary because it is only one of two such scenes. The other involves a dirty old man who shows up at Sandstone with a sex van full of vibrators, mirrors, and stirrups and is more than happy to show anyone who asks how all the gizmos work. Giggling nervously, a young female Sandstone member agrees to be strapped into place while the nameless pervert shines a spotlight on her vagina. The gynecological exam is mercifully brief and one is left wondering who let this guy onto the retreat grounds. Like the father-daughter swinger team, this character seems to be an outlier, or so one hopes.

Much of the movie is dedicated to couples explaining the benefits and challenges of Sandstone's sexual opportunities. One lengthy scene is dedicated to interviews with married couples, shot off of Sandstone grounds. Here, one wife explains how anxious the idea of going to Sandstone makes her, and how unnerved she would be to find her husband having sexual encounters with another woman. Another couple describes how liberating the experience of Sandstone has been as it allowed the husband to have extramarital relationships without guilt and without compromising his marriage. The scene is prolonged and uncomfortable, largely because it feels that there is an awful lot of compromising and marital negotiating to make the Sandstone experience work, none of which seems especially liberating, relaxing, or natural, particularly for the wives. Another sequence depicts the stress between Tom Hatfield, one of Sandstone's managers, and Nancy, the daughter introduced in the film's opening scene, who have coupled up, but experience strain in their new relationship when Nancy continues to sleep with other men as she does not want a "primary relationship." Tom experiences great distress and talks to anyone who will listen about how upset he is. Conferring with John and Barbara, all while in the buff, Tom seems hard pressed to accept John's advice to "pull it together."[45] Domestic life might be fetishized in theory, and monogamy old-fashioned, but, in practice, it was still sacred turf.

The climax of the documentary is the filming of one of Sandstone's notorious sex parties, where the adults gather in the main house for a buffet dinner, some clothed, some naked, many discussing everyday things like food, school, and work. There is drinking but it appears moderate, certainly by the standards of the mid-1970s. Then, the residents and guests gather in the basement where some mingle and others get busy on the mattresses laid out for this very purpose. Some are well aware of the cameras, others seem surprised. While sexually explicit, it is not especially pornographic; it is not meant to arouse the viewer but to showcase what liberated sexuality can mean. After it is all over, the film depicts couples playing games of charades. The effect is to make the sexual revolution seem pedestrian, a little boring, and a fair bit of emotional work. *Sandstone* closes with John Williamson finishing the hopeful thought he had articulated at the beginning, that there will be "considerable acceptance of pluralistic styles" as traditional marriage, monogamy, family, and the American work ethic "don't work and won't work." He ends the film with great optimism that the world was changing in a way that would revamp American domestic arrangements and accept Sandstone's paradigm of sexual community.

While the movie openly displayed the sexuality of Sandstone to whoever had the opportunity to see it, and Tom Hatfield spread the message of Sandstone far and wide in his popular memoir, *Sandstone Experience*, the Williamsons had been purposefully vague in the local press, with John telling the *Los Angeles Times*, for example, that "it's a private club doing things we'd rather not discuss."[46] The opacity was the result of trouble with both Los Angeles authorities and neighbors who, in the years following Sandstone's opening in 1969, saw the retreat as yet another example of the sixties generation's outrageous sexual permissiveness. When Ed Lange faced down the courts in the fracas over the 1970 "growth center" licensing ordinance, Sandstone was also named in the case. Whereas Lange refused to apply for the license, and instead fought the courts on the basis that the ordinance interfered with the constitutional right to assemble, John and Barbara Williamson, frightened by the threat of arrest and fines, did apply.[47] The arbitrariness of the process, which was part of Lange's case, was borne out when the Williamsons were denied the license for which they had applied by the County Public Welfare Commission and then promptly cited when John appeared before the Malibu Justice Court to plead to the misdemeanor offense for not having a license.[48] This circular logic was what had brought down Fraternity Elysia and imprisoned Lura Glassey in 1940 and was the impetus behind creating the licensing ordinance in the first place.

Sandstone's application for a license was rejected in the wake of the same charged public meeting in October 1970 when citizens' groups in Topanga Canyon came out loudly in favor of the growth center licensing ordinance and full of vitriol for both Elysium and Sandstone. Distressed owners of homes and businesses loudly complained that hordes of drug-addicted hippie sex freaks had invaded their suburban neighborhood. Representatives from the Topanga Canyon Baptist Church and the Topanga Chamber of Commerce voiced concerns that orgies with "psychedelic overtones" and "free-wheeling sex" were unduly influencing "impressionable children" and destroying housing values.⁴⁹ The sexual revolution had come to the Canyon and residents were not having it. Concerned citizens from the San Fernando Valley charged that "the hippie-oriented Esalen Institute near Big Sur is the mother group for the growth centers" and that these immoral places would "influence impressionable children to experiment with nude clubs." Even worse, according to one Northridge housewife, these centers were conspiring to drag "down our system of free enterprise, freedom of religion, and the morals of youth. They are all tied in together to break down our normal inhibitions."⁵⁰

Free and natural living was not just troubling for its liberated sexual expression but, for some Americans, it represented freedom from organized religion, anti-materialism, and threatened the nation's youth. Given how easily appropriated the free and natural lifestyle was by consumer capitalism, and how inherently at home it could be found in suburban contexts, the moral outrage seems, at the very least, dated and more concerned with maintenance of housing values. Just as in the 1930s, social nudity in the era of the sexual revolution was a metonym for communalism, a perceived threat to the American "way of life."

While the Topanga Canyon anti-growth-center contingent freaked out about the specter of naked Manson-crazed dope-fueled free-loving youth openly having sex on their front lawns, the reality was that the new sexual permissiveness of the 1960s and 1970s reduced the numbers of people interested in nudism at all. Pornography was widely available and people experimented on their own; they didn't necessarily need a nudist experience to shed their American sexual hang-ups. If anything, nudism seemed kind of staid, which is one of the reasons Ed Lange had gone to such lengths to distinguish Elysium from the traditional nudist camp. Growth centers like Elysium and Sandstone became greatly resented by nudist camp owners like Ernie Miller, proprietor of Samagatuma, in Ramona, California, who complained to the press that these "nonconformist camps," as he put it, "like pseudo-nudist magazines, are driving many away from legitimate nudism." As the owner of Oakdale, in San Bernardino, Mel Hocker, bluntly phrased it, "the sexual revolution is killing us."⁵¹ By 1970, both Hocker and Miller, as well as other nudist camp proprietors, reported deep cuts in their membership numbers and speculated that the reason was that people were either fearful that nudist retreats *were* sex camps or figured they were *not*, and thus sought a more libertine naked experience elsewhere. Hocker further worried that "for years legitimate nudist organizations have fought to achieve a good image. These people now come along and give nudism a bad name."⁵²

It didn't help curry favor with traditional nudists, either, when Ed Lange invited Bob Guccione's *Penthouse* to feature Elysium in a piece on nudism. The magazine was very clear that, unlike Sandstone, Elysium was no sex camp, explaining that "touching and sensuality are stressed and encouraged here, although a distinction is made between this and 'sexuality.' Actual . . . activities leading to orgasm are not done in the open." Lange further clarified that "he [saw] nothing wrong with sex out in the open but [felt] we [were] not sociologically ready for it yet."[53] *Penthouse* and Lange may have seen a sharp distinction between sensuality as therapy and open, public sex but this was not a subtlety appreciated by traditional nudists struggling to keep their camps and retreats afloat.

The sexual revolution did not kill off nudism, but it certainly changed and more deeply marginalized it. Indeed, the expansion of the print pornography business in the 1970s decimated the nudist magazines so essential to nudist culture. As pornography moved toward hard-core imagery, the courts grew less lenient, culminating in 1973's *Miller v. California* in which the US Supreme Court case reaffirmed that obscenity was not protected by the First Amendment and invited more conservative standards by shifting the jurisdiction over the definition of obscenity from a unified national one to more repressive local ones. The decision fueled new laws, mostly enacted on the local level, forbidding the sale of magazines with explicit sexual imagery, and especially the blatant display of pubic hair, on newsstands, giving rise to the adult bookstore.[54] In defiance of *Sunshine Book Company v. Summerfield*, the *Miller* case judged nudist magazines erotic and relegated to the same triple-X store as hard-core pornography. Since nudist magazines no longer offered thrills that could compete with the newly raunchy publications, nudist magazines simply grew obsolete.[55] In 1985, a sociological study of adult bookstores in New York found that only 1 percent of magazines sold featured nudism.[56] Today, there are only two published in this country, and they are by subscription only.

Sandstone did not survive past 1976, when the Williamsons sold it and tried, and failed, to raise the money to set up a much larger retreat center in Montana, although the couple continued to host workshops and encounter sessions at their new home in San Francisco. Despite having had a much shorter life than Elysium, and far fewer participants, Sandstone has had a larger cultural presence that cemented the Williamsons' project in the American popular imagination as the apex of the sexual revolution's excesses.[57] In the early 1980s, thousands of single and married white residents of Eastern Seaboard suburbs were still placing nude, sexually explicit ads seeking partners for private sex parties but, by the middle of the decade, the mortal realities of AIDS and other STDs had stifled the open celebration of suburban middle-class swinger culture.[58]

○   ○   ○

If the sexual revolution, and the changes in obscenity law that helped spur it on, eroticized both nudism and suburbia, it also brought the free and natural lifestyle into domestic space in new ways as Americans continued to experiment with the relationship between the built environment and the body. But instead of the emphasis on privacy that was such a key feature of the domestic DIY sunshine architecture of the 1950s, by the late 1960s and 1970s, suburban homes reflected newly relaxed attitudes about family nudity, and not just in nudist families. For example, instead of bathrooms and dressing areas fortified with locks and protocols for the utmost in personal privacy, sprawling, heavily carpeted, open-plan living spaces encouraged families to wander around the house naked, bathe and toilet together, and play in the nude. Wall-to-wall mirrors produced the illusion of space while encouraging both body scrutiny and self-affirmation. Those who could afford it began to build saunas and steam rooms into their homes, taking inspiration from Scandinavian, Japanese, and Native American bathing practices, and ancient hot springs culture, constructing bathrooms that allowed the whole family to use it at one time. This "living bath," according to historian Barbara Penner, "reflected more relaxed social mores, especially the easing of prohibitions around nudity."[59] Meanwhile, the immense popularity of wood paneling helped emphasize the natural design theme of bringing the outside in.

More than any other household installation, the popularity of the hot tub reflected the ubiquity of the free and natural lifestyle, including its nudity, health claims, and casual sexuality, as hot tubs were not just built for bathing but for entertaining. As many a hot tub enthusiast would report, "the experience is good for the circulation, for inducing [sleep], for bringing body and soul together, and for providing a sense of warmth and community with others."[60] In case naked entertaining got out of hand, DIY guides to building one's own alerted homeowners that while hot tubs encouraged naked health and sociability, and enhanced one's living space, they were potential death traps if mixed with drugs and alcohol. Not only did the hot tub become an architectural staple in many a suburban house, it became a cultural phenomenon with its own Venice Beach–based periodical, *Wet: The Magazine of Gourmet Bathing*, which by turns fetishized and mocked the sexuality of domestic nudity. And in a gesture toward subverting the wholesomeness of heterosexual marriage while embracing nudism's cult of natural authenticity, Los Angeles artist Robert Alexander made headlines nationwide by officiating at hot tub nuptials as a hippie rite of passage.

Sexy suburbia did not stop with hot tubs. If early millennial suburban sexual fantasies like *Desperate Housewives* offered a counterweight to self-consciously urban soaps like *Sex in the City*, in Los Angeles's San Fernando Valley the "sexy suburbs" fantasy produced a global multibillion dollar pornography industry. Housed temporarily inside ordinary tract homes or, sometimes, posh gated communities, pornographers and their stars and staff stage erotic dramas in mundane settings. Alongside breakfast nooks, kiddy pools, and two-car garages, the majority of all American triple-X films are shot for an enormous international audience. But as Laura Kipnis argues in her work

FIGURE 40. "A thirteen-classroom Montessori school in Santa Monica is converted into a hot tub club where patrons can melt their cares away. Two women play backgammon on a floating game board, 1980." Photograph by Mike Mullen. *Herald-Examiner* Collection, Los Angeles Public Library.

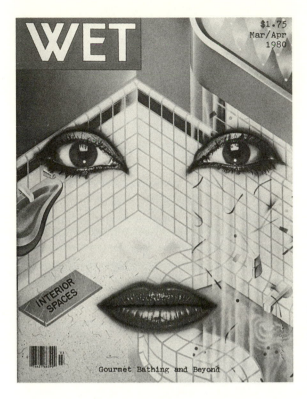

FIGURE 41. The body and the bathroom become one in *Wet: The Magazine of Gourmet Bathing,* March–April 1980. Collection of the author.

on pornography and the politics of fantasy, what these suburban film sets promise, ultimately, is the eroticism of the banal.[61] It becomes less a convenience that pornography is made in the suburbs and more a necessity of a sought-after aesthetic in which the everyday, even as quotidian as a suburban backyard, promises unfettered experiential sexuality. It is within the candor of triple-X pornography that domestic fetishism finds its true home.

Perhaps no one captures the marriage of the free and natural lifestyle with the aesthetics of suburban erotica better than photographer Larry Sultan. Sultan, who grew up in the San Fernando Valley in the 1950s and 1960s, made a career capturing the sublime tension between the dignity of his human subjects and the overly bright landscapes of suburban tract housing, manicured lawns, plush interiors, and immaculate patios. Indoor-outdoor living is so perfectly executed in Sultan's frames that, at first glance, it is not always clear if you are seeing indoors or out. A man practicing his golf swing is featured on a shag carpet so plush it resembles a championship green while a backyard is shot through a sliding glass door so clean that it takes a minute to process that it is there. On the one hand, there is a cold artificiality about the setting and posture of the people that could serve, by now, as a fairly cliché indictment of cheesy suburban life. But, on the other, the familiarity of the scenes is so touching and warm that the viewer feels comforted, almost swaddled, by the overwhelming domesticity of Sultan's world. In perhaps his most famous series, shot between 1997 and 2003, Sultan photographed the off-stage moments of pornography shoots in the Valley, the quintessential trope of Southern California suburban living. Porn actors lounge on plastic lawn chairs, blow-up mattresses, and sofas, waiting for their cue. Production assistants nap between scenes while naked actors share a laugh or grab a glass of water from the kitchen. The images are weird and anxiety-producing but also funny and inclusive. The viewer, whether she likes it or not, fits right in. Sultan himself has commented on the unsettling nature of his "Valley" series:

> It is common for adult-film companies to shoot in tract houses—the homes of dentists and attorneys and day traders whose family photographs can be seen in the background, and whose decorating tastes give the films their particular look: It's as if one family went on vacation for a few days, leaving everything in the house intact, and another family, an odd assembly of unrelated adults, has temporarily taken up residence. . . . In these films, lazy afternoons are interrupted not by noisy children but by the uncontrollable desires of delivery boys, babysitters, coeds, and cops. They crowd in the master bedrooms and spill out onto the patios and into the pools that look just like our neighbors' pools, like our pool. And by photographing this I'm planted squarely in the terrain of my own ambivalence—that rich and fertile field that stretches out between fascination and repulsion, desire, and loss. I'm home again.[62]

Another feature of Sultan's work that both unsettles and intrigues his viewers is the blurry line between public and private with which he plays. Being in someone's home is an intimate act, as is having sex, but somehow filming sex in someone else's home becomes strangely distant and public. It is a commercial venture that relies on a paying public and Sultan's photographs invite in the public gaze. Yet an element of personal intimacy remains, less in the porn actresses waiting for their cue than in the carefully trimmed house-plants that the homeowner has left on the kitchen counter in the hope that someone, between scenes, might remember to water them.

The Williamsons may have brought suburban sexual fantasies to life at Sandstone by marrying the free and natural lifestyle to the sexual revolution, but the American sexual imaginary had long seized on the suburbs as a fertile environment where social repression could breed sexual desire. *Because* of its intimate domesticity, not despite it, the free and natural lifestyle took hold in the American suburbs and laid the path for an integration of nudity, sexuality, domesticity, and environmental artifice in which the filming of pornography becomes, well, natural.

○   ○   ○

While Sandstone was at its peak popularity in the early 1970s, and the sexual revolution under the scrutiny of Gay Talese, and other cultural observers, proponents of free and natural living were not just swinging in the privacy of the suburbs; thousands were also taking to the nation's beaches and city streets to make a claim to naked living in public space. Nude beach activism would draw from traditional nudist culture, although many traditional social nudists resented all the negative publicity, and it would draw, too, from the gay, feminist, environmental, and civil rights movements. While the sexual revolution involved changes in how Americans lived their intimate lives, it was also deeply political, as in the fight for reproductive rights, which resulted in 1973's *Roe v. Wade*, and in challenges to regressive nudity laws that historically could condemn an innocently naked person to imprisonment on felony sex offender charges. "Freeing" beaches for safe and legal nudity became a rallying cry as the sexual revolution, social justice activism, and social nudism coalesced around the meaning of being "free and natural" in public. Once again, the naked body would take on political significance but, this time, the fight would be on a national stage, would permeate local and state politics and, on occasion, become violent. At stake, increasingly, was the right to self-expression in public and the right to claim public space as appropriate for a free and natural living experience that was, in fact, free.

CHAPTER 5

HOW TO FREE A BEACH

On July 10, 2012, many readers of the *New York Times* were surprised to learn that not only was there a nude beach in Mazomanie, Wisconsin, but that it had been a state-sanctioned public nude beach since the 1980s with as many as seventy thousand visitors a year. The reason Mazo Beach, found on the Lower Wisconsin River, ended up on the front page of the national section of the paper was because state and local authorities were issuing growing numbers of citations for lewd and lascivious behavior, with as many as forty-two arrests in 2011. More surprising, perhaps, was that the tickets were not written up for the nude sunbathers and skinny-dippers who had traditionally occupied the beach; instead, what attracted the attention of the Wisconsin Department of Natural Resources and the local cops was drug use and sexual activity on Mazo itself, and in the surrounding woods. The problem had apparently grown so troublesome that rather than have a resource-strapped police department deploy more patrol officers the state closed public access to almost seventy acres of forest.[1]

For nude beach activists led by the Oshkosh-based Naturist Society, what made the citations and arrests most worrisome was that the arbitrary line between indecent and simple nudity, a line long negotiated by nudists and local authorities, had become, once again, ambiguous. As a result, long-accepted nude sunbathing and swimming could be redefined as lewd under the law and prohibited. Equally upsetting, Mazo had historically been a discreet place, perhaps mythic in local lore, but generally left alone by authorities. It was in the 1970s that nude beaches attracted large crowds and achieved notoriety as places where hippie youth acted out the sexual and psychedelic excesses of the counterculture. That time had long since passed, and yet Mazo Beach was attracting national attention decades later for similar problems. The main reason for the increase in traffic at Mazo, in fact, was the internet; beaches quietly visited by locals had become easier to find through nudist websites and Google maps, encouraging use by those uninitiated into the protocols of public nude recreation.

Apart from private resorts, many of which have their own beaches, there are only a few legal public nude beaches in the United States. What exists instead is a thicket of complicated local laws and customs, which are constantly renegotiated as the cultural and political landscape bends and shifts. Some nude beaches are technically illegal but so remote that no one cares. Many nude beaches are accepted by local authorities, who essentially turn a blind eye, but complaints from other beachgoers can result in unpleasant encounters with police and citations or arrests. A handful of nude beaches, such as Haulover Beach in Miami, have legal designations but only for part of the beach, which can create tensions if there is spillover onto the non-clothing-optional sections. The battle to establish legal nude beaches in the United States has been deeply contentious, pitting developers, police, and social conservatives against beachgoers and nudists, often with dissatisfying outcomes for everyone. Nevertheless, hundreds of American beaches remain nude by custom and a distinctive part of the civic imagination and collective memory of cities and towns across the country.

A look back at over fifty years of free beach activism reveals a large social movement dedicated to personal freedom, sexual liberation, open access to public space, and a return to a state of natural being in the thick of modern urban environments. While nudity and sexuality, both straight and gay, were often the initial cause for consternation, concern and, ultimately, repression among the opposition, the struggle over nude beaches reflects deeper strife over social control, sexual surveillance, property rights, and the line between public and private citizenship rights, all of which have long been characteristic of policy debates and power dynamics in American cities and suburbs. The goal to live naturally, seemingly so easy in theory, ran into trouble once the naked body became the site for the meaning of "freedom." For nude beach activists, "freedom" meant public nudity in designated zones but not necessarily pursuing naked living in other parts of their lives. For organized nudists, "freedom" was a life lived in the nude without legal hassles, onlookers, or pot-smoking hippies messing everything up. While nude beaches still exist all over the United States, there is nothing like the summers of 1972 or 1974 when tens of thousands took to the beaches in the nude with the hope of legalizing their bodily exposure. Meanwhile, organized social nudism continues in private camps, retreats, and suburban communities, while an expensive resort culture caters to sexualized "lifestyle" nudism. Much like many urban struggles throughout the United States, free public space has been replaced by private sites that encourage both consumerism and surveillance.

The most active era of nude beach activism in the United States was in the 1970s as the nation seemed simultaneously poised to accept public nudity along with relaxed sexual mores and prepared to tamp down on anything appearing the slightest bit licentious. In writing about the history of pornography, Whitney Strub states: "a peculiar ambivalence regarding sex and sexuality marks American history. Oscillating between repression and indulgence as various configurations of power form and dissolve, this American ambivalence toward sexuality made pornography a salient issue for politicians."[2] Nudism in general, and the issue of public nudity specifically, occupied a similarly ambivalent place within the American psyche but, given the right context, could blow up into a fraught political dispute eagerly seized upon by politicians seeking a hot button issue. The complexity of nude beach politics is further highlighted by beaches' sexual geography; historically, they have been sites for both gay and straight cruising, a fact that runs afoul of nudists' claims to a nonerotic body culture. While beach nudity and beach sexuality may, in fact, be distinct, their coexistence has contributed to strained public relations and a recent national surge of legislation against beach nudity. One of the key challenges for activists has been that once spaces are "freed" for the body, they are also eroticized, altering the spaces' initial purpose and audience, and often ending their public availability because of the misuse of a few.

Nude beach advocates are well-organized, nationally situated, and legally well-versed in public land-use regulation; First Amendment constitutional rights; local and federal sex and obscenity laws; and coastal accessibility disputes, which often mirror non-nudist beach access fights. While the ambiguous meanings of the naked body should make it an unstable foundation for a social movement, one of the most sustained and tenacious examples of American popular environmentalism and embodied political activism has been the effort to liberate public beaches for nude suntanning and recreation.[3]

The struggle to establish legal nude beaches in the United States has also proven a point of contention within organized nudism, creating a split, sometimes ugly, sometimes negotiable, between nude beach advocates who claim the beach as natural, public space, and social nudists who prefer to keep their practice on private property and away from the glare of politics and media. In fact, most social nudists do not consider naked beachgoers nudists at all, given that they live clothed most of the time. Meanwhile, free beach activists have argued since the 1970s that their movement, with its celebration of "freedom and spontaneity," in the words of sex therapist and naturist, Leon Elder, represented a welcome "break from the tradition of the old-time nudist colony."[4] There has always been overlap between card-carrying nudists and nude beach activists, but they are often mutually exclusive with differing goals and political strategies. A paradoxical characteristic of social nudism in the United States is, in fact, its practice in private. While being out-of-doors is important to the nudist lifestyle, since full body exposure to sun and air is one of the main objectives, it is primarily a subculture practiced behind closed doors, gates, and membership fees. It is not difficult to become a member—most clubs simply ask for identification and annual dues, occasionally a background check—but the properties are private and membership revocable. In contrast is public nudity, a controversial and generally illegal practice, with the media associating "public" and "nude" with streaking, flashing, exhibitionism, or the otherwise lewd behavior of social outliers.

Public nudity, however, has an equally legitimate history as a cultural and political practice in the United States and its proponents have struggled to characterize it as a natural and progressive act and one that should have legal protection. It has been an uphill battle, however, because it is next to impossible to control its visibility, or how this visibility is interpreted by onlookers, and it *is* impossible to control who participates. This is part of the appeal of beach nudism—that it is economically "free" as well as physically "free"—but this open public nudity is also accompanied by overt sexuality and voyeurism. The most common complaints against nude beaches, in fact, are that they encourage public sex and attract onlookers, from the casual passersby to pornographers with cameras. Waxing rather philosophical in their graphic 1977 account of the sexual politics of nude beaches, sociologists Jack Douglas, Paul Rasmussen, and Carol Ann Flanagan write that "like so much of life, the nude beach naturalness and casualness appear to have limiting conditions," concluding that it was next to impossible for public nudity to occur in isolation from erotic display, sexual competitiveness, and body scrutiny.[5] Free beach activists like Leon Elder, however, continued to assert that rather than a charged sexual site, "a free beach is a place where people find liberation from the trappings of civilization and share the common denominator of being their simplest selves."[6]

Drawing on the social movements of the 1960s, nude beach activism has been of a piece with gay rights, feminist politics, burgeoning environmental concerns, and an anti-racist agenda to desegregate all aspects of American society. As nude beach activism radicalized, proponents preferred to call it a "free beach" movement, implying a popular environmentalist impulse to expand public access to natural spaces in the United States, nude or otherwise. This was, and continues to be, a marked break from traditional social nudism, which has favored keeping access to their camps, retreats, and resorts private, largely because of its beleaguered history of harassment and litigation. Nevertheless, as nude beach politics, and clashes with police, accelerated in the early 1970s, establishing many of the legal and practical precedents for future struggles to free American beaches, the American Sunbathing Association (ASA) came out in support of free beach activism by actively publicizing where free beaches could be found and providing maps to members. The ASA defined "free beaches" as "all natural swimming facilities that are easily accessible to the general public, are fairly well known locally, and are relatively free from official harassment. And by 'natural' we mean ocean beaches, inland beaches, rivers and lakes."[7] Thus, to "free" a beach meant that it had to be publicly accessible, it had to have a natural water feature, and it had to be safe from aggressive patrolling. The fight to free beaches would continue until the present day, with little sustained agreement between local authorities and nude beachgoers.

Beaches, of course, have racialized histories as segregated spaces of white privilege and as tourist sites for what Catherine Cocks calls the "tropicalization" of the body, whereby the intentional taking-on of color through leisure serves as a marker of social status.[8] In the early 1970s, for example, "free the beaches" became the rallying cry of Revitalization Corps, the social activist group founded by Ned Coll to fight poverty, structural racism, and segregation in New England. Connecticut's system of privatized beaches and exclusionary zoning ordinances kept beaches white and wealthy while the state's large black population was relegated to the remaining public beaches, which were often polluted and poorly maintained. Coll, an Irish American, challenged the system by bringing busloads of mostly African American kids from the rougher parts of Hartford to Connecticut's wealthiest communities, "unannounced, demanding access to the beach, and challenging vacationing families and local residents to do their part in the making of a more equal, integrated society."[9] These protest actions provoked resentment and fierce resistance from Connecticut's rich homeowners because, as Andrew W. Kahrl puts it, "this was how Jim Crow worked in the Northeast, through ostensibly color-blind and race-neutral land-use regulations and the privatization (in fact if not in name) of public space."[10] The stakes were much higher for anti-racist activists putting their safety on the line to break Jim Crow than for nude beach activists, but along with the slogan "free the beach," they shared the convictions of public space and free access at the pivotal moment in American urban history when both were being lost.

It is impossible to trace when Americans first sunbathed and swam nude. What people do in secret or in secluded areas elude the historian's eye, and even how they define nakedness, a seeming absolute, can vary.[11] In the eighteenth century, Europeans and Australians of means made use of bathing machines, small wooden rooms on wheels into which a patient climbed, undressed, and then was rolled into the sea to be dunked naked into frequently freezing salt water.[12] For this therapeutic bathing, it was important for women to remain unseen, but nude male bathing and swimming became increasingly normative in Great Britain and Europe well into the nineteenth century.[13] The United States did not adopt the practice of the therapeutic beach to the same extent but what is clear is the nude beach has been a clandestine part of American culture for well over a hundred years. An examination of national newspapers reveals numerous reports of illegal nude bathing and the fines incurred as a result. In 1904, for example, two Japanese immigrants swimming nude in Long Beach, California were arrested and fined $5 apiece.[14] In the early 1930s, rich white skinny-dippers accompanied by servants attracted unfriendly attention in Santa Monica before taking off in a chauffeured automobile, while in Redondo Beach, two youths, one the son of a public defender, were hauled up before a judge who fined them $100 each for swimming naked at one in the morning.[15]

These few examples, all from Southern California, spoke not just to the illegality of nude bathing in the early twentieth century, but also to the complex shortcomings of tying a city's economic fortunes to the body. Long Beach, for example, had, since the 1880s, marketed itself as a seaside resort for people of refined tastes by building high-end health sanitaria and bathhouses. One such venue, the Wilmore City Bathhouse, combined the health of the body with the cultivation of the soul and spirit as orchestras, opera singers, and other high art performers were hired to play to the bathers below.[16] As the city grew, and the new track of the Pacific Electric Railway that connected Los Angeles to Long Beach spurred more oceanfront development, a new bathhouse opened in 1902 that attracted large numbers of working-class customers. Almost immediately, the city government put in place an ordinance regulating the wearing of bathing suits on public thoroughfares so that wet and sandy bathers would not brush up against well-dressed passersby. City trustees argued that the ordinance was not about morals or decency but simply protecting its wealthy guests.

By the early 1920s, however, the political climate had grown ever more conservative and Long Beach authorities stipulated that "no person over the age of six shall appear on any highway or public place or on the sand or beach or in the Pacific Ocean in Long Beach clothed in a bathing suit which does not completely conceal from view the trunk of the body" and allowed only for limited arm and leg exposure based on precise measurements of individual bodies. With stiff fines and jail time as punishment, Long Beach was pretty serious about its bathing suit laws; however, without a platoon of tape-measure-wielding fashion police, these exposure laws were difficult to enforce.[17]

Long Beach was not alone in having bathing suit regulations; other cities in the United States implemented similar legislation during the 1910s and 1920s. While skirting bathing suit laws and beach nudity proper was punishable by fines and jail time there were health professionals and urban planners who favored beach nudity. Having already experimented with heliotherapy in response to the pioneering work of Auguste Rollier, American doctors not only saw modern architecture as a way to expose their patients to the sun but beachgoing too was promoted as a cheap and effective way to cure some of the worst diseases of the industrial era, an idea that was carried through the Great Depression.[18] Chicago's health commissioner, Arnold Kegel, recommended in 1930 that sex-segregated nude beaches be established on Lake Michigan.[19] Similarly, Lewis Mumford included nude beaches in his 1938 planning project for Honolulu.[20] Despite such professional support of the health and social benefits of legal nude beaches, none were established in the United States until the 1960s, and most of these have remained in contention ever since.

One of the major claims of American nudists to the beach is its role as a public space that leaves it open to dialogue and negotiation. As some geographers have argued, disputes over beach access are not capricious fights over recreational space but, rather, are serious conflicts over public claims to a landscape of inclusion and belonging.[21] To have public access to any beach signifies a kind of mass civic ownership not controlled or limited by the property interests of the rich and powerful. In fact, beaches always have been especially charged social spaces, claimed as they have historically been by the unclothed, barely clothed, the cruising, and the gay, thus positioning them as part of many a city or county's sexual geography and easily targeted for censure and harassment. As much as we may tend to think of the beach as part of nature, it is useful to think of beaches as extensions of larger metropolitan areas and part of any city's zoning and containment concerns.

As part of a metropolitan sexual geography, the nude beach is also an unofficial zone of shared codes and community, cordoned off as it is by virtue of its unorthodox corporeality. For a site to be inscribed as a sexual space can actually be liberating for those operating within it.[22] Frequently, however, the body is subjected to the same local and federal policies that mark specific urban spaces as socially problematic such as the ghetto, the red-light district, or the slum. In these cases, the social forces affecting the city also mark the body in such a way as to render it marginal, outside acceptable understandings of the civic, and pushed to the far reaches of the political and economic mainstream. In urban sex districts, for example, the bodies for sale through prostitution and pornography can become metaphors for a degenerate neighborhood already coded as a pathological spatial body representing the bad stuff "down there."[23] Nude beaches, with reputations (earned or not) for public sex, have been equally pathologized as troubled metropolitan districts. Not all people who visit nude beaches, of course, seek an illicit sexual encounter, but the public nature of beaches highlights the interpretative significance of nudist display.[24] As nude beaches became more contentious, the bodies on them were increasingly derided as bad and degenerate or characterized as good but aggrieved by naked interlopers. Nude beach activists had to delicately balance the argument that nudism allowed for individual freedom of expression which, for some, might be sexual, while demonstrating that their practice of nude beachgoing was family-friendly and benign. It was no coincidence that the most active era to legalize nude beaches was the same historical period as the urban crisis, when American cities suffered at the hands of neoliberalism and misguided postwar urban policy, and the early culture wars when major battles over pornography, adult entertainment venues, and red-light districts were fought out in the courts. In all these cases, public spaces and the bodies that occupy them, were subject to policies and laws most concerned with relegating presumed degenerate subjects to the far margins of American society with little concern for the socioeconomic factors predetermining the so-called degenerate behavior in the first place.

While free beach activism is not limited to the West Coast, California with its enormous coastline, massive public beach system, nude-friendly climate, notorious health and body culture, and deep roots in the counterculture protests of the 1960s was, and remains, ground zero for the most organized and litigious nude beach actions in the country. The first documented effort to establish a legal nude beach in the United States was XB-58 (Experimental Beach 1958), a carefully orchestrated public relations event organized by American Sunbathing Association members Stan Sohler, Ed Lange, and Sol Stern. On June 29, 1958, on a stretch of coastline twelve miles north of Santa Cruz, California, approximately one hundred men, women, and children, all invited families, gathered for a pretty typical day at the beach. For months, Lange and Stern had been unable to secure permission from either State of California or county authorities to designate a beach in central California legally "free" so they negotiated with local district supervisors and the county sheriff's office to rent the Davenport Landing beach for a weekend-long nudist outing. This particular piece of coastline was agreed-upon by both nudist activists and local authorities because it was private, monitored by gate access, and not especially visible from Highway 1 above. A consistent complaint of police from the 1950s to the present day is that the problem with nude beaches is not so much the naked people on them as the lookie-loos who gather to watch.[25] The geographical location and logistics of Davenport Landing significantly reduced this problem, which is one of the main reasons local authorities allowed XB-58 to take place. The ASA apparently had been more nervous than the sheriff's office, insisting that its own emissaries organize the event to ensure the beach would be used in "compliance with American Sunbathing Association principles."[26] Despite it being heralded a banner success by those who took part, more radical nude beach advocates did not consider it a "free" beach because of its private nature, foreshadowing activist arguments about public and private space to follow in the 1960s and 1970s. Nevertheless, other, similar organized weekends took place without major incident in San Luis Obispo and in parts of Los Angeles and San Diego Counties.[27] Though there were few arrests, and local police generally ignored what were relatively uneventful family outings, this moment of postwar nude beach experimentation was one of the few times organized nudism directly ventured into free beach politics, preferring instead to turn inward, putting its energies into the national expansion of nudist clubs and the publication of nudist lifestyle magazines.[28]

Nude beach activism would thus have to come from other quarters, notably the counterculture, student movements, and sexual activism of the 1960s.[29] Hippies had drawn attention to public nudity through various naked political, cultural, and aesthetic activities on communes, in public parks, and at beaches

FIGURE 42. Photograph of model Diane Webber, participating in XB-58. Photograph by Ed Lange. Courtesy of the Southern California Naturist Association.

and lakes around the country while the Sexual Freedom League mixed nudity and free love. In 1965, Sexual Freedom League founder, Jefferson Poland, organized a "wade-in" at San Francisco's Aquatic Park to "draw attention to the right of citizens to use at least a portion of the public beaches for nude swimming and bathing."[30] For their efforts, Poland and his two female coconspirators were arrested and charged with violating local morality codes and sentenced to not insignificant ninety-day suspended sentences and six months' probation.[31] The "wade-in" attracted national attention in the press but did little to galvanize broad public support for legal nude beaches in California or the United States writ large.

The following year, in 1966, Darrell Tarver, a young Southerner, veteran of the Air Force, and a San Francisco State graduate, founded the "Committee for Free Beaches" after spending most of 1965 experimenting with nude swimming and sunbathing on Northern California public beaches.[32] Taking along some friends, Tarver's strategy was to park at a public beach, hike a couple of miles along the coast to find a less accessible area with more privacy, and strip there. If people walked by, Tarver and his friends would either put their bathing suits back on or leave them off and wave cordially. For the most part, no one cared too much about well-behaved naked people on secluded beaches. And, in fact, many passersby would take off their clothes and join the group. Tarver reported to Jefferson Poland that "the most eager participants were from local nudist parks. Although these families advised us to be more cautious, they often remarked that the environment we had created did not suffer from the social cliques, racial barriers, and emotional blocks often found in nudist parks."[33] This statement from 1965 nicely articulated the general sentiment shared today by nude beach proponents that their activism represents not only a different type of nudism, one that is practiced in public, rather than in private, but also one that is more progressive politically. Tarver described conversations among nude beach participants that included new ways to think about education, drugs, individual freedom, and how to encourage women's participation in nudist culture by stopping male harassment.[34] While it is important to take purported Sexual Freedom League feminism with a grain of salt, it is useful to see that, early on, nude beach activists defined their practice as more progressive, inclusive, and more in line with the social movements of the 1960s than the restrictive protocols of traditional social nudism.

Once Tarver put together the Committee for Free Beaches, the group began trying out various Northern California beaches in search of a public stretch that was accessible but not overly visible. The committee settled on San Gregorio, a secluded beach twenty-five miles north of Santa Cruz and just south of San Francisco, past Half Moon Bay, on Highway 1.[35] Together with the East Bay Sexual Freedom League, and ads for carpools placed in the *Berkeley Barb*, the committee's Bay Area publicity campaign resulted in hundreds of hippies, bikers, students, and families, nude and clothed, gathering at San Gregorio. The fun, however, would not last as the event was poorly organized. Garbage and sewage piled up, there was inadequate crowd control, the naked kept wandering out of the designated area, irritating neighbors, and, much to Poland's frustration, participants refused to take responsibility for anything and "refused to unite and organize."[36]

The claiming of San Gregorio by the Committee for Free Beaches in the spring of 1966 earned a certain degree of notoriety, its lack of organization notwithstanding, and inspired Southern California nudists to "free" other sites like Black's Beach in La Jolla, Pirate's Cove in Malibu, and Venice Beach, all three of which were especially popular with gay men but also attractive to large numbers of straights and families.[37] These ventures were technically unsanctioned by authorities at any level but Justice John Merrick's 1968 historic overturning of Los Angeles County's anti-nudity ordinance in the Elysium case pointed toward a more liberal attitude in California toward nudity in general.[38]

The generative actions of the Committee for Free Beaches and the change in the legal climate triggered more organized action on the part of nude beach advocates. In 1969, Ed Lange petitioned William Penn Mott Jr., director of the California Department of Parks and Recreation to establish San Onofre Cove in Gaviota State Park (the northwestern corner of San Diego County) as a clothing-optional beach. Lange sent his letter at the behest of Neil Blum, chairman of public relations and education for the American Sunbathing Association, which was again taking interest in nude beach politics despite its retreat in the late 1950s. Blum hoped that Lange could organize another beach experiment (this time XB-68) in conjunction with the state authorities. Blum's call to arms from the ASA headquarters in Mays Landing indicated that the free beach agitation in California had caught the eye of American nudist leaders.[39]

FIGURE 43. XB-58, Davenport's Landing, Santa Cruz, California, June 1958. Photograph by Ed Lange. Courtesy of the Southern California Naturist Association.

The summer of 1971 marked a watershed in the numbers of nude beach-goers in Southern California and increased surveillance by law enforcement. Malibu, with its combination of spectacular coastline, bohemian vibe, and enormous wealth, was a primary focus for cops (patrolling undercover in Bermuda shorts and bathing suits) who arrested sixty-eight people on Topanga Beach in August. Complaints about nude men seemed to be the main concern; women were far less of a problem. According to one local homeowner, "we've been enjoying topless women around here for three years."[40] Despite complaints filed about nudity, only one resulted in a charge for indecent exposure. The majority of the arrests were prompted by alcohol and drug use and, as would ultimately prove a useful legal argument for aggrieved homeowners, trespassing. Since the late nineteenth century, California law allowed for public access to all beach below the high-water mark. It was customary for California homeowners to allow beachgoers access to the sand above the high-water mark but Malibu's elite worked hard to prevent public use of the beach. Encouraging the police to patrol the beach in search of law-breaking naked swimmers and sunbathers significantly cut down on the crowds, nude or otherwise.[41]

Santa Barbara became the next county to experience the "freeing" of beaches along another idyllic coastline host to great wealth, a historic downtown, and Isla Vista, a student neighborhood adjacent to the Santa Barbara branch of the University of California. A string of beaches had grown popular with upwards of five hundred nudists on any given weekend and, while it was patrolled regularly by police, seemed to be trouble-free.[42] In the fall of 1971, the local Santa Barbara paper reported that there were generally very few problems with nude sunbathers; the concerns raised by homeowners and local law enforcement had more to do with backed-up traffic, parking hassles, and worries that the constant flurry of publicity would simply bring more people, nude or clothed, to what was otherwise a quiet beach community.[43] Santa Barbara district attorney David Minier weighed in to reassure both homeowners and nude beachgoers alike that, while trespassing was a violation of the state penal code, and any uninvited guests on private property could face prosecution, nudity was not. "Basically," he said, "if there is no one offended by it, there is nothing in the law that says it is illegal." Hedging his bets, Sheriff John Carpenter stated that his deputies would issue citations, rather than make arrests, unless nudists refused to put on their clothing. In that case, Carpenter argued, "we are going to enforce the nudity situation any time we have complaints—and we have had complaints."[44]

By the spring of 1972, the situation in Santa Barbara had grown significantly more unpleasant. Sheriff Carpenter began aggressively arresting nude sunbathers all along the coast from Summerland, Shark's Cove, and Isla Vista north to Gaviota, about thirty-five miles of beach. By the summer, over eighty people had been arrested, sometimes in handcuffs, at Summerland alone.[45] Most of the encounters with police occurred after three o'clock in the afternoon, so it became customary for beachgoers to pack it in for the day ahead of any impending conflict. District Attorney Minier switched his position and decided to prosecute beach nudity as illegal under the punitive California Penal Code section 314, which prohibited all public nudity.[46] Groups like the Earth Institute in Woodland Hills, part of the San Fernando Valley, organized and launched its own Free Beach Defense Strategy, a bulletin warning of forthcoming arrests and encouraged concerned citizens to gain injunctions to prevent further harassment by the Santa Barbara County sheriff.[47]

The public response to the police sweeps was mixed. Many complaints had less to do with nudity than with commerce; as a resort town, Santa Barbara relied on tourist dollars and business owners worried they would lose summer rentals if naked sunbathers crowded the beaches or if permitting nudity encouraged more licentious activities like public sex and drug use.[48] Others seemed acclimated to the culture of nudity on their beaches, participated themselves, or found the aggressive presence of law enforcement to be more offensive than naked suntanners, writing to the papers that they were "sure glad the police have so much time on their hands."[49] Outspoken support for the growing number of cited and arrested nudists came from the American Sunbathing Association and Elysium. ASA president Robert Johnston sent delegate Tom Caldwell from the headquarters in Mays Landing, New Jersey, to Summerland to report on the effects of the busts on beach attendance, which apparently had taken a hit because of the arrests. Ed Lange vocally supported the establishment of free beaches in Santa Barbara, and throughout the United States, and reported in the press that he hoped to work with state and local officials to create a clothing-optional policy that would stop the police sweeps.[50]

After the hundreds of arrests and citations in Santa Barbara County during the spring of 1972, with one hundred arrests between March 31 and April 2 alone, Superior Court Judge Charles Stevens granted a temporary writ of prohibition ordering the municipal court to take no further action in the cases where people, arrested in the nude, were charged with indecent exposure and disturbing the peace.[51] Some of those arrested took a deal whereby they could forfeit their bail in exchange for an outright dismissal of the indecent exposure charge, which, if they were convicted, meant lifetime registration as a sex offender. Many refused the deal, however, preferring to fight the charges, arguing that nudity did not automatically translate into lewd behavior in practice or under the law.[52] Frustrated by their inability to stop nude sunbathing, County Supervisor Frank Frost and Sheriff Carpenter announced their plan to ban it entirely because the problem was no longer "pure nudity" but an "increasing amount of homosexual activity." Arguing that naked men (rather than naked women) were potential sexual deviants, Santa Barbara passed the first anti-nudity ordinance in the state in over thirty years and began a homophobic panic that would drive much of the public discourse surrounding beach nudity in the years to follow.[53]

Much of the agitation during the summer of 1972 was provoked by a landmark California Supreme Court case, *Chad Merrill Smith v. California*. In 1970, Chad Smith was arrested in San Diego County for sleeping naked on a beach. Though charged with indecent exposure and convicted, Smith was exonerated on appeal by the California Supreme Court, which ruled that lewdness required sexual intent and acts beyond mere nudity.[54] The ruling stated that "absent additional conduct intentionally directing attention to his genitals for sexual purposes, a person, as here, who simply sunbathes in the nude on an isolated beach does not 'lewdly' expose his private parts within the meaning of section 314" (the section of the California Penal Code that prohibits indecent exposure, rules it a sex crime, and has been virtually unchanged since its enactment in 1872). Since Smith had no intention of exposing himself for sexual gratification (the beach was deserted when he undressed; people gathered while he was sleeping), the court believed that his nudity was not a crime.[55] The ruling in June 1972 struck down Smith's conviction, which had come with a hefty sentence including being placed on probation and being required to register as a sex offender anywhere he chose to live.[56]

With the *Smith* decision, popularly interpreted as "nude does not mean lewd," California came to host the most liberal nudity laws in the country and the effects were immediately felt in the courts. In Van Nuys and West Los Angeles, for example, judges promptly dismissed indecent exposure charges against several women arrested for going topless in Venice Beach. In tossing out the cases, Judge Dan Kaufman stated that while he personally did not sanction nudity on public beaches, "mere nudity [was] not a violation of the indecent exposure law." Unhappy with the outcome, the city attorney's office issued several statements arguing that *Smith* only addressed nudity on secluded beaches, not any public beach, and that topless women had been "foisting themselves on an unwilling public." City attorney David Schacter, a strong opponent of nude beaches, prophetically stated that "nudity on the beaches will increase until the higher courts are finally forced to decide where individual nudity rights end and public welfare rights begin."[57]

With all the national publicity surrounding the *Smith* decision, the new permissiveness of the sexual revolution, a well-organized gay rights movement, and a new environmental consciousness with a cultural priority on being "natural," free beaches in California exploded in popularity. Up and down the coast, San Gregorio, Bonny Doon, Black's Beach, and San Onofre, among others, became more crowded, more controversial, and there were more arrests. Within days of the *Smith* decision, the Los Angeles Sheriff's Department clamped down on Pirate's Cove in Malibu, just south of Point Dume State Beach, where nude attendance had grown into the thousands, arguing that nudism was a nuisance that attracted audiences of problematic peepers and that *Smith* was open to legal interpretation. Captain Donald Foxen argued that the court's ruling meant that a sunbather may be naked on an *isolated* beach and that Pirate's Cove was not considered as such.[58]

Free beach activists disagreed and, strengthened by their numbers and emboldened by the successful Supreme Court ruling, took issue with the escalating police presence and continued to show up at Pirate's Cove in growing numbers. It was clear, for the first time, that nude bathers were fighting back. Law enforcement responded aggressively and, in August 1972, Pirate's Cove became a site of physical conflict when twenty-five deputies from the Los Angeles County Sheriff's Department, brandishing rifles, drove onto the beach in jeeps and dragged away six nude sunbathers charged with trespassing.[59]

Out of the escalating clashes with law enforcement at Pirate's Cove emerged a collaborative friendship between lawyer Peter Hartmann, ASA officer Neal Blum, and aerospace industry analyst Eugene Callen, who together launched a class-action suit, *Callen and Blum v. Beverly Hills Land Development Company*, Los Angeles Superior Court Case, #37439, contending that the police harassment of nudists in Malibu was actually stemming from private concerns over land values and private property—not nudity.[60] Though they dropped the suit once it became clear that the local cops were backing down in the face of growing numbers of activists and several successful court injunctions against citations and arrests at Pirate's Cove, what emerged instead was "Beachfront USA," the West Coast's largest and most active nude beach advocacy group.

Founded by Callen, an articulate, outspoken, and flamboyant free beach activist, Beachfront USA focused public attention on the hundreds of arrests at beaches along the California coast. Callen urged those arrested for indecent exposure to take their cases to court rather than accept guilty pleas for lesser charges. Even though *Smith* settled the issue insofar as nudity without lewd intent was not a sexual offence, how to define "lewd intent" was often in the hands of prosecuting attorneys and the police. Since an indecent exposure conviction came with such harsh sentences, many who were hauled up before a judge accepted a lesser charge of disturbing the peace even if they felt they had broken no law. Having pushed back successfully against the egregious interference of the Sheriff's Department, which officially ceased its campaign of arrests and citations at Pirate's Cove in May 1973, Beachfront USA turned its attention to Venice, where the significant gay population lent fuel to the fire as the uptick in police sweeps along the coast continued.[61] The Venice police dealt especially harshly with the famous beach area, arresting over 150 people that summer for indecent exposure, among other charges.[62]

Venice, a longtime site for bohemians, artists, and the city's gay community, had especially drawn the ire of the Los Angeles Police Department. Police crackdowns on coffeehouses, galleries, and flophouses for fostering "subversion" were notorious in the mid-1950s while the attraction of tourists to the area made the hippie stronghold a favorite place for police surveillance from the 1960s forward.[63] Venice was also the home of the second incarnation of Muscle Beach, a modest outdoor gymnasium next to the boardwalk that came to host some of the most famous bodybuilders in the world, even serving as the home base for a young Arnold Schwarzenegger in the 1970s. Crowds used to gather in the 1930s and 1940s at the original Muscle Beach in Santa Monica, where the Works Progress Administration had installed exercise equipment, to watch amazing gymnastic displays of strength and agility, performed by women and men, but it was the sculpted, greased, and tanned male weightlifters that drew much of the attention. Fueled by fitness impresarios Bob Hoffman, Vic Tanny, and Joe Weider, and their myriad pictorial magazines, male bodybuilding became both a popular cultural trend and big business. The body, in fact, became a site for building good American patriots during the Cold War and a vessel for commodity consumption as savvy entrepreneurs like fitness guru Jack LaLanne and nutrition specialist Paul Bragg soon figured out. Federally funded exercise programs, a new heart-health consciousness, and televised calisthenics became hallmarks of 1950s body culture as Americans became concerned about the ill effects of suburban life and convenience foods on their waistlines while the military worried that physical weakness made the nation vulnerable to communist infiltration.[64] The bodies admired at Muscle Beach, first in Santa Monica, and later in Venice, reflected what fitness historian Jonathan Black has called a "robust masculinity . . . [one that] hints of homosexuality and the occasional charge of promiscuity."[65] Venice, unlike Pirate's Cove, San Gregorio, or any of the Santa Barbara beaches, was expressively flamboyant, distinctly urban, and long associated with sex and a highly visible physical culture.

It was thus not surprising that during the summer of 1972, when beaches all along the California coast became subject to increased surveillance, Venice seemed especially repressive and its gay sexual geography had no small role to play in the skirmishes between nude beachgoers and the cops. Sergeant Arvid Keidser of the Venice Division of the Los Angeles Police Department stated that "many times when police find a person sunbathing nude alone, they will merely advise the person to dress. However, with drinking and homosexuality often attendant factors in Venice nudity, the police contend that most of their arrests involve sexual activity which would be considered lewd."[66] In response, organizers of the gay nudist group Lavender People took to the sand. Sandy Blixton, free beach activist and member of the Lavender People, described one afternoon as beautiful, warm, and well-attended: "It wasn't only the gays," said Blixton. "There were lots of straight couples with kids. They loved it. It's the most beautiful natural thing."[67] Unfortunately, Venice's notoriety and tourist crowds also attracted onlookers, many of whom stared or took pictures. Blixton explained that "we hated that more than the pigs." For the Lavender People, explained head organizer Mike Miller, the gawking spoke to the very reason why public nudity was important: "If a person's sexual outlet is so limited that he's bound to jump at the first opportunity to drool, that shows something about sexual oppression. We're trying to break down sexual mores that are outdated, outmoded, and oppressive."[68]

The summer of 1972 would go down in American nudist history as the most violent moment in the free beach movement, with the largest numbers of arrests and police repression, but the beachfront activism and sheer numbers of participants would produce momentum. Thanks largely to the still murky, but promising, effects of the *Smith* decision, free beach activists stopped the police aggression in Pirate's Cove and began significant negotiations with the Los Angeles City Council to free Venice. In short, it felt for many that a groundswell of support for public nudity had grown, largely in response to changing social mores, the sexual revolution, and the gay and women's rights movements, and it was time to get serious about legally sanctioning nude beaches once and for all.

In an effort to mitigate the tension between the increased numbers of naked people on Venice Beach and law enforcement, the Los Angeles City Council worked with Beachfront USA from 1972 through 1974 to set aside a section of legal nudist-friendly beach. Callen reported to Cec Cinder, nudist activist and free beach historian, that the activity in Venice was the result of well-coordinated efforts and plenty of planning. In the fall of 1973, Beachfront participants staged what Callen characterized as "little nude-ins" at Venice Beach, making it clear to local authorities that in the absence of anti-nude bathing laws, Beachfront would fight any arrests. Beachfront's activism also included flooding Venice with thousands of nude sunbathers recruited from Pirate's Cove.[69]

By the spring of 1974, things looked bright for Beachfront USA, which had created a "nude beachhead" in Venice with thousands of nude bathers, "dramatizing in the eyes of the general public for the first time the full range of the coming impact of the free beach movement. We believe we have thus accelerated and intensified a process that otherwise might have taken several years."[70] Then, in late June, the city council voted 9 to 4 to legalize a "clothing-optional zone" at Brooks Beach alongside the Venice boardwalk.[71] Unfortunately, that initial vote was not adequate to pass the ordinance because it was not unanimous; the clothing-optional zone was thus subject to a second vote and, in the interim, the city council folded before public pressure to pass an anti-nudity ordinance much harsher than anything the city had seen since the 1940s.[72] The ordinance, introduced by Councilman Arthur K. Snyder, prohibited nudity in all city-owned recreation areas, including parks and all beaches. On the fourth of July, thousands of nudists converged at Venice Beach hoping to lend support to the cause but the clothing-optional zone's days were numbered; on July 5, the council voted 6 to 5 for "a total ban on beach nudity."[73]

Councilwoman Pat Russell, one of the five who had voted against the total ban, a representative of the city's Sixth District and a liberal advocate of wilderness protection and freedom of expression, supported the legalization of municipal nude beaches. According to the Beachfront's board of directors, under Russell's original plan "each Los Angeles resident would have been given the freedom to choose a cover-up or to sunbathe in a natural, non-prurient fashion. In addition, those preferring the textile alternative were to be given exclusive use of most of the beach areas. They would have been permitted to enjoy the beach in the attire they chose without ever encountering sunbathers who decided not to wear clothing. This ordinance therefore presented a rare opportunity in local government, whereby regulation of freedom of expression would have been expanded and the friction normally existent in preserving such a fundamental freedom of expression would have been removed."[74] Russell, along with her fellow council members, received hundreds of phone calls and unusually heavy mailbags full of letters from the public in support of freeing beaches in Los Angeles generally and Venice in particular. Most argued that "there is nothing lewd or dirty about the human body and those feeling so should be able to express that feeling" and that "no matter what some uptight people say, nudity is not harmful; the city has not gone down the drain since people have been nude on the beach."[75] Some tourists were horrified by the police crackdowns, writing to the press that they couldn't "believe that in 1974 California taxpayers are going to allow their money to be spent on such ludicrous waste. All over the world people are pulling free from the dangerous shackles of mental attitudes that say the body uncovered is a corruptive threat."[76] Local Angelenos suggested "the freedom from clothing at Venice Beach is significant because it affirms the beauty of the entire human body without arbitrarily excepting parts of it." Thousands showed up to support the freeing of Venice, with the press corps left blinking at the sea of "glowing posteriors, like a constellation of moons turning pink in the sun" but also to point out that the apparently spontaneous exhibition of neighborhood solidarity was an angry response to a proposed city ordinance that would confine nude bathing to certain municipal beach areas, a restrictive rather than a permissive move as it was not yet, in fact, illegal to be naked on beaches in Los Angeles.[77]

The city council, however, also received letters along the lines of one from J. Edward Gibbons, resident of Pacific Palisades, who in the wake of the nude beach ordinance's defeat, wrote that he found it distressing that the council would have even considered allowing nudity on public beaches in the first place. Gibbons's main concern was that if given a section of beach, and "nudists 'get their foot in the door,' there will be no controlling the situation at any beach." He further suggested that if nudists wanted to indulge in naked sunbathing, they should buy their own private beach.[78] But what makes this letter especially revealing about broader attitudes toward the free beach movement and the climate of sexual permissiveness for which the 1970s is notorious, is its concluding fair warning: "One last word—if you have doubts about what would happen with nude bathing, I would suggest you spend a few days at the beach. You will find that even now, you will be approached by homosexuals, prostitutes and other dregs of humanity. The activities in which you see couples engaged (both mixed couple and couples of the same sex) do not leave much to [the imagination]. Many times my family and I have had to leave the beach on a sunny afternoon in sheer embarrassment and disgust."[79]

In ways similar to the panicked passage of the 1939 anti-nudity ordinance, when movies, burlesque, and dance clubs were too permissive for Los Angeles County and apparently much of the rest of the country, the action taken by the city council in 1974 to ban nudity anywhere in public came on the heels of other repressive local legislation intended to help stem the national tide of shifting sexual mores. In July 1973, the Los Angeles County Superior Court ruled that strip clubs like the Classic Cat, the Pink Pussy Cat, and The Losers had failed to prove they were legitimate theaters and thus could be prosecuted and shuttered for staging nude entertainment. Under previous anti-nudity laws, theaters in Los Angeles County and City had been exempt from nudity restrictions. The previous May, however, Judge David A. Thomas aggressively opened the door for the prosecution of adult entertainment venues by dissolving injunctions preventing the arrest of nude bar employees in forty-four outstanding court cases. Though the clubs argued that they *were* theaters, featuring nude versions of well-known productions like *Cabaret*, the California Supreme Court upheld the local anti-nudity ordinances' constitutionality and the ruling went into effect on May 30.[80]

Then, in March of 1974, Los Angeles City Council's Fire and Civil Defense Committee moved to ban the sale of pornographic magazines from vending machines and to prohibit the display of photographs or drawings of *any* nude human bodies on sidewalk news racks if visible to passersby, a move backed by the Catholic Church and the conservative group "Coalition of Fathers," which vaguely claimed to represent local PTAs, service organizations, and parents.[81] To repress any public depictions of nude human bodies by assuming them pornographic was in violation of most obscenity law and stunningly regressive.

Though the deputy city attorney doubted that the courts would uphold it, the city council voted 12 to 1, Councilman Ed Edelman dissenting, to pass another citywide ordinance stating that no genitals, breasts, buttocks, or pubic hair could be displayed on news racks. Even though the city attorney's office believed that publications in news racks fell outside the definition of Chapter 7.6 of California Penal Code Section 313, which defined "harmful matter" as materials showing a shameful and morbid interest in nudity or sex, the ordinance was signed by Mayor Tom Bradley on May 9, 1974. A suit challenging its constitutionality was promptly filed by the American Civil Liberties Union, which had already been granted court orders restraining bans on news racks in other municipalities like Burbank and Lynwood.[82]

On the day of the final reading of the nudity ban before the city council, Robert Opel, already famous for streaking at the 1974 Academy Awards, stripped and addressed the council, daring them to oppose the clothing-optional beach in Venice.[83] Perhaps the last straw, previously pro-nude beach advocates like Edelman and Russell bowed to the pressure and on July 11, 1974, the city council again voted 12 to 1 against having public nudity on Los Angeles beaches.[84] This time the lone dissenting vote was from an African American councilman, David Cunningham, of the Tenth District who "refused to succumb to pressure and letter writing campaigns to change his vote."[85] In a brave statement given on the floor of the city council, Cunningham argued that his colleagues were supporting an anti-nudity ordinance not because they thought it was the right thing to do, or because they were even representing their constituents, but that they were afraid of the aggressive campaigning of the conservative right. The second point Cunningham raised was that the reason the issue was before the council at all was because the Los Angeles Police Department has asked the Police, Fire, and Civil Defense Committee to devise an ordinance banning nudity anywhere in the city and the committee had agreed but voted to set aside a designated area where people could swim and sunbathe without clothing. Not getting their way, Cunningham argued, the police together with other citizens' groups upped the ante to ban all nudity and initiated what Cunningham angrily felt was a "flat-out effort by the Police Department to control what this Council does."[86] He concluded with the statement: "If we could get out from under the hysteria, the organized protests and the pressures that have been engineered by the police and perhaps some members of this Council, and thought seriously about what we are doing, we would only need to ask ourselves one question. That question is, what is wrong with having a place on the public beach where people who want to, can swim and sunbathe without their clothes on? That is the only question."[87]

Despite Cunningham's pleas to commonsense, the city council reversed its previous support for a clothing-optional section of beach in Venice and, instead, provided the police with an enforceable code to prevent a nude presence in pretty much any public area in the city. Dismayed, Cunningham told the *Los Angeles Times*, "all of us are concerned about morality and crime in our city but crimes involving guns and violence are far more important than those concerning nudity. I don't know yet of any nudity that killed anybody."[88]

Los Angeles thus adopted the following ordinance on July 18, 1974, which banned all public nudity from any beach, park, or recreational area under the jurisdiction of the municipal government, and it was enforced by Los Angeles police officers in shorts and t-shirts patrolling one hundred miles of coastline. As an "urgency measure," it went into effect the following day:[89] "No person shall appear any place under the jurisdiction of the Board of Recreation and Parks Commissioners . . . in such a manner that the genitals, vulva, pubis, pubic symphysis, pubic hair, buttocks, natal cleft, perineum, anus, anal region, or pubic hair region of any person, or any portion of the breast at or below the upper edge of the areola thereof of any female person, is exposed to public view or is not covered by an opaque covering. Subdivision (x) further provides: 'This subdivision shall not apply to children under the age of 10 years.'"[90] That the human body should have been broken down into so many specifically outlawed parts was a stunning reminder that free and natural living—and the public display of the naked body—remained deeply vulnerable to legal and social restriction. The clinical anatomy of the city measure spoke to a new degree of neurosis about corporeal exposure and a disturbing specificity about what was constituted sexual.

One case, *Eckl v. Davis*, was brought by free beach activists to the California Court of Appeal to try to overturn the measure on the basis that it was discriminatory to single out women whose breasts could not be exposed while those of men could. The appeal fell on unsympathetic ears. In response to Maureen Eckl's claim that the ordinance denied women their constitutional right to equal protection under the law, the presiding justices wrote "nature, not the legislative body, created the distinction between that portion of woman's body and that of a man's torso."[91]

While the courts may have felt they had settled the issue of nude bathing in Los Angeles, Venice remained a contested urban beach. Police continued to cite women for going topless and men for wearing garments that exposed their buttocks, but it was rare to find entirely naked sunbathers.[92] In 1986, Dave and Suzy Davis, founders of the Nudist Information Center, organized a nude beach walk on Venice Beach during Labor Day weekend to challenge California's anti-nudity laws on public beaches and their efforts were met with prompt arrests.[93] The event itself attracted media attention and became part of a case that Beachfront USA brought in 1990 to again try to overturn the 1974 ordinance. And, again, in 1992, the appeals court upheld the anti-nudity law. A frustrated Cec Cinder stated in the press that "we don't think that municipalities have the right to establish dress codes and back them up with a club and a gun."[94]

For four straight years, from 1972 through 1975, free beach advocates in Southern California organized and fought high-profile battles both in the courts and on the beaches to allow nude sunbathing and swimming without harassment from law enforcement. The demands were relatively simple: to have clothing-optional zones where nudity was legal and beachgoers would have access to the same facilities (lifeguards, toilets) as those on any other public beach. While the beaches of Los Angeles ultimately proved impossible to free despite support from the public and local government officials, nudist activism did have success at the national level, with the founding of National Nude Beach Day, and in San Diego, with temporary establishment of Black's Beach as the first legally nude beach in the United States.

In May of 1974, in the midst of the Los Angeles municipal and county beach fights, a San Diego city ordinance established Black's, in the well-heeled town of La Jolla, as the first legal nude beach in the country. The ordinance was explicitly based on the *Smith* decision that ruled that nudity without lewd, sexual intent was permissible by law in remote and semiremote areas. Black's Beach is secluded, isolated as it is by vertical cliffs, and notoriously difficult to access; the only way to get there from the neighborhood above is by cutting across a field and climbing down a long, steep and slippery cliff path. Within San Diego lore, Black's had been a nude, and gay cruising, beach for decades dating back well before World War II. Despite San Diego's political and social conservatism, few were especially concerned about Black's Beach largely because it was so hard to get to; it was, and remains, mostly a preserve of dedicated nude sunbathers and surfers. Once the San Diego City Council passed the ordinance in May of 1974, it ensured that signs clearly marked the narrow "swimsuit optional" zone, the Department of Parks and Recreation posted several lifeguards, and naked sunbathers soon crammed into the small strip of legal nude beach. But, as was the case in Santa Barbara, Pirate's Cove, and other freed beaches in the 1970s, the growing numbers of participants drew the ire of local residents and law enforcement. On May 24, 1975, for example, the first anniversary of "freeing" Black's, over fifteen thousand people showed up to celebrate the American free beach movement's greatest success and the dawn of what one social scientist referred to as a national "body freedom social movement."[95] The mood at Black's on any nice summer day was playful, with families, kids, gay and straight couples, and singles participating in usual beach activities.

Was it a sexualized space? Yes, but according to lifeguards and patrol officers, no more than most beaches. Observers noted men looking at women in bikinis but rarely ogling women in the buff. A culture emerged, too, of regulars versus newcomers with the regular visitors to Black's keeping an eye on potential voyeurs or harassers, especially of single women. As one lifeguard reported, "If I see something happening to a woman and she doesn't like it, I'll go over and arrest the guy."[96] A combination of camaraderie typical of subcultures, vigilance, and surveillance kept Black's Beach safe. It is unclear how racially mixed Black's was at its peak popularity; police and lifeguards' reports that there was "no racial tension" could reflect a homogeneous scene as much as it might suggest a tolerantly diverse one.[97] The San Diego police remained remarkably laidback about the clothing-optional zone and certainly restrained in comparison to law enforcement officers in Los Angeles and Santa Barbara. While keeping an eye out for drug use and nudity outside the clothing-optional zone, one police officer told the papers that at Black's, "we have more problems with dogs being off leashes than with the people being nude on the beach."[98]

FIGURE 44. Black's Beach, ca. 1977. Union Title Insurance Company Photograph Collection. © San Diego History Center.

Black's seemed so successful that San Diego County Board of Supervisors proposed establishing another legal clothing-optional beach a few miles north in the bohemian enclave of Encinitas, between the famous surf break "Swami's," named for its proximity to Paramahansa Yogananda's Self-Realization Fellowship temple, and Moonlight State Beach. The idea was another clothing-optional beach would ease some of the pressure at Black's and legalize the activities of the already hundreds of nude sunbathers who already gathered there. The problem, however, was a new condominium project that would end the secluded nature of the six-hundred-foot strip of beach.[99] Nevertheless, nude sunbathing continued near Swami's and northward along the San Diego coastline all the way to San Onofre State Beach. State Parks and Beaches Area Manager Jack Welch reported that no one at any of the dozen or so free beaches had been arrested; patrolling officers just asked nude sunbathers to put their clothes back on.[100]

Though things seemed peaceful and progressive on the surface, trouble was brewing. Homeowners in La Jolla Farms, the exclusive community overlooking Black's grew increasingly irate about who they called the "kooks" in their midst and the traffic that came with weekend crowds. Some began investigating whether or not the City of San Diego should have sought a permit from the California Coastal Commission before legalizing the nude beach while others began demanding to have the trail down to Black's named a protected resource under the Environmental Bill of Rights and blocked to visitors altogether.[101] Others disliked the fact that the beach had, in fact, become a major tourist attraction, especially with large numbers of military men: "Black's is now the biggest liberty port in town," complained a local realtor. [102]

Disgruntled residents proceeded to get organized. In 1977, an anti-nude-beach group calling itself Save the Beaches, urged the San Diego City Council to put Proposition D on the ballot in the fall, when over three hundred thousand voters were expected to show up for the city primary. Proposition D was essentially a referendum to end the legal basis for Black's and forbid nudity on all beaches in San Diego. Made up of local residents, property owners, business interests, and churches, including the bishop of the San Diego Roman Catholic Diocese, Save the Beaches complained of the large numbers gathering at Black's, including the twenty-five thousand who showed up on the Fourth of July and outdrew both Sea World and the San Diego Zoo. The group also maintained that Black's was an unfair tax burden, a message it spread with billboards stating "Don't Pay for Their Play. Yes on D." Echoing Anita Bryant's Save Our Children, the powerful antigay activist group that, in 1977, successfully downed a Dade County, Florida, ordinance to prohibit discrimination against lesbians and gay men in employment, housing, and public accommodations, Save the Beaches' strategy also smacked of homophobia.[103] The group made a point of suggesting that nude children on Black's Beach were vulnerable to pedophiles, unwelcome photography, and exposure to "unacceptable sexual activity" taking place on the beach.[104] The connection between Save the Beaches and Save Our Children was not lost on the pro-nude beach faction: "I think they're the same kind of people, and if they're victorious here, their next target will be gays," speculated Robert Jacobs, president of the Nude Beaches Committee.[105]

Despite the best efforts of the free beach movement, Proposition D passed in the citywide primary and on October 5, 1977, the San Diego City Council repealed the three-year-old resolution that had legalized the clothing-optional zone at Black's Beach. The voting was relatively close, with opinion polls reporting that 73 percent of voters eighteen to thirty-four supported nude beaches but the majority of those actually voting were older, more conservative, and decidedly opposed.[106]

To celebrate the fourth anniversary of Black's Beach, despite its recent failure at the polls, Beachfront USA, now led by Charles Finley, and the Nude Beaches Committee, headed by Robert Jacobs, hosted a party at Black's on Memorial Day weekend in 1978. According to *Beachhead*, the newsletter of the American free beach movement, over forty-seven thousand showed up in the buff and well-prepared for the police. The Nude Beaches Committee placed lookouts armed with whistles across the beach. If anyone saw a patrol officer, the alarm was sounded and everyone pulled on his or her clothes. It was an effective system, so much so the cops took a decidedly laissez-faire approach to the whole event. San Diego's police chief, William Kolender, in fact, stated that "little if anything will be done if people decide to take off their clothes."[107] Apart from swimming, sunbathing, and festive body painting, the main activity of Memorial Unity Day, as the Nude Beaches Committee dubbed it, was signature-gathering to get the beach back in the November 1978 local election.[108] Though they got close to the 37,425 valid names they needed to qualify for a spot on the ballot, their efforts fell short when the deadline arrived in September.[109]

Though Black's Beach's life as the one legal nude beach in the country was short, its notoriety continues to the present day. While rare for it to attract crowds in the tens of thousands, as it did in its mid-1970s heyday, it is still used by surfers and gay and straight nude sunbathers. Throughout the 1980s, the crowds dipped in number largely because of difficulty in accessing the site. The already dangerous trail grew more slippery and steep because of landslides and erosion and several people were killed in falls. An obvious solution was to build a stairway and stabilize the cliff and San Diego city councilman Bill Mitchell championed the cause, but to little effect.[110] Once the general public downed the clothing-optional zone in the 1977 election, and wealthy residents fussed about the large crowds, the city lost interest in maintaining the beach. Not only was a stairway not built, but in 1982, the city pulled the lifeguards and closed the trail altogether. People, of course, continued to go to Black's and, in 1983, a man drowned in an incident that could have been prevented if a lifeguard had been present. This led to a restoration of lifeguard patrols, a service that still continues. Black's remains the largest and perhaps most famous nude beach in the country but, like so many, is not legally sanctioned. Rather, nudity is tolerated on the part of the beach managed by the state park system.[111]

Black's brief legal status inspired free beach activists nationwide. In the summer of 1976, Eugene Callen, who was, by this time, terribly ill with bone marrow cancer, joined forces with another nude beach activist, Lee Baxandall, member of the Free the Free Beach Committee in Massachusetts. Baxandall's group had organized in 1975 in response to efforts of police and the National Park Service to ban nudity on the traditionally clothing-optional Truro beaches in Cape Cod.[112] The result of their collaboration was National Nude Beach Day held on Sunday, August 8, 1976. In the middle of bicentennial celebrations, thousands of free beach activists across the country took to the sand as part of the first bicoastal beach liberation strategy.[113] Activists used the opportunity to get petitions signed, stage peaceful nudist "happenings," and launch a public relations campaign that would reshape public perceptions of the nude beach issue from hordes of troublemaking drugged-out hippies to a righteous quest for public space and individual expressive freedom. As one observer wrote, "it is conceivable that those who want to wear bathing suits will have special areas set aside for their use by the end of this decade, since vast numbers of people of all ages consider bathing suits unnecessary. They presently wear them to keep out of jail, but when given a choice, they strip happily. Modesty is not a concern in this bicentennial year when personal freedom is being touted as a basic American right."[114]

Within the free beach activist community, National Nude Beach Day was proclaimed an enormous success attracting, as it did, huge crowds and lots of free media attention, with marches and gatherings held all over the country. This collaborative feat led to Baxandall and Callen spearheading National Nude Weekend, now Nude Recreation Week, which still takes place every July, but with its current focus less on free beach activism and more on celebrating nudist culture writ large. Privately owned camps, resorts, and retreats are jammed with visitors and for many proprietors it's their most lucrative week financially and for participants, it represents a now decades-old annual gathering of the nudist tribe. As National Capital Beachfront, a free beach group in the Washington, DC, area put it, "[we'll] be there to promote understanding of the clothes-optional recreation movement as a natural solution to many problems of modern living."[115]

But the future of National Nude Beach Day for Los Angeles nude beaches was less rosy than organizers could possibly have realized at the time. Pirate's Cove, in particular, took a big hit, literally. In the fall of 1978, a fourteen-by-ten-foot crack opened in the side of a cliff overlooking the strip of beach privately owned by the Reco Land Corporation. The Los Angeles County sheriff's office declared it a public health hazard and ordered it dynamited by a local demolition expert.[116] Two years later, in 1980, after the state's Department of Parks and Recreation had purchased the 33.5 acres of property for almost $5 million, the California Coastal Commission voted unanimously to close Pirate's Cove completely to people and allow it to become a natural sanctuary for seals and sea lions.[117] While ostensibly a report by the California Department of Fish and Game that indicated that the beach would be used by sea lions if humans vacated the spot led to the commission's vote, the papers noted that the decision was strongly supported by Malibu homeowners and retired police chief Ed Davis, who was running for state senate. Davis's deputies, of course, had led many of the raids on the Malibu beaches in previous summers. Davis reported to the *Times* that he supported closing the beach because it attracted "people with binoculars and long-range cameras, whether they're looking at seals, whales, or naked humans."[118] The Clothing Optional Society, led by Lynn and James Hensley, submitted a proposal to the Department of Fish and Game, with copies circulated to the major media outlets in the Los Angeles area, suggesting ways of meeting everyone's needs. Chiding the sheriff's department for patrolling for nudists but not for voyeurs, vandals, and other petty criminals who had made trouble on the beach throughout the 1970s, the Hensleys suggested closing Pirate's Cove but leaving the adjacent Big Dume open as "a Clothing Optional Preserve (something like a seaside botanical garden) protected and kept in its natural state, so all users could view nature firsthand without disturbing it."[119]

FIGURE 45. "Kathryn Cummings, left, with Free Venice sign, was among 19 demonstrators who left on a protest march from Will Rogers State Beach to Venice," 1978. Photograph by Chris Gulker. *Herald-Examiner* Collection, Los Angeles Public Library.

For a few months, it looked as if nudists would keep the beach open despite the urging of Governor Jerry Brown to turn Pirate's Cove into an ecological reserve. But complaints from homeowners about misuse of the beach, especially the unpleasant discovery of human feces, trash, and debris on the rocks, and ongoing arrests for public drinking, marijuana use, and public sex lent strength to the argument that the tiny strip of beach would be better served by seals seeking refuge for breeding.[120] As a result, in August 1980, a health inspector and four sheriff's deputies closed the beach for being in violation of Section 427.5 of the California Health and Safety Code.[121] Throughout the summer of 1981, when the state decided not to close the beach, nude beachgoers showed up in large numbers leading to the arrest or citation of 1,096 people on Malibu beaches, many of whom, according to residents, were engaged in drinking and public sex, including gay couples, who seemed to prove the biggest affront.[122] The surge in arrests led to a jamming of the Malibu and Santa Monica municipal courts as hundreds were brought before judges, one of whom dismissed many of the cases because the county ordinance on nude bathing was too unclear to reach a judgment. In the judicial fray, two judges were dismissed, including Judge John Merrick, a longtime resident of Malibu and the jurist long sympathetic to the nudist cause in Los Angeles County.[123]

Though only a handful was ultimately found guilty and sentenced, the effect of the bad publicity, both the arrests and news of badly behaved beachgoers, was to significantly reduce the numbers in the Point Dume area for years to come. Lynn Hensley, the chairperson of the Clothing Optional Society, reported in the press that she agreed with the sheriff's department that the numbers in 1982 were well in decline, although she noted that nude sunbathers had moved north to Leo Carillo State Beach on the Ventura County line. The police argued that in the wake of the arrests, there were far fewer nudists because of "voluntary compliance," which meant that if sheriff's deputies asked them to put on their clothes, they did so to avoid citation or being taken into custody.[124] Much like police crackdowns on vice in any urban neighborhood, the effect was to move the offenders into other parts of the city rather than actually stop the behavior. Hence the aggressive police presence to elicit compliance with the vague local anti-nudity ordinances.

The increase in the numbers of beachgoers was one of the problems created by the popularity of the Nude Beach Days publicity blitz. The other was a change in how nudist information traveled. The point of the event was to draw supporters and publicize nude beachgoing in the mainstream media in a way that highlighted the practice's fun and family-friendly energy. And it worked. Tens of thousands flocked to clothing-optional beaches nationwide, most major media outlets covered the story while even more enthusiasm was generated by underground youth newspapers, which were sure to publish press releases alerting the world to a huge public nude gathering.[125] But as The Naturist Society member Mark Storey points out, "by the 1980s, such publications were less common, and news of the [National Nude] Weekend had to be issued through mainstream news agencies like the AP and UPI. This still worked, but now the news was transmitted by the press as titillating reading for a more conservative readership."[126] Concern about how free beach activism would be portrayed in the press, and a desire to archive the efforts of what was by then a national movement, also led to Baxandall and Callen founding the Free Beach Documentation Center in Oshkosh, Wisconsin, Baxandall's home base. Not only did the center store the primary materials of the free beach movement, it also published an annual newspaper, *Free Beaches*.[127] Having some sort of control over the image and message of nude beach activism had been a pressing concern since the earliest days of XB-58 and it would continue to be so as the events got larger, prurient public fascination became greater, and the tensions between the free beach folks and the private nude camps and colonies grew more abrasive. As early as 1972, when the free beach movement really took off, older nudists took note of the change in demographics, especially age, and the shift in context. One observer, Madeline Johnson, told the papers that "card-carrying nudists are becoming the conservatives of the unclothed world. The public has gone far beyond our regimented background," she said in reference to the growing trend among young adults to take it all off on public beaches. In addition, the proliferation of erotic entertainment and openly marketed pornography "goes far beyond anything you find in a nudist camp."[128]

While tensions between traditional nudists and the free beach movement grew, the actions of nude beach activists continued to have widespread political and cultural effect. Early in 1979, rumors spread that California was about to legalize eight nude beaches including San Onofre in San Diego County, Pirate's Cove at Point Dume, Hazard Canyon in San Luis Obispo, Andrew Molero Beach in Monterey, Pomponio Beach in San Mateo County, Red Rock Beach in Marin County, Lake Natomas in Sacramento, and Millerton Lake in Fresno.[129] In April, Russell Cahill, director of the California State Department of Parks and Recreation, despite opposition from Governor Jerry Brown, scheduled three public hearings on the issue of clothing-optional zones in the state system.[130]

On June 1, 1979, after hearing the many sides of the issue, Cahill decided that while no nude beaches would be designated within the park system, he found "proponents' arguments that a few miles of beach be set aside for their use were persuasive." The problem, he articulated, was that designating nude beaches would focus opponents' ire in such a way as to create conflict that would be difficult, and expensive, to patrol. Cahill's issue was not with nudity, what he called a "victimless crime" but monitoring the opposition. Thus, he concluded it would be "the policy of the Department that enforcement of nude sunbathing regulations within the State Park System shall be made only upon the complaint of a private citizen. Citations or arrests shall be made only after attempts are made to elicit voluntary compliance with the regulations. This policy should free up enforcement people to concentrate on other pressing duties."[131] In short, if no one complained, nude beachgoers were free to disrobe on designated strips of coastline. The "Cahill Policy," as it came to be known, was celebrated by free beach activists for strengthening *Smith*, if not actually securing legal nude beaches. As David Irving, an activist from San Diego put it, "On the isolated beaches we've been using for years, nobody ever complains. In fact, you could probably get away with it on most regular beaches without running into the occasional asshole who would go find a ranger to complain to. Furthermore, since the policy says they will try for voluntary compliance first, and only issue citations when nudists refuse to dress, then there's no risk of getting busted."[132] It would be upheld in 1988 by Deputy Director Jack Harrison and remained the unofficial policy in California state parks for the next twenty years until crackdowns on nude beachgoers at San Onofre State Beach in San Diego County in the first decade of the twenty-first century that resulted in the rescinding of the Cahill Policy. The resultant citations, arrests, and aggressive police presence have continued to effectively close nude beaches used without incident for the better part of thirty years.[133] Legal challenges from national groups like the Naturist Action Committee (NAC), who filed an action in the California State Court of Appeal, in 2009, to reinstate the Cahill Policy failed to get a sympathetic hearing.[134] In the wake of aggressive state action at the beach, involving multiple citations and arrests over several months, the Naturist Action Committee sued the Department of Parks and Recreation. A California Superior Court ruled in NAC's favor but an appellate court overturned the ruling. The Superior Court refused to rehear the case. In its newsletter, the NAC expressed anger and frustration that the American Association for Nude Recreation (AANR) not only refused to help the NAC's case but also obstructed it by taking the Department of Parks and Recreation's side, asserting that there was a "problem" at the San Onofre site.[135]

As the nude beach movement grew, so did political friction between the free beach people and the social nudist people. Unlike the campaigns to legalize nudism in the 1940s and 1950s, which pivoted on legal definitions of obscenity, the free beach movement articulated its position in relation to space, access, freedom from surveillance, and nature. In its manifesto of August 1975, the Cape Cod Free the Free Beach Committee lambasted the National Park

Service, and evoked the language of the anti-war movement and the new environmentalism, for scarring the landscape with its "ecology-churning" jeeps, the "militarization of the beach," and destroying the beach in order to save it.[136] Beachfront USA argued that free beach activists were to fight for "a return to the natural" and to restore the "rational bathing habits of thousands of years of human history."[137]

Free beach activism also expressed a more finely tuned consciousness about racial equality than the earlier social nudist movement, understanding that even if nude beachgoers had a tough time of it, their whiteness offered easy access to most beaches while nonwhites had to fight ugly civil rights battles to use the same public spaces.[138] The struggle of Ned Coll and the Revitalization Corps to free beaches for black people in Connecticut, for example, was loudly publicized by free beach advocates in the Midwest and on the East Coast.[139] In 1976, as part of National Nude Beach Day, Lee Baxandall's *Green Mountain Quarterly* issued the following statement under the banner, "Freedom of Beach": "Even the access to beaches has different levels of denial. Whites generally have access to get their tans. But tan and black people aren't allowed onto long stretches of coastline [such as here], in Connecticut, where a long campaign is being waged to break the grip of tight white towns which deny access to non-property owners."[140]

Another difference was free beach activism's feminist critique. Naturism and the free beach movement emerged at the peak of feminism's second wave and it influenced its politics. Women involved in the free beach movement argued that naturism freed nudity from commodification, an important step in liberating women from sexual objectification. They were sharply critical of social nudism for its complicity with troubling social norms by hosting beauty pageants at its resorts, a type of pageantry in line with Miss America and the cruder Miss Nude America Contest.[141] But women participating in both traditional nudism and free beach activism argued that getting rid of clothing and the superficial trappings of gender norms encouraged acceptance of one's own body, a better ability to relate to men and women, and a more physically liberating way of moving through the world. To not have to focus on clothes, bras, jewelry, makeup, and posture could free women to engage in more fulfilling and collective roles.[142] In defining themselves in opposition to social nudists, naturists distinguished between the older generation who traveled to isolated camps and paid gate fees for admission and a younger generation inspired by feminism and the civil disobedience of the Civil Rights Movement.[143]

It became clear to leaders of the new free beach movement that as much as they may have shared culturally, social nudists and the American Sunbathing Association represented private, property-owning clubs, which were anathema to free beach philosophy. If free beach advocates were going to gain legal traction, they needed to build a group specifically focused on the issues of public space, beach access, and environmental sustainability. The result was the founding of The Naturist Society in 1980 by Baxandall and colleagues in San Francisco.[144]

It is no coincidence that the split between traditional nudism and free beach activism took place in 1980. Nudism had attracted a fair amount of attention from academic circles in the 1960s, with some of the most positive studies coming out of psychology and sociology. These studies generally concluded that nudism promoted a healthy psyche and sexual identity, even if there was some naïveté in believing entirely in the nonsexual nature of exposing one's body to others.[145] But, by the late 1970s, regressive concerns about urban vice were resurrected and effective campaigns were launched to close down strip clubs and disperse red-light districts using anti-nudity ordinances and zoning concerns as the weapons of choice.[146] These campaigns were compounded by moral panics about child abuse and anti-pornography campaigns that together created a climate in which nudity in general seemed perverse and degenerate.[147] These panics infected academic work and studies were produced during the 1980s that suggested exposing children to nudity, including parental nudity, constituted subtle forms of abuse. As with the legal debunking of the McMartin satanic preschool charges, these studies were challenged by credible psychiatric and sociological evidence that concluded that children exposed to nudity in healthy social circumstances grew up to have an equally healthy sexual identity and ego.[148] Nevertheless, as Richard Mason, head of the South Florida Free Beaches put it, it was clear to nudists "that the newly forming Christian religious right [was] going to target nudists and naturists as part of their strategy to attack the nude nightclubs and the non-related pornography industries. The promotion of anti-nudity legislation, nationally, soon followed and has consumed time and money of the Naturist movement ever since."[149]

Women, too, both within the nudist movement and without, were concerned that the pictorial representations of nudists, especially women and children, were either pornographic or subject to pornographic interpretation by pedophiles and sexual deviants. As Brian Hoffman points out, the late 1970s proved a flashpoint as anti-pornography feminists Andrea Dworkin, Catharine MacKinnon, and Susan Brownmiller worked to suppress pornography as tantamount to sexual violence while civil libertarians won major legal battles to market and consume hard-core porn.[150] With the pornography battle lost, there was a new focus on the vulnerability of children and women in this, for some, newly liberated sexual landscape and for others, a horrifying cesspool of perverted deviance. This would have political implications far beyond nudist culture but is significant here for the wedge it drove between traditional nudism, which had long relied on pictorial magazines as the main organ of cultural expression and information and free beach activism, which relied more on publicity and public outreach. Baxandall responded to feminist criticism of pictorial representation of nudism by publishing essays on the issue in The Naturist Society's flagship magazine, *Clothed with the Sun*, and encouraged publishers of nudist magazines, like Ed Lange, to tread carefully and sensitively when printing photographs of kids. But this would not undo sexist tensions already endemic within nudist culture. Hoffman notes that "despite naturism's liberal sexual values, feminist critiques of pornography, child sexual abuse, and sexual violence provoked sexist responses from many naturist leaders and members."[151] While free beach activism tried to manage a delicate relationship with anti-pornography feminism, traditional nudism, under the auspices of the American Sunbathing Association, issued strong public statements about their place within the pornography debate. At a conference in Las Vegas in 1985, ASA general counsel Robert Page, stated, "We must not curtail our legitimate activities, or the photographic portrayal of them, just because a small percentage of people find the pre-adult a source of sexual interest. But we are all responsible citizens of a larger community, we believe in social family nudism, and most of us are, or have been, parents. We therefore have a collective responsibility that prevents us from taking the easy way out by not dealing with the issue up front. One hopes it is quite clear that organized nudists do not seek support for broadening of any form of censorship. Rather, our aim is to do what is reasonable, feasible and conscionable to prohibit and prevent sexual abuse of children."[152]

As hostile a cultural and political climate as the 1980s fostered, the founding of The Naturist Society ushered in an active era of grassroots organizing glued together by cheaply produced newsletters, zines, and beach events. The Gay and Lesbian Naturists formed in 1981, South Florida Free Beaches was founded in 1980 and successfully won a clothing-optional designation for the now famous Haulover Beach Park, just north of Miami Beach, and Michigan hosted the Nude Beach Advocates.[153] Washington, DC, had National Capital Beachfront with its own newsletter, "The Capital Sun." San Diego hosted FAIR

(Friends of Alternatives in Recreation) and Topanga Canyon nudists formed
B.A.R.E., "a political action to attain a LEGAL nude beach," with its newsletter "Nudesbriefs." Newport Beach organized the Friends of Freedom and Free
Beaches, publishing "Orange Country Nude Beaches Newsletter" while Central Coast Beachfront out of Lompoc, California, published a handy "Hassle
and Voyeur Index" to grade the degree of surveillance of nude beaches from
Santa Barbara to San Diego. The effect of the organizing was to draw public attention to both nudist culture and the issue of beach access with the intention
of securing legal clothing-optional areas on city and state beaches. Despite its
discomfort with the publicity, in 1985 the American Sunbathing Association
sanctioned an interest in public land accessibility and promised to support the
efforts of The Naturist Society.[154] In 1990, The Naturist Society founded the
Naturist Action Committee (NAC) to serve as the legal arm of the larger organization and it has since grown into a national body for the creation and protection of clothing-optional areas. As recently as 2013, the NAC called on the
State of California to formally designate specific beaches as clothing-optional.
Interestingly, the American Association for Nude Recreation refused to sign
the petition, preferring to maintain the sharp division between social nudist
culture and free beach activism.

FIGURE 46. The Western Sunbathing Association makes an appearance at the
Occasional Pasadena Doo Dah Parade, ca. 1990. Photograph courtesy of Pamela
Roberts.

The story of nude beaches follows broader American socioeconomic and cultural shifts. As the Mazo Beach, Wisconsin, example highlights, new mapping technology and the web have caused trouble for nude beachgoers as the number of visitors grows in size. In California, naturists have encountered the same problems other visitors have as the state struggles with budget deficits and keeping public beaches open at all. These economic problems combined with cuts to law enforcement and heightened tensions between the California Coastal Commission's restrictions on private development and wealthy Californians' claims to beach space that is, in fact, public has led to regressive measures and a clamping down on nudist beach use. Meanwhile, Fire Island, New York, long a gay mecca and home to one of the state's only legal nude beaches, received notice in February 2013 that the National Park Service, which has no ban on nudism on beaches, would be enforcing New York State anti-nudity laws. Similar to the Mazo Beach problem, the newspapers reported that "with the growth of social media sites promoting the libertine pleasures of Lighthouse Beach, the crowds have become larger and the behavior coarser."[155] And, as when red-light districts or other sexualized urban areas are forcibly shut down, participants just go elsewhere. In the case of Fire Island, the sense is that beachgoers will move over to a smaller, and before now, trouble-free legal nude beach in Sandy Hook, New Jersey, with the likelihood that similar problems will soon arise. From the vantage point of the twenty-first century, it appears that the hypersexualized landscape of online culture has made the ability to shape real world spaces for a socially naked experience difficult and the possibility of a free (unpaid) one that much more so. For a new generation seeking a free and natural lifestyle, the lines between public and private are unclear and the boundary between nudity and sexuality that much harder to decipher. Capitalism, however, offers a solution in the form of "lifestyle consumerism," in which nakedness retains nudism's claim to feeling good in one's skin while offering a range of niche-marketed naked options for each and every free and natural consumer.

CHAPTER 6

NAKED LIFESTYLE CONSUMERISM

Today, "naked" is one of the most marketed of terms and one infused with a panoply of related meanings including clean, honest, real, raw, healthy, natural, sexy, simple, organic, and authentic. What naked does not mean, however, is free. To drink Naked® juice, wear Naked and Famous® jeans, smoke Buck Naked® e-cigarettes, apply Naked® eyeshadow, wash with Herbal Essences Naked® shampoo, hire Naked® marketing representatives, seek the protection of Naked Security®, shop for sexy underthings at Naked Wardrobe®, or take Bold and Naked® yoga classes is to engage as wholeheartedly in the consumer marketplace as if these commodities were named Baroque®.

Given that nudism's rejection of fashion has been one of its strongest challenges to capitalism, it is ironic how often "naked" is used to sell clothing and beauty products. But even if advertisers can't interest nudists in adorning themselves, or make them anxious about their bodies, nudism's philosophies of honesty and authenticity, their "naked truth," if you will, have become very attractive to marketing executives.[1] Among the myriad fashion and beauty products peddled as "real" or "natural" are American fashion magazines themselves, which have recently nodded to public pressure by having more realistic and natural-looking models and lots of articles on feminist empowerment.[2] The February 2018 issue of *Allure* magazine revealed this new appropriation of the free and natural lifestyle when the editors featured actress Dakota Johnson, star of the *Fifty Shades of Grey* movie franchise, and the tagline, "The New Naked," on the front cover. Interestingly, Johnson is not naked at all, but wearing matching beige underwear under a sheer dress. The "new naked" is more of a reference to the articles found inside on wellness, self-exploration, and personality analysis, such as "Losing Clothes, Finding Zen," which recounts a visit to Esalen, and "Naked Person," which lists characteristics that make someone more "naked," including the ability to buy organic food. While *Allure* does feature a few glances of unretouched nudity, a bit of bare breast here, and a sideways shot of an unclad hip there, in the middle of the "new naked" issue is an essay titled, "The Body, Shopped," where readers can learn of the newest plastic surgery technology, such as TissuGlu, which seals skin back together after a tummy tuck. The takeaway is that the "new naked" can be liberating, but only if one looks really good naked while pondering one's authentic self at a luxurious retreat spa. *Allure*'s editors deserve kudos for the elegance of the layout and the tempting embodied experience promised within: it is pure free and natural lifestyle consumerism complete with Esalen credentials.

The *Allure* example of contemporary beauty advertising highlights the inroads marketers have made into the same body positivity and self-esteem concepts underlying much of the free and natural lifestyle. Sometime in the late twentieth century, there was a perceptible shift, particularly in the marketing of beauty products to women, from the narcissistic celebration of self as in L'Oréal's "Because I'm Worth It" campaign, introduced in the 1970s, to Oil of Olay's "Love the Skin You're In," which implied that while there was nothing that *needed* improvement, a little skin cream couldn't hurt. Meanwhile, Dove's "Campaign for Real Beauty," launched in 2004, with its eye-catching billboards with almost-nude atypical models (women of color, older women, slightly heavier than average models) was heralded in the mainstream media for its radical portrayal of "normal" women. Feminist critics, however, found the advertisements disingenuous as Dove is owned by Unilever, the body product company responsible for its hypersexualized advertising of cologne-based gels and sprays to adolescent boys. In response to its critics, Dove established the "Self-Esteem Project," an educational nonprofit supported by the research of "independent academic experts" whose mission "is to ensure that the next generation grows up enjoying a positive relationship with the way they look—helping young people raise their self-esteem and realize their full potential." Most importantly, "the Dove Self-Esteem Project was created from a vision where beauty is a source of confidence, not anxiety."[3]

The upshot is that consumer capitalism is no longer simply making you so anxious about your body that you buy products, and lots of them, to improve yourself. That is very twentieth century. Instead, consumer capitalism now affirms how awesome you already are. In fact, you are so awesome, so natural, that just a few more products will help you stay that way. Not everyone, of course, is buying the self-esteem altruism of cosmetics companies and there are innumerable blogs and websites excoriating these companies and their advertising. Yet naked products and an almost decade-long trend toward "nude" color palettes in clothing, underwear, and makeup continue to rack up huge sales indicating that consumers, and especially female ones, are attracted to the idea of appearing naturally naked while unnaturally clothed and cosmetically enhanced. Matching one's actual skin tone to the products that claim to be "nude" or "naked" can be frustrating since there are millions of different skin tones and, seemingly, about a million nude foundations that do not match them. "Loving the skin you're in" suddenly seems not so silly; in fact, it is downright seductive.

It is thus not surprising that learning to "love the skin you're in" is the catchphrase for myriad body positivity therapies, handbooks, encounter groups, blogs, and body-focused feminist philosophies. It is also a mantra for black women and other women of color who participate in online forums tying self-love and anti-racist body politics to a rejection of white beauty standards. While not necessarily tied to nudity, whether personal or social, "love the skin you're in" modalities generally emphasize the naturalness of one's body, self-acceptance of the body one has, and explicitly, or implicitly, foster the idea that a healthy self-image will produce a healthy sex life and sexual identity.[4]

Inherent in the quest for self-love through body acceptance is a search for an authentic corporeal experience. What does it mean to accept oneself, feel empowered sexually, reject oppressive beauty standards while creating one's own sense of beauty, and somehow feel natural and effortless in performing one's identity? Nudists, of course, for almost a hundred years have loudly proclaimed that shedding one's clothing and not hiding behind its false signifiers is the ticket to authentic living. As the Western Sunbathing Association wrote of Americans who have experienced a nude beach or a nudist resort, "so now you know the pure, clean feeling of a world without clothes. You know that how you feel *inside* is the true measurement of yourself as a person, and not how much your clothes cost or where you got them."[5] To focus on the inside, rather than focus on the outside, and challenge the social status quo, speaks to one way that nudists could neutralize the ideological gap between traditional nudism's private orientation and free beach activism's emphasis on public spaces. Indeed, the historical division between the two camps has been neatly exploited by consumer capitalism, which markets ever more expensive private nudist experiences, while it simultaneously shrinks the public sphere, further marginalizing free beach activism.

One nudist group that has resisted both the split between advocates of private and public nudity, *and* capitalism's exploitation of it, is the Southern California Naturist Association (SCNA) based in Calabasas, in the San Fernando Valley. Unlike many of the historical nudist groups discussed in this book, and those extant today, the SCNA is not a "landed" club in that it owns no property of its own nor is it associated with one specific resort or camp. Instead, through a monthly newsletter, political organizing around the issue of free beaches, and an action-packed agenda of weekly, monthly, and annual events, the SCNA has sustained a presence on both local and national levels of organized nudism for almost twenty years. The SCNA, which formed when Ed Lange's Elysium folded and the land sold, has been actively involved in the continuing fight to free beaches in Southern California, battles to permit nude hiking along nature trails in the region, public outreach to educate Californians about nudism, and the assimilation of nudism into common urban and suburban social activities.

The SCNA reports on the state of legalized nudity and the constantly shifting terrain of nudity laws throughout the United States, organizes its own political presence on contested nude beaches, especially Bates Beach, and continues the Elysium tradition of distributing nudist literature independently published by the Ultraviolet Press. The SCNA, which has its roots in the sexual freedom and liberated expression of 1960s and 1970s nudism that Lange celebrated at Elysium, today is more focused on including women in its ranks, with events like women-only gatherings, sustaining the culture of naked living outside of commercial resorts, and body acceptance. The SCNA helps sponsor events like "International Women in Naturism Day" and "Love the Body Positive," a nudist theatrical performance that encourages the nudity of the audience. The play by Johanna Adams has, at its core, "a vital message about body image and acceptance."[7]

The SCNA is affiliated with both The Naturist Society, the Wisconsin-based nudist organization dedicated to fighting anti-nudity laws and freeing American beaches and the American Association of Nude Recreation (AANR), the contemporary incarnation of the American Sunbathing Association, which is both the largest nudist organization in the United States and the major affiliate for nudist resorts and landed clubs. As such, the SCNA straddles the two main nudist streams, public activism and resort culture, participating in protest activities like "Free the Nipple" actions to legalize public female toplessness and encouraging membership at private nudist camps and travel to nudist hotels. But it is in the booking of venues like bowling alleys, art galleries, and recreation centers for naked socials that the SCNA stands out for resituating the nudist concept of the natural body in urban and suburban arenas. There are strong echoes in SCNA promotional literature of nudism's long-treasured tenet of freeing the body of the expectations of American consumer culture and the acceptance of nudity as a natural expression of our humanness. Keeping their connection to mainstream nudism through their affiliation with AANR, the SCNA nevertheless retains the free and natural vibe of Elysium and a lighthearted, though well-organized, approach to naked living. By not having its own property and maintaining its focus on political activism and body acceptance, SCNA retains the authentic aims of the American nudist movement and feels less like a consumer lifestyle and more like a fun social activist group. SCNA's contemporary form of social nudism is very much in line with "love the skin you're in" body positivity and feminist self-love. SCNA's organizational and philosophical strategies seem to be working, too. The group's May 2018 newsletter put out a call for as many volunteers as its membership could round up to help meet the growing demand for more nudist events and gatherings in Southern California.[8]

Another example of naked lifestyle consumerism is the current popularity of naked yoga classes in the United States. But here, the private quest for internal calm and well-being has been neatly absorbed into capitalism's exploitation of the free and natural lifestyle. Yoga has long been a featured practice of the free and natural lifestyle but its naked variant, while having ancient origins, is experiencing a contemporary renaissance. An internet search for naked yoga will get hundreds of hits, most of which fall into three categories.

1. Pornography that uses naked yoga as the ruse to have sex on film (in the old days, it was pizza delivery or plumbing mishaps, but in today's marketplace, why not yoga?). Even when not showing explicit sex, these sites feature pornographic bodies, complete with airbrushed skin, surgically enhanced breasts, and hairless mons pubis in yoga positions highlighting these eroticized physical features. Cable networks and streaming services also feature naked yoga films, which are generally amateurish and focused on how many crotch shots can be crammed into a scene. *Natural and Nude Yoga Techniques*, available on Amazon Prime, is a case in point.[9]

2. Sleekly marketed yoga studios that either offer regularly scheduled naked yoga classes or specialize in the genre, with celebrity teachers

like New York's Aaron Star, who also runs a swift business in naked, and erotic, yoga videos. These studios are, for the most part, directed toward gay men and often restricted to male participants.

3. Women-friendly nude yoga classes that are usually mixed-gender and oriented toward yogis and yoginis interested in achieving an enhanced body awareness and experiencing the physical freedom of nudity in a safe environment. These classes often claim deep roots in nude yoga's ancient Tantric and sadhu traditions evoking nudity as the key to yogic authenticity and the sacred feminine.

Naked yoga is generally practiced in mixed-gender groups, although sometimes in single-sex classes, and is often organized through social networking sites such as Facebook and Meetup. While the SCNA vigorously promotes naked yoga classes, most are not specifically nudist, instead drawing curious yogis from already established yoga communities in urban centers. Naked yoga classes can be exhilarating bonding experiences but can also leave practitioners, and especially women, open to competitive body scrutiny and unwelcome sexual overtures. Moreover, naked yoga's online imagery is disconcertingly close to pornography, with its artificially enhanced bodies and keen eye for exposed genitalia.

The expectation that yoga, unlike swimming or aerobics classes, for example, is a natural fit for a naked body practice has ancient origins in India and more recent historical roots in American social nudism. Modern yoga and nudism emerged in the United States as closely coupled body practices harnessed to pursuits of health and natural living but there is confusion within the current practice of naked yoga as to where the liberated body ends and the sexualized body begins, reflecting broader societal hang-ups about nudity and sex that yoga alone cannot remedy. The problem is less that yoga is an inappropriate site to work these issues out; rather, we are asking a lot of a body practice, albeit a sophisticated one, to resolve the social fallout of misogyny, the competitive scrutiny of capitalism, and body commodification. The nature of consumer economics has increasingly made yoga a commercial enterprise with the same strategic niche appeal as any other commodity. As enterprising yogis trademark competing products like AcroYoga®, CorePowerYoga®, YogaFit®, BROga® and YogaLean®, the commodification and sexual objectification of the body within yoga culture intensifies.

The uncomfortable relationship between sex and yoga has surfaced recently in disturbing media scandals about abusive student-guru relationships, sexual harassment, and rape within international yoga schools, as well as in feminist scholarship critiquing contemporary yoga's objectification of young, white women and exclusion of women of color. The commodification and concomitant sexualization of asanas (physical postures) is interpreted as a problematic deviation from yoga's meditative origins, its healing potential as a therapeutic tool for body and spirit, and the presumed goals of community, enlightenment, and embodied self-acceptance. The website Yoganonymous's ongoing discussion about the prevalence of online "selfies" that privilege the extraordinarily fit, young, and nimble is one example, as is the criticism of former model-turned-yoga-teacher, Tara Stiles, for her emphasis on the body beautiful in her bestselling book, *Slim Calm Sexy Yoga*.[10] Judith Hanson Lasater, founding coeditor of *Yoga Journal*, made waves in 2010 when she publicly criticized the current incarnation of the magazine for using sex to sell yoga: "I am confused because I do not understand how photos of naked or half-naked women are connected with the sale of practice products for asana, an important part of yoga. These pictures do not teach the viewer about yoga practice or themselves. They aren't even about the celebration of the beauty of the human body or the beauty of the poses, which I support. These ads are just about selling a product."[11]

While yoga is held up as a spiritual and meditative practice that transcends material and physical desires, it has had a long and conflicted relationship with human sexuality. Anthropologist of religion Joseph S. Alter explains "until the beginning of the twentieth century—and in sharp contrast to what it has become over the course of the past hundred years—hatha yoga was magical, mystical, structured with reference to the physiology of sex, and concerned with embodied immortality. It was inherently physiological rather than metaphysical, even in its most philosophical articulation."[12] Yoga's physicality was inherent to its practice, as well as the cosmology that supported it, so much so that Alter argues "yoga fetishizes the body as a whole and parts of the body in relation to one another."[13] Sexuality and its denial, whether explicit or subliminal, *and* the fetishism of the body, are deeply interwoven into the corporeality of asana practice. In our contemporary moment, this historical confusion plays itself out as a dialectical tension between a yearning to link yoga seamlessly to a past, however checkered, in order to uphold its spiritual authenticity, and the hope that tethering yoga to modern body culture will somehow transcend Western society's profound and paradoxical anxieties about sex.

Naked yoga has the potential to address this tension by shedding the worst elements of our competitive body culture, encourage healthy intimacy, and prompt us to love the skin we're in; however, its overt corporeality sexualizes the space in which participants practice and clouds yogic interpretations of physicality and community. In jettisoning the markers of commodity fetishism by forgoing the clothing, jewelry, and decorative props ubiquitous in contemporary yoga culture, naked yoga also leaves the body bare and vulnerable.

Just like clothed yoga, which draws from Indian, European, and American cultural traditions, naked yoga has no one continuous route from the ancients to the present but neither is it a twenty-first-century invention nor a consumer novelty. Digambara Jain monks, members of one of India's, indeed the world's, oldest religions, do not wear clothes and follow a series of vows and duties that resemble Patañjali's *yamas* and *niyamas*, the ethical commitments of yoga.[14] Dasnami ascetics, the *naga* sadhus, are holy men who live naked and are easily recognizable by their long dreadlocks and ash-and-paint-coated bodies.[15] To many British colonials in the nineteenth century, it was these naga (naked) ascetics who represented yoga, indeed, India, and appeared to be practitioners of a kind of black magic with their bodily contortions and seeming otherworldly ability to live without food, water, or even air.[16] Indian nationals in the early twentieth century placed distance between these ascetics and modern asana practitioners in what would be a successful effort to "clean up" yoga for an international market, which, in the exchange of Eastern spirituality for Western capital, could challenge British colonialism.[17] Nudity was thus intentionally severed from the modern yoga practices that would leave India to find a welcome audience in the West, and particularly in the United States. But unlike the contemporary practice of naked yoga in the West, which aspires to liberate and encourage self-realization, Philip Carr-Gomm points out "the nakedness of the Jain saints [was] designed to demonstrate their renunciation of physical attachments and pleasures rather than their celebration."[18] The goals and demography of contemporary naked yoga bear little resemblance to its Jain origins in deeply religious, celibate asceticism; nevertheless, it is useful to remember that nudity and yoga are intricately linked historically and that the very nakedness which draws sensational attention to the material body now originally signified a *renunciation* of material and sexual desires.

One of the earliest references to naked yoga in the United States was in a 1938 essay in *The Nudist* entitled "The Mental Element in Our Physical Well-

Being" by Marguerite Agniel, a yoga enthusiast and author of the successful yoga guide, *The Art of the Body: Rhythmic Exercises for Health and Beauty* (1931). Her essay featured nude women in a variety of yoga postures along with Agniel's suggestions for focusing attention on breathing to improve concentration and foster a healthier relationship between one's thinking and spiritual selves.[19] The marriage of nudism and yoga made perfect sense: both were exercises in healthful living; both were countercultural and bohemian; both highlighted the body; and both were sensual without being explicitly erotic. Moreover, in both practices, the health and beauty of the body were paths to better living but not necessarily ends in themselves.

While yoga had been first introduced to rapt American audiences in 1893, when Swami Vivekananda lectured at the Parliament of the World's Religions at the Chicago World's Fair, it was in the 1950s that modern yoga took shape as a popular physical practice in the United States and when it became especially attractive to female practitioners.[20] Fascination with the *Bhagavad Gita*, Hinduism, and the meditative benefits of raja-yoga, of course, has a much earlier American history, going back to Ralph Waldo Emerson, Henry David Thoreau, and the nineteenth-century intellectual and cosmological pursuits of the transcendentalists.[21] The creative and elite vanguard of the 1920s and 1930s also experimented with yoga, following the teachings of such celebrities as the flamboyant guru Pierre Bernard, his handsome and serious nephew, Theos, and the mystic leader Jiddu Krishnamurti, but it was in the wake of World War II that yoga asanas became a regularly practiced form of exercise.[22] Paramahansa Yogananda's wildly successful *Autobiography of a Yogi*, and his ingenious mail-order yoga courses, embedded yoga in American popular culture along with other postwar consumer fads like paint-by-numbers and coonskin caps. And it was Indra Devi's Hollywood studio, famous clients, and bestselling publications like *Yoga for You* and *Forever Young, Forever Healthy* that solidified the physical practice of yoga in the postwar United States as a key to keeping fit, staying slender, and achieving an overarching sense of well-being, particularly for women.[23]

The 1950s were, in fact, ripe for anything Americans could interpret as a new kind of exercise; the decade was laden with messages generated by the federal government, US military, and medical doctors that Americans were growing soft as a result of postwar prosperity. As Shelly McKenzie argues, freeways, car culture, and suburban homes full of conveniences and convenience foods were making Americans lethargic and overweight while a male business culture of cocktails, smoking, and stress was causing a lethal "cardiac crisis" with men in its sights. Together, doctors and Eisenhower's President's Council on Youth Fitness promoted physical exercise as a way not just to prevent soft bodies but also any political ideologies that might be "soft on communism."[24]

Women, of course, were also caught in the crosshairs of the new postwar fitness market. If they were to be good American suburban housewives and keep their husbands satisfied enough to return to the family home, they had better keep their girlish figures. Between Jack LaLanne's televised calisthenics and nutritional tips and Indra Devi's popular books and LPs for cultivating a home yoga practice, white, heterosexual, middle-class women were expected to be thin and in shape. While there were plenty of spurious gadgets on the fitness market in the 1950s (the electric slimming belt being one of the most famous), LaLanne's scissor kicks in leotards and Devi's clear directions for stretching, twisting, and balancing were inexpensive and easy to replicate. By the time white suburban housewives were practicing *suptabadacanasana* in their living rooms, American yoga had been pretty much shorn of its spiritual and meditative qualities. It had also been feminized, but only to the extent that yoga was a conduit to shaping a sexually appealing female figure.

By the early 1960s, yoga was a regular feature in *Sunshine and Health*. Along with home modifications for suburban nudist living, readers could further expand their quest for health and well-being as nudism and yoga came together in a syncretic modernist exercise in natural living through the body. Ads for a mail-order "Yogism Course" promised "power is the secret of success. In Yogism, now adapted to needs of Western Man, is the power you've always wanted! Banish anxiety, worry, fear, and frustration! Take vitality from the air . . . cleanse mind and body of defeatist poison. . . . Strengthen your spine and nervous system, control your emotions." For twenty-five cents, an interested reader could order Lesson 1 from the Insight School.[25] A 1961 *Sunshine and Health* pictorial displayed women practicing yoga poses at a nudist camp while the 1962 issue of *Nude Living*, which featured the interview with architect Richard Neutra, made a point of explaining that the interviewer, Audre Hardy, was a nudist and a practitioner of "Hindu yoga."[26] In each of these examples, what was foregrounded was *not* that yoga needed to be practiced naked to be beneficial but rather that yoga's meditative and physical tools had a sympathetic overlap with nudism's goals of health, mental and emotional well-being, and progressive social change through a corporeal practice.

Yoga and nudity became more intrinsically entwined with sex in the 1970s when yoga became an integral part of the Human Potential Movement, the

New Age outgrowth of both the counterculture and popular psychology that taught that ultimate happiness and fulfillment could be reached through the self-actualization of one's true talents and desires. In 1972, Malcolm Leigh published a short, heavily illustrated guide to postural yoga featuring nude women; and, in 1974, the short film, *Naked Yoga*, written and directed by Paul Corsden, fully captured the aesthetics of New Age yoga nudity, with jelled lenses creating a psychedelic aura, flowing water, and ethereal female yogis evoking the early twentieth-century nymphs of Fidus fame.[27] A German symbolist painter and practicing theosophist, Fidus (Hugo Reinhold Karl Johann Höppener, 1868–1948) depicted a phantasmagoric art nouveau world of nudity, sex, and nature popular with early nudists and yogis in Europe and, later, the American counterculture.

Esalen was the most famous of the Human Potential Centers, where naked yoga classes have been led since the 1960s, but Elysium, Ed Lange's retreat in Topanga Canyon, was also an early adopter of yoga for health and relaxation as part of its therapeutic offerings.[28] Yoga, like Elysium's other activities, could be practiced nude or clothed but, unlike the yoga described in *Sunshine and Health*, at Elysium, yoga's benefits were tied to its nakedness. To reach one's full potential, one had to be comfortable in one's skin and the key was to allow oneself to feel vulnerable and absorb the vulnerability of others. While some of Elysium's yoga offerings suggested that participants would be more comfortable wearing clothing, others, like "Energy, Breath, and Movement" and "The Body Learning Workshop," were purposefully naked and promised "through a process of sensory awareness, therapeutic touch and gentle movement exercises, the learner will have the opportunity to answer questions regarding sexuality, healing, stress, pain, and the connection between mind and body."[29] No one who attended these classes expected to have sex, or if they did, they were sorely disappointed. What the Elysium workshops did do; however, was integrate nudity and yoga in ways that expressly promoted healthier sexuality through mind-body awareness. Nakedness, and the sensuality it generated, was thus integral to this New Age variant of yoga.

Today, yoga is a multibillion dollar industry that has been assimilated into medical, therapeutic, fitness, and fashion cultures in ways unimaginable a generation ago. Why yoga has become such an economic juggernaut and hugely popular cultural trend is widely debated, but the major reasons can be tied to innovations in yoga marketing specifically, and broad developments in globalized lifestyle and wellness consumerism more generally. As the body increasingly carries the status signifiers of wealth, health, and well-being, yoga

FIGURE 47. Relaxation workshop, Elysium, ca. 1980. Photograph by Ed Lange.
Courtesy of the Southern California Naturist Association.

has proven an exceptionally malleable commodity: a marker of urban hip-
ness, a badge of alternative lifestyle pursuits, a sign of socially progressive political leanings, evidence of a spiritual quest, and a ticket to fitness. A Marxist
cultural analysis of the body under global capitalism would suggest that our
social relations have become so tied to commodity consumption, and their
concomitant signifiers, that we have completely naturalized the labeling of the
body. We derive "common sense" from how people look no matter how hard
we work and how much we spend to produce a desirable body.[30] We know
the perfectly sculpted body is artificial and yet we derive intrinsic knowledge
from it. Yoga, both as corporeal practice and a commodity, also naturalizes
these relationships, which can be hierarchical and unjust. Indeed, yoga's pre-
vailing link to physical fitness makes it difficult to separate from the surveillance and categorization, indeed, fetishism, of bodies in American culture.

Yet, despite their concerns about contemporary yoga's privileging, and
marketing, of young, fit, white, and thin female bodies, feminist scholars, yo-

gis, and activists alike also see yoga as liberating and empowering, and the disproportionate number of women in yoga classes certainly upholds that view. Indeed, challenges to yoga's commercialism bloom in communities all over the United States including Long Beach's free daily "yoga on the bluff" program organized by Dharma Shakti's Yogalution, which also runs the city's only donation-based studio, and organizations like the Yoga and Body Image Coalition and Off the Mat, Into the World, which encourage the application of yoga principles to social and economic ills. While we cannot escape the essential embodiment of the yoga experience, we can use it to challenge restrictive societal norms and take our bodies back.[31] The contemporary practice of naked yoga can challenge the commercialism and sexism of modern asana practice but naked yoga's sensuality and hypercorporeality make it more complicated than a simple stripping of yoga's flashy trappings.

The naked yoga studio that has received the most press is New York City's Bold and Naked, founded by Joschi Schwartz and Monika Werner. Offering co-ed, male-only, and Tantric massage classes, Bold and Naked's website states that "naked yoga changes and reshapes your muscles and gives them more endurance and flexibility, but you will agree, one of the coolest things about it is that it changes your perception and understanding of your own body. Join us and have fun! Pierce the illusion of whatever holds you back to reveal that you can accept, appreciate and celebrate yourself."[32] Perusal of the studio's website and accompanying blog makes it clear that Bold and Naked is positioning itself as a serious yoga center for studying meditation and yoga philosophy, while simultaneously exploring varied elements of human sexuality. Bold and Naked's owners are also actively focused on attracting gay men to the studio. While the nudity of their classes is not supposed to be about sex—rather, "it's about being comfortable in your own skin and the amazing confidence that comes with it"—the studio explicitly promotes naked yoga as beneficial for sexual health.[33] Within the visual online context of Bold and Naked, a high-end urban yoga studio, being naked is sexy and the inherent promise of a Bold and Naked physical practice is a body that others will find sexually appealing. The offering of naked (male) Tantric massage certainly drives home the point that feeling good in one's body is a sensual and erotic enterprise. Yet the Bold and Naked blog also puts forth a pretty straightforward feminist self-loving credo: "Part of yoga is to honor and connect with your body. Practicing yoga naked frees you from negative feelings about your body and allows you to be more accepting of your physical imperfections. You will find a deeper connection with yourself and the world around you."[34]

There is nothing wrong with Bold and Naked's yoga offerings; in fact, the studio's website and the press's positive coverage promise a safe, exciting, and athletic yoga experience that likely can go a long way to making yogis—male or female, gay or straight—feel good in their skin. Its New Agey "Create the Life You Want to Live" mantra is right in line with most yoga practices in the United States.[35] The troubling tension, however, is that Bold and Naked's framing of yoga as both liberating and sexy is symptomatic of contradictory messages within contemporary popular culture that confuse liberated bodies (those that are free of signifiers, categories, judgments, and scrutiny; Bold and Naked even states it bluntly: "You can't do anything without being labeled")[36] with bodies that are sexually desirable. A key part of marketing *any* element of our body culture, whether fashion, fitness, or health, is tying the commodity to sex appeal, making the enterprise of body improvement fundamentally a narcissistic one. This process fetishizes the body, sublimating anxieties about sex, aging, and death, and instead foregrounds the body's desirability as the main signifier of successful socioeconomic relations. By making the body itself a commodity fetish, and not simply a vessel for selling other commodities, our cultural economy collapses the distinction between liberation and sex.[37] Of course, the two can be mutually inclusive, but they are not the same.

For many women, for example, feeling liberated in one's flesh is to *not* feel sexualized. Feminist critics of beauty culture in the United States have debated for decades over whether or not participating in the consumer economy of beauty and the body allows the agency of choice or is simply an exercise in sublimation and gender oppression intrinsically tied to the body's sexual objectification.[38] Indeed, one of the great attractions of nudist culture for women has been the opportunity to relinquish the social pressures to lose weight, wear makeup, and squeeze into restrictive clothing.[39] Women express delight at being naked without fear of sexual advances or body shaming and articulate it beautifully when describing the pleasures of the "nude world versus the rude world."[40]

The conundrum for contemporary yoga is that it is presumed to be outside the sexual corporeal realm; yet as has been noted by many observers critical of how yoga is currently marketed, its popularity and growth as both a cultural movement and a consumer market is inherently tied to the body, both its perception and its performance. In the United States and, indeed, in most of our globalized world, it is increasingly difficult to untether the corporeal from the sexual. Yoga offers an opportunity to at least try, although yoga is itself subject to sexual fetishism, as is made evident in recent online posts about the sexiness of yoga pants, an uptick in labiaplasty to rid one of "camel toe," or the staging of Australian *Yoke* magazine's provocative cover of a young, topless female yogini posing in *uttanasana*, with her polka-dot-underpants-clad posterior in the air.[41]

While Bold and Naked is an example of how contemporary yoga can combine sexuality and asana, other naked yoga classes and studios are more women-centered, less commercial, and less focused on athleticism and fitness. Their relationship to sex and the eroticized body, however, can vary. Katrina Rainsong is a performance artist, nudist, and model who teaches naked yoga classes in Scottsdale and Tempe, Arizona. Her branded practice, R. A. W. Nude Yoga (the acronym standing for revealed, authentic, and wise) encourages us to think of our bodies as "living temples." She argues "to feel our own nudity in a non-sexual, non-medical construct can be new and very healing. To perceive other people's nudity in a non-sexual setting can be healing not only for the individual, but also for the collective."[42] In her artistically produced book, *R.A.W. Nude Yoga: Celebrating the Human Body Temple*, Rainsong features a combination of black and white photographs of male and female yogis, a brief but thoughtful history of nude yoga, poetry, descriptions of the postures, and treatises on the significance of practicing nude. For example, she writes "nude yoga allows your whole body to breathe; to feel the air on every inch of your skin. It allows you to indulge in your physical perceptions. And while it is sensual, it need not be erotic. In practice we consciously engage all of our senses, all of our chakras, our entire being."[43] In fact, the images are not erotic. The yogis are young, attractive, fit, and have extraordinarily glowing skin but Rainsong states in her introduction that the photographs have not been digitally altered or airbrushed; the people are real. The yoga postures are impressive and tastefully shot and the sense of empowerment emitted by the photographs is that of remarkable grace and physical control.

Megan Leigh Kobzeff, a protégé of Katrina Rainsong, also teaches naked yoga classes in Tempe. Twice a week, she leads a series called "Love the Skin You're In," a yin (gentle) yoga practice that is clothing-optional for participants. With a more modest promotional style than that of Rainsong, Megan Leigh presents images of herself lying peacefully on the floor under a string of Tibetan prayer flags. With long dreadlocks, tattoos, and a beautiful Earth Mama physique, this naked yogini imparts a feeling of authentic pleasure in her own body and a yoga practice that approaches something natural and uninhibited. Rather than even evoking the issues of sex or sensuality, in an online interview, Megan Leigh states "both practicing and teaching naked yoga have transformed me into a more body-positive and self-loving person. It is beautiful to see a group of people of varying body types, age groups, and cultures all feeling comfortable enough in their own skin to strip away their ego and their clothing."[44] Here, naked yoga really does seem healing. Fitness, the body beautiful, and sexual health are not part of the conversation in the way they are for Bold and Naked or even Katrina Rainsong's more women-focused practice.

Naked yoga, while perhaps a gimmicky way to compete in the ever-changing fitness marketplace, is nevertheless an old practice, dating back to yoga's Indian source and the sexual rituals of Tantra.[45] The contemporary interest in practicing it is pretty much severed from its religious origins but today's naked yoga still speaks to a similar impulse to make the body vulnerable in a socially prescribed ritualistic setting and thereby reach a higher state of being, whether it be excitement, meditative bliss, or deep relaxation. In this way, the practice of naked yoga in hipster urban settings is not dissimilar from the huge surge of popularity in tattooing, piercing, and other physical body modifications that have, in the past thirty years, moved rapidly from centuries on the social margins to mainstream social acceptance. While trendiness, fashion, and being cool are no doubt major reasons for the widespread visibility of body modification in contemporary American culture, it still speaks to an ancient urge for ritual and community forged through the body and an urge to mark one's body as unique. However tied to the consumer marketplace body modification might be, one still pays for a piercing, branding, or tattoo in pain, as well as money, which is largely part of its cultural appeal to millions of practitioners. No matter how enmeshed in lifestyle consumerism we are, and no matter how commodified the body, the impulse to authenticate one's physical experience of living is still very powerful. It is not necessarily free or especially natural but it *is* ancient and part of a desire to love the skin we are in, whether we like it or not.

Another commercial example of the contemporary search for authenticity through the body, and the overt marketing of the free and natural lifestyle as a consumer practice, is the popularity of nude tourism. In the twenty-first century, nudism has evolved from a marginal subculture into an international travel activity for those with years of experience as well as for the newly curious. Nude beaches and resorts are the main destinations although nude cruises and nude hiking are other popular choices. A cursory flip through any one of the nude travel guides on the market will show naked tanned adult bodies relaxing poolside, sitting in natural hot springs, lounging on gorgeous beaches, and definitely loving the skin they are in. The most popular and widely read guide, *The World's Best Nude Beaches and Resorts*, copublished by the nudist British press, appropriately named Lifestyle, and The Naturist Society (TNS) in Oshkosh, Wisconsin, reports that "today, nude beaches are a regular part of holiday life in Europe and America, with some of the most beautiful locations and the smartest facilities imaginable. Long gone are the days when nude beach lovers had to hide themselves away on remote stretches of coast. Now you can choose from an almost endless list of allover bathing experiences, from the glorious tropics to the invigorating Arctic."[46]

However one feels about naked bathing in the Arctic, the marketing of nude tourism as not only a legal mainstream activity but as a status-enhancing one tied to leisure time and disposable income contrasts significantly with its origins in The Naturist Society's radical activism that organized the hippie skinny-dippers William Hartman and Marilyn Fithian regretted not interviewing in their landmark study, *Nudist Society*. Free beach activist Lee Baxandall, together with other national free beach leaders, founded The Naturist Society (TNS) in 1980 to "promote and defend nude recreation on appropriate public and private lands."[47] TNS grew directly out of the radical activism of the 1970s and its mission moving into the conservative 1980s was to publish guides to nudist living, monitor anti-nudity agitation, and sustain communication and cooperation among the many different regional nudist groups active across the country. Its first "Gathering," as TNS referred to its meetings, was held at Elysium in October 1980 where two major concerns within the nudist movement were addressed. The first was trying to breach the wall between the private, landed clubs which wanted to avoid legal trouble or the attention of the media and the more loosely organized free beach people who understood nude recreation as a political act. This was not simply a logistics issue—there were real philosophical differences between how social nudists understood their body practice. The other concern was the sexism of social nudism and motions were made to rid the movement of the nude beauty pageants popular at nudist camps since the 1940s.[48]

That same year, Baxandall published the first edition of the *World Guide to Nude Beaches and Recreation*, which has remained in print ever since. Notably, in 1995, TNS changed the word "Recreation" to "Resort."[49] The effect of the *World Guide* was to retain the nudist social and political network found in the United States and take it global. If the numbers of people claiming nude beaches grew around the world, free beach activism might become a thing of the past as nude recreation was absorbed into the cultural mainstream. It also alerted nude beachgoers to which places were free of surveillance, and which ones might attract surly citation-writing authorities. Within the nudist movement, the *World Guide*, together with Baxandall's other new publication, the magazine *Clothed with the Sun*, also served "to present the growing trend of clothing-optional beach use to recreation managers and law enforcement officials as being led by people who were organized, well informed, and able to articulate a coherent mission."[50] In short, it was important to present free beach activism as not just made up of hippie troublemakers but law-abiding people who simply wanted to be naked on beaches. In 1989, TNS intentionally changed *Clothed with the Sun* to *Nude and Natural* to circumvent new concerns about sun-caused skin cancer and to emphasize the free and natural lifestyle behind social nudism. Today, the magazine is simply called *N: The Magazine of Naturist Living*, which allows readers to insert whatever signifier "N" holds for them. TNS has thus carefully negotiated the contested space between nudist clubs and beach activists, between nudists in general and legal authorities, and between a nudist practice in "nature" and a nudist practice comfortably ensconced in consumer culture.

The easiest way to do all this negotiating was to encourage nudism as a travel lifestyle and *The World's Best Nude Beaches and Resorts* and *N* magazine certainly have helped. In 2014, the American Association for Nude Recreation (AANR) reported that nude tourism generated more than $440 million a year in the United States alone. Mom-and-pop nudist camps that survived the upheavals of the 1970s and 1980s are now closing and being replaced by upmarket nude resorts with health spas, high-end restaurants, and other fancy amenities. Nude cruising has also become big business. Nancy Tienmann of Bare Necessities Tour and Travel, a nude cruise line, reported to *The Economist* in 2014 that they had grown exponentially from their first cruise of thirty-six passengers in 1990 to a three-thousand-passenger Caribbean cruise in 2013.[51] By 1992, Bare Necessities was already fetching $1800 to $5200 per passenger per week.[52] Even the *Journal of the Senses*, Ed Lange's magazine promoting Elysium, had an article in 1991 proclaiming the mainstreaming of nude cruising.[53] In a nice quid pro quo, *Forbes* magazine returned the favor and mentioned Elysium in an essay about the enormous profits generated by nudist tourism.[54] Part of the explanation for the remarkable uptick in naked tourism is the aging of nudists in general, the fact that these aging nudists tend to be white, retired, with disposable income, and that the public nude beaches that originally generated the interest in naked travel have largely been legislated out of existence.[55] Haulover Beach remains the nation's biggest, and most famous, public nude beach whose visitors generate over $1 billion a year for Miami's tourist economy.[56]

Not all nude tourists, however, are white. Wealthy African Americans are also indulging in the delights of free and natural consumerism. *Griots Republic*, a travel and lifestyle magazine for black yuppies, recently featured "Black Nudists: Embracing the Skin You're In," a short piece on the Black Naturists Association, which was founded in 2016 to "advocate nudity through naturist environments . . . to help promote healthy body image and self-esteem for those in the black community."[57] Directly challenging the misconception that nude beaches, in particular, were "only for older white people and those with beach bodies," the Black Naturists Association emphasizes the naturalness of nudity but also the importance of private resorts for preventing "public sexual activity or unwanted advances of a sexual nature."[58] The group thus organizes quarterly meetups at the most exclusive private nudist resorts in the world, with its first gathering at a rented mansion at Miami's Haulover Beach. This is not free beach activism; it is for-profit beach tourism, but the segregationist legacy of organized nudism in the United States, as well as the long history of racially segregated beaches, justifies the desire of young black nude tourists to have control over the environment in which they choose to experience the free and natural lifestyle.

With most of the big money in nude tourism coming from retirees, it behooves those profiting from it to attract younger customers, much like the tobacco industry. Both AANR and TNS reported in the early years of the twenty-first century that their membership rolls had ceased growing and there was concern that social nudism would ultimately die out in the United States. Nudism simply did not hold the same appeal for Generation X, and it certainly did not for millennials. Public nude beaches still had appeal, if they could be found, but one new avenue has been forged by young nudist groups like Florida Young Naturists and Vita Nuda, who organize through social networking sites and are supported by AANR and TNS-affiliated nudist camps and resorts. In 2011, for example, Nudepalooza in Kissimmee, Florida, attracted a few hundred twenty-somethings to the Cypress Cove Nudist Resort and Spa that usually catered to an older clientele.[59] In 2015, *Playboy* magazine reported a new trend in New York City of young nudists gathering at "nudie spas," privately booked restaurants, or apartments in cool neighborhoods. Other activities involved covering oneself in full body paint and riding around the city in double-decker buses. As *Playboy* put it, "Yes, nudity has a whole new look. Once a subculture stereotyped as droopy baby boomers baring all at Indiana retreats, nudism is attracting a hipper, perkier audience."[60]

Other millennial nudist events include Bodyfest, which takes place each year at established nudist clubs, such as the long-standing Lupin Lodge in Los Gatos, California. The relatively small gathering resembles a music and yoga festival, but with everyone in the buff. It draws fans of Burning Man and other alternative hippie-New-Age-super-festivals, many of which began as underground gatherings of art freaks in the desert and have evolved in the twenty-first century into massive commercial ventures. The hope among Bodyfest organizers is that their enterprise will grow too. With that hope in mind, Bodyfest also runs PhotoNaturals.com, which encourages the participation of the young and beautiful at nudist events and circulates the images online. Participants who are photographed for PhotoNaturals.com are compensated. As one Bodyfest/ PhotoNaturals.com model put it, "If I'm going to be naked on the Internet, I better get paid for it."[61]

While bringing young people on board to increase AANR membership numbers and sustain American nudist culture into the foreseeable future may be the goal of the outreach efforts, Bodyfest and senior nude cruising are not overlapping experiences. Even though nude cruises might not attract the nudist faithful as much as the curious and leisured retiree, and they are most certainly part of free and natural lifestyle consumerism (it's hard to find a better example), they nevertheless remain defiantly *nudist*. The cruises advertise leisure, sun, health, and socializing in a laid-back environment much as nudist camps have for decades. The millennial nudist festivals, urban nudist gatherings, and nude modeling, however, have a decidedly more cynical bent. Sure, it's all about being free and natural, but it is also about being young and beautiful and getting paid for it. It is less lifestyle consumerism than it is self-commodification. These are free and natural bodies for sale.

Something else is up with millennial nudity. *Playboy*, the very magazine carrying the Bodyfest story, and the print juggernaut of the sexual revolution, stopped publishing nude photographs altogether in February 2016 and for one year was a nudity-free magazine. Leading up to the decision to cut the pictures of naked women, which had built the *Playboy* empire, the *New York Times* reported that "with its circulation down to about eight hundred thousand, *Playboy*'s chief content officer, Cory Jones, and Scott Flanders, the company's chief executive, are setting out to leverage the *Playboy* brand and stay relevant in an era where sexting is commonplace and nude photographs in magazines are almost quaint."[62] With free pornography accessible everywhere and free and natural lifestyle consumerism pervading most of American popular culture in one way or another, nakedness had become harder to market as a commodity unto itself. Taking away the soft-core images, however, did not help *Playboy* regain readers or advertisers and, in the spring 2017 issue, *Playboy* put the naked women back.[63] It remains to be seen how the venerable girlie magazine American audiences read "for the articles" will fare in the years to come. Part of the problem is that Americans do not really read *any* magazines anymore, since online sources fill the specific niche markets magazines used to fill, and online advertising is cheaper than print. But part of the problem for *Playboy*, as the *New York Times* noted, is that print nudity is simply a dated form. Even if it is more explicit than anything *Playboy* would show anyway, a printed pornographic image does not carry the rarified shock value it used to—especially for a generation of young people with unprecedented access to pornographic videos of others, and sometimes of themselves. It makes sense that young people might become fascinated with nudism as a free and natural option beyond pornography and a relic of another era, but it also makes sense that they would have trouble understanding it outside of consumer culture. Frankly, why would they?

In a 2002 article highly critical of modern nudist culture, Ellen E. Woodall contrasted early nudist practice (collective, inexpensive) with the contemporary version she argued was brashly commercial, sexist in its promotion of mainstream representations of women (young, white, thin), and ultimately just another part of the corporate hotel and entertainment industry.[64] These changes were certainly afoot but today the generational divide within nudist culture and social shifts in how public nakedness is understood are also a result of the ubiquity of hand-held camera-phones that can not only snap pictures but also produce video and upload it to millions of viewers in a matter of seconds. Whereas nudists originally relied on children to prove the natural wholesomeness of social nakedness, in recent years, social panics over pedophilia, as well as the difficulty in controlling who has cameras—long banned from nudist camps—has led some resorts to simply ban children. Many members of the organized nudist community believe adults-only nudist resorts feed the problem of flagging numbers by suggesting there is something prurient about nudism and by catering to random visitors rather than familiar dues-paying members.[65]

The movement of the free and natural lifestyle from outside American capitalist interests to becoming entirely enmeshed in it has had the effect of making the body ever more present as a marker of status, desirability, and health. Free and natural lifestyle consumerism also includes wellness practices, which have the cultural effect of intensifying the individual responsibility to thrive and glow. It thus makes sense that the old, the aging, and the young and uncertain about the future, would find naked body practices exhilarating experiences that hold the promise of finding the authentic self, a feeling of freedom, and a ritualistic, or even primal, return to nature. For many people, to be naked is to feel good. But naked wellness, whether on a cruise or in a yoga studio, has become big business and, because of the limitations on where one can be socially naked, as well as the private expense of pursuing the opportunity, free and natural living has become contained and niche-marketed. Trademarks of the free and natural lifestyle, from organic foods to detox manuals, alternative health practices to seminars on loving the skin you're in, are now ubiquitous, but we are not more free and natural. In fact, the free and natural lifestyle is expensive and cut off from anything recognizable as "nature." In this cycle of escaping consumer capitalism via consumer capitalism, it is the privatized naked body that carries the promise of natural authenticity while the public naked body's constant legislation, surveillance, and containment sustains its ability to shock.

BODIES OUT OF PLACE

As the dapper British actor, David Niven, stood before a massive television audience, and about a beat before he introduced Elizabeth Taylor, who would announce *The Sting*'s Oscar win for Best Picture, a slender, white, and very naked young man jogged out from behind the background curtain and ran off the stage. As the live audience at the Dorothy Chandler Pavilion in downtown Los Angeles burst into laughter, Niven cracked, "Well, ladies and gentlemen, that was almost bound to happen."[1] With that very brief tele-visual moment, the April 2, 1974, Academy Awards, and the streaker, Robert Opel, were cemented forever in the American popular imagination. Even if people do not remember Opel's name, there remains a collective memory of *that* Academy Awards ceremony. Opel was not arrested for the Oscar gag, but later he would be sentenced to four months in jail when he stripped at the Los Angeles City Council hearing on municipal nude beaches on July 11, 1974.[2] Opel, a gay man involved in free beach activism, and a creative artist provoca-teur, left Los Angeles after serving his sentence, and opened a homoerotic art gallery in San Francisco called Fey-Way Studios in 1978.[3] Fey-Way hosted one of Robert Mapplethorpe's first West Coast shows, and featured the gay fetish art of Tom of Finland.[4] Tragically, on July 7, 1979, thirty-nine-year-old Opel was shot and killed by junkies robbing his gallery. Though his life was full of political activism, a range of interesting jobs, acting, and lots of art, Opel is best remembered for being America's most famous streaker.[5]

While certainly notorious, Opel's nudity at the Academy Awards is even more remarkable for the nation's cavalier attitude about the incident. Opel was not arrested and, while Niven could have been thrown off by the distraction, he ad libbed brilliantly. Demonstrating the self-assurance of a seasoned actor, certainly, but Niven's "bound to happen" comment also revealed that someone running naked across the most watched stage in the country, if not the world, was not unanticipated. Rumors have long since circulated that Oscar organizers invited Opel to do it, but given that these are difficult to substantiate, it is more productive to think about why an American audience was so unfazed by the startling appearance of a naked man on the stage of one of the nation's most public, and formal, events. Indeed, the fact that Opel streaked between the very proper Niven and the glamorous Taylor might lead one to think that people would be irate that such a precious national institution had been reduced to a fraternity prank. Instead, the audience seemed to find it hilarious and, with the intentional media blackout to discourage further streaking incidents, the whole thing was rendered pretty inconsequential.

In fact, 1974 was the year that streaking, defined as running naked in public, hit peak popularity, particularly among American college students. The press went nuts with tales of naked young people while jokes, cartoons, and "Streak Freak" buttons permeated popular culture. As Bill Kirkpatrick argues, some were offended by the rampant public nudity but, for the most part, "the consensus among mainstream social observers in 1974 was that streaking was nothing more than a silly diversion."[6] Indeed, what the reaction to Opel's stunt revealed most of all was that streaking, though still shocking, was pretty trivial stuff. Kirkpatrick makes the argument that streaking actually had been originally tied to political activism, such as students organizing to impeach Richard Nixon, but by 1974, a concerted effort was made on the part of the mainstream media, university administrations, and conservative politicians to render streaking apolitical and a return to childish innocence. Though not all streakers were white and male, the fact that many were, and associated with college fraternities, helped further the case that streaking was just "kids being kids" and that the radical campus activism of the 1960s was long over.[7] In part by depoliticizing it, and in part by reporting on it as such a dumb thing to be doing in the first place, mainstream America rendered streaking impotent and the trend, the occasional naked and drunk sports fan notwithstanding, was over by the end of the year. That streaking would be presented publicly as a silly kiddie fad at the peak of the free beach movement's most radical and violent protest era suggested that public nudity still carried just as much cultural weight as it ever did. Nudity could certainly be commodified and sexualized, but naked bodies out of place were not so easily depoliticized. The spaces where nudity occurred still *mattered*, thus imbuing naked bodies with enough shock value to still be useful for social protest.

○   ○   ○

Most participants in naked living experiments in the United States stress that their desire to live nude is one of individual choice to be free and natural in their bodies and to be left alone to shape their private world around their pursuit. The privatization of most naked spaces, including suburban housing developments, nudist clubs, and tourist resorts has, for the most part, resolved the significant legal and social pressures experienced by nudists in the United States. For others who channel political struggle through the naked body, nudity is a public concern tied to the claiming of public space and the redefinition of social meanings of "natural." The naked body becomes a means to talk publicly about sexuality, race, and experiential authenticity. Pushing the naked body beyond being the *cause* of social protest to being the *site* of social protest takes nakedness outside the nudist cause of free and natural corporeal display to a far more political realm. While certainly an ancient form of protest, the assertive display of the naked body in order to force social change has become more common in the twenty-first century, largely because at the same time that nudity is more prevalent in American popular culture, it is also more carefully contained. Thus, the spaces in which one experiences nudity matter greatly and designate whether the nudity is appropriate or deviant.

The body laid bare in unexpected places upsets social normativity, disrupts the usual circulation of bodies through space and, in the case of urban nudity, evokes anxiety about unexpected intimacy, dirt, and touching.[8] Indeed, naked bodies that move outside of appropriate zones into public space can be incredibly unsettling. As vulnerable as the naked body may be to the elements, its unexpected presence, its visible, overt rejection of social norms, and its imposition in public spaces which, by law, it is usually not allowed to occupy, imbues it with cultural and political power that has been harnessed to social protest movements as varied as free beaches, gay rights, gender equality (the right of women to bare their chests as men do; public breastfeeding), and animal rights (the notorious "We'd rather be naked than wear fur" campaign by People for the Ethical Treatment of Animals [PETA]).

A now familiar example of nakedness as social protest is found in the contemporary environmental movement where annual nude bike rides are particularly colorful examples of nudity in unexpected places. In a press release for the World Naked Bike Ride in New York City, organizers explain that "the annual (and undoubtedly cheeky) event is actually a very serious environmental effort, where folks from all around the world bike in their birthday suit to protest the world's dependence on oil and other nonrenewable energy sources. Note: The motto for the ride is 'as bare as you dare.'"[9]. One of the best known of naked social protests, the World Naked Bike Ride has grown exponentially, with cities now providing permits and police with little fuss or fury. Mainstream environmentalism, by focusing on "Earth First" principles and evading the racial and class issues of environmental social injustice, such as fieldworkers' pesticide poisoning or the crises of inadequate housing, is well-poised to use the naked body as a political tool because most of those participating are all already relatively empowered; the world annual nude bike ride is not a social protest of the world's poorest, most marginalized people.

My purpose is not to critique the generally white middle-class environmentalists who ride their bikes naked once a year, although I am unconvinced that the protest action, nude or otherwise, will do much to stop the burning of fossil fuels or slow the effects of climate change; instead, the bike ride brings positive attention to nudism, whose practitioners joyfully celebrate the free publicity. I am far more interested in thinking about what public nakedness means in the twenty-first-century United States when the organized nudism of the 1930s and 1940s might seem quaint and naïve, the sexualized nudity of the 1960s and 1970s appears a countercultural free love relic, and most public beaches remain "unfree." Meanwhile, suburban nudism continues as a practice linking body to built environment, nude tourism is a high-end commercial interest and, via social media and online pornography, we have more access to nudity than at any time in modern history. It would appear on the surface, perhaps, that nudity has grown quotidian. Indeed, it is in the very stripping of shock value from nakedness that nudism empowers those who practice it and differentiates nudism from other kinds of nakedness.[10] Naked protest, however, by virtue of its surprise factor and its placement of nude bodies in unexpected places restores shock value to the exposed body and, in turn, burns an image of nudity connected to a social concern into the brain of the viewer. Nudism thus sublimates the fetishism of the exposed body while naked protest exploits it.

Even if this is how two forms of nakedness (nudism and naked protest) function in contrast with each other, neither resolves the paradox of using the modern body to express naturalness. Nudism claims to authenticate a natural human experience by dispensing with the artificial markers of gender and class—namely, clothing. Nudists argue that to live naked is to live as nature intended and have historically used the naked body-as-natural trope in their treatises, legal briefs, and public relations. But nudists generally do not live anywhere near "nature," and, as we have seen in the previous chapters, have worked hard to allow naked living in the most unnatural of places. As much as displaying the naked body is a central tenet of American nudist culture, images of naked bodies perched on sofas indoors or playfully frolicking in six feet of snow undoes the assertion that being naked is so natural as to be mundane. Naked protest, however, gets its performative power from the very fact that it is actually deeply *unnatural* to view naked people in the selected protest site. This further makes naked environmental protests like the nude bike ride unintentionally ironic because as much as the event might be intended to protect the natural realm, and the association of the naked body with the protest meant to underscore the natural theme, if it felt at all natural to see hundreds of naked people on bicycles, there wouldn't be a protest. No one would notice. The presumed naturalness of the naked body is neither resolved, nor actually explained, in either case; what is different between nudism and naked protest is how the bodies are contextualized in space.

As much as being in nature is culturally constructed as freeing, oppositional to the excesses of the modern age, and a form of leisure, the very notion of embodied nature pushes bodies, in the words of geographer Phil Macnaghten and sociologist John Urry, "to do very unusual things, to go to peripheral spaces, to place themselves in marginal situations, to exert themselves in exceptional ways [or] to undergo peak experiences."[11] While not necessarily naked, bodies purposefully placed out-of-doors are the vessels of modern selves also seeking authentic experience and a sense of liberation. Along with the contradiction that modern bodies must intentionally seek out and perform exceptional acts in order to be free in nature, those same bodies are also subject to scrutiny, monitoring, and exclusion. Being in nature often involves leisure time and economic resources, strict limits on where one can go ("stay on the trail"; "don't bust the crust"), and abiding local laws, such as anti-nudity ordinances.[12] These conflicting experiences of nature, like so many embodied experiences, have everything to do with the specific geographic contexts in which they take place. Lounging by a lake in an urban park is a different experience of freedom and control than a backwoods hike miles from the nearest highway; however, neither is completely natural nor unfettered. The lake might be artificial, while outdoors, but one can simply walk to it and put down a blanket. The backwoods trail is perhaps sublimely pristine but the hiker is likely strapped to thousands of dollars' worth of equipment and performance wear. Critic Sarah Jaquette Ray argues further that by constantly fetishizing certain types of bodies as "making sense" in nature, such as those of privileged white wilderness athletes, bodies of color, immigrant bodies, and disabled bodies are rendered "unnatural" and reify the socially unjust hierarchies that already marginalize them.[13] Thus, the very concept of the body in nature, as well as any modern notion of the natural body, is highly contingent.

If social nudism and naked protest actions cannot make the naked body "natural"; if indeed, to a certain degree their success relies on the naked body not being natural in most settings, they have an even bigger problem resolving the tension between nudity and sexuality. As this book has traced since the early twentieth century, nudism emerged in part as a reaction to the sexualization of the body in the public sphere and strived to decouple sex from nakedness, with limited success. Part of the problem, according to scholars David Bell and Ruth Holliday, is that for all of social nudism's emphasis on nonsexuality, "Some naturism advocates recognized the sexual potential of being naked in nature, constructing a vision of the countryside as a 'pre-cultural' site for free love."[14] While Bell and Holliday focus on the origins of British nudism, the point they make is important for the American context in that the presumed naturalness of being naked was often tied to sexual health, *not* asexuality. A typical treatise on the subject appeared in *Natural Herald* in 1950, arguing that the sex shame of the non-nudist world created obsessive preoccupations with sex while nudists, and especially their children, could "learn the truths of life in a wholesome way."[15] Nudism, by virtue of being natural, could make sex healthy and natural too. By the tenets of the American nudist movement, healthy sexuality born of naked living was very different from the lewd erotics of pornography that both commodified and sullied the body. This is one of the reasons why photographing nudist culture was so important to the movement and why placing the body out-of-doors in natural scenarios was critical to nudism's ideological aesthetics.

Naked social protest movements, however, play with both sides of the sexuality issue by either heightening the sexiness of nudity or asserting nudity's asexuality. For example, in the print media variant of PETA's "We'd Rather Be Naked" campaign, nubile nude celebrities, such as former *Baywatch* actress, Pamela Anderson, and porn star, Jenna Jameson, lounge languidly or otherwise pose provocatively, purposefully evoking the seduction of pinup girls and centerfolds. In the street theater component of the campaign, young naked women are out-of-doors, on their hands and knees, and in cages. The political point is to raise the specter of the dire condition of caged and trapped animals. The visual effect is more complicated as the image of caged, naked women is itself a form of sexual fetishism.[16] PETA has long been one of the most provocative, and controversial, of contemporary naked social protest movements largely because of their overt sexualization of the nude and vulnerable female body to sensationalize the horrors of animal cruelty. By deploying sexualized nudity, PETA helps naturalize the objectification of women. Sexual nudity in this context is not simply deployed; it is exploited.

In contrast, participants in the naked protest movement, "Free the Nipple," who campaign to legalize women's right to go topless in public rely upon the argument that nudity is *not* sexual. The "Free the Nipple" campaign, which grew in popularity in the wake of a 2012 docudrama of the same name, has become an international movement for gender equality, with organized topless protests held all over the world. In its most basic argumentative form, allowing women to do the same thing as men, in this case, publicly bare their chests, toplessness does appear to be a simple case of desiring gender equality under the law. If men can do it, why can't we? Not surprisingly, the consistent problem for the United States courts has been one of context. It has, for example, been legal since 1992 for women to be publicly topless in New York City but as the "Free the Nipple" campaign has grown and become more visible, local authorities have become concerned. In 2015, New York City mayor Bill de Blasio moved to cite "nipple" activists in Times Square, where young women in thongs, showgirl headdresses, and with American flags painted on their breasts, mingled and accepted cash tips from passersby. Given Times Square's pre-Giuliani history as the center of the city's sex industry—and Times Square's recent reconfiguration as a family-friendly tourist destination—it was a provocative choice for a protest site if the point was to underscore how *not* sexual urban female toplessness is.[17]

A peculiar merger of New Age spirituality and female topless activism is GoTopless.org, a group founded in the United States in 2007 by French journalist, Claude Vorilhon, who is better known as "Raël," the leader of a 1970s UFO cult. Followers of the "Raëlian Movement" believe scientists from another planet arrived on Earth and made all living things, including us.[18] While recruiting cult members is Raël's main concern internationally, GoTopless.org has taken on a life of its own in the United States with a sophisticated website mapping topless legality (and illegality) nationwide and well-publicized female topless marches and rallies. Whereas "Free the Nipple" activism emphasizes the asexuality of women's breasts, GoTopless.org claims women's constitutional and inalienable right to be as topless as men in public. While it is hard to see GoTopless.org as much more than a recruitment tool for the Raëlian Movement, it nevertheless articulates a clear body politics and a loud claim to the appropriateness of public nudity. In this literal example of a cult of the body, authentic corporeal experience is tied to a bizarre religion, yet GoTopless.org demonstrations are refreshingly lighthearted, channeling as they do a combination of Mardi Gras parade and social protest performance art.

A related naked social protest issue also tied to the legality of female nudity is public breastfeeding. The feeding of offspring is often expressed as natural and nonsexual by breastfeeding activists (or lactivists), who also pitch the issue as one of personal choice or as a challenge to public stigmatization. The public discourse, which rages on hundreds of blogs, websites, and social media networks, tells of humiliating stories of breastfeeding women forced into bathroom stalls, escorted off planes, and prevented from feeding their children at work.[19] Facebook itself contributed to the controversy when, in 2008, it began pulling photographs of women breastfeeding their young from the site.[20] While there is no question that there are important labor and childcare politics wrapped up in public breastfeeding debates, the public *discourse*, as it currently exists in American popular culture, is more concerned with the naturalness and asexuality of breast exposure. In fact, "Free the Nipple" activists often cite breastfeeding as the definitive reason for the asexuality of bare breasts. In the words of one activist, "breasts aren't sexual at all. Naturally, they're for babies."[21] Feminist scholars, however, take issue with the asserted obvious naturalness of breastfeeding, pointing out that this equation works to shame women who, for various reasons, cannot breastfeed and subsequently resent the insinuation that the quality of their maternity is in question for bottle feeding their young. Such scholarship similarly problematizes the asexuality of exposed female breasts by pointing out that this falls neatly in line with the misogynistic cultural assumption that properly maternal bodies ought to be asexual ones.[22]

The association of nudity and sexuality, while disrupted by these varying forms of naked politics and protest, are not decoupled nor, perhaps, should they be. Sexuality can be powerful too. Seeing naked bodies that do not fit standardized and commercialized beauty norms, yet understanding that some may find them sexually appealing, finding them attractive ourselves, or simply accepting that these bodies might behave sexually in a separate, more private setting, can also be a deeply empowered experience. Encountering people who are entirely comfortable in their skin is simultaneously a delight and a culturally subversive experience as so much of late capitalist body commodification is precipitated on the production of corporeal anxiety and insecurity.

While public nudity retains the potential to shock us—sexually, culturally, and politically—we are now also expected to be cooler about it than in previ-

FIGURE 48. GoTopless.org protest rally, Venice Beach, 2015. Photograph by Ron Mercer. Courtesy of the Southern California Naturist Association.

ous, more uptight eras, but only if it is contained in very specific ways. One of the best contemporary examples is the work of American artist, Spencer Tunick, who is internationally known for gathering large numbers of naked people together in one place and photographing them. Some of his photographs have hundreds of people, others thousands. In his largest work, Tunick photographed eighteen thousand naked people in Mexico City's Zócalo Square in 2007. The photographs are displayed in art galleries, and sold for art market prices, but Tunick has also profited handsomely from published catalogs of his work and the publicity reaped from three HBO documentaries that track the complex orchestrations to get thousands of people in the right place at the right time. His work is very popular and Tunick very famous for producing it. He has, in interviews, insisted that his work be referred to as "installations" rather than photography, implying an ephemeral kind of artistic experience such as a 1960s be-in or nude human mandala, but the work is posed for the camera and it is collectable.[23] Tunick's work involves a global public which registers on his website as potential models for upcoming projects by filling out a form requesting one's gender, age, and skin tone, as depicted on a seven-point color array.[24] The fan-based website Spencer Tunick Experience features testimonials from hundreds of participants who derive a great deal of free and natural pleasure from taking part in the projects.[25] Clearly, getting naked in public retains a certain thrill as does collaborating in the making of an attention-getting work of public art.

Tunick's art also has been infused with social significance. Greenpeace commissioned Tunick to photograph six hundred naked volunteers on the Swiss Aletsch Glacier to heighten awareness of global warming and AIDS activists encouraged Tunick to bring attention to World AIDS Day by having nude HIV-positive men and women pose in Manhattan. Mia Fineman, associate curator of photography at the Metropolitan Museum of Art, has pointed out that "Tunick's shtick, though conceptually thin on its own, is supremely well-suited for this sort of political publicity stunt. Here, public nudity is invested with real meaning, whether as a symbol of the fragility of the environment or as a visible reminder of the hidden politics of illness."[26] Especially timely political significance has also been invoked, as when Tunick posed a hundred naked women outside the 2016 Republican National Convention in Cleveland.

But, for the most part, all this carefully orchestrated public nudity is essentially aesthetic and, because of the often huge numbers of participants, the bodies on display are rendered anonymous and unnaturally gathered. Indeed, in Tunick's 2016 "Sea of Hull" installation, over three thousand blue-dyed bodies lying close together in the streets of the east Yorkshire city evoke thoughts of World War II concentration camp corpses or, at the very least, some sort of zombie apocalypse. These publicly naked bodies present a provocative image, but the disruption is planned, even welcome, and it is unclear what is being protested, if anything. Fineman also notes that Tunick's installations easily lend themselves to high-end advertising as in his 2008 Art Basel Miami exhibit that features "500 people cavorting in the hotel's pool on fluorescent pink and green floats, standing on the hotel's art deco balconies, and popping open bottles of champagne. They're all naked. Wow."[27] Ultimately, Tunick's work represents the apex of contained, controlled nudity that is anything but free or natural and is easily commercialized. In short, viewers are not rendered uncomfortable by what they see. This is not the same as naked social protest that intentionally shocks and disrupts to make a political point.

○   ○   ○

The body exposed can be empowering for women and men. As the historian and social theorist Donald M. Lowe has simply put it, "sexual energy is power."[28] This specific form of empowerment, in our globalized, late-capitalist world, is closely tied to patterns of consumption, the visual, sexualized power of advertising, and the objectification of the body. Because claiming the body as a site of personal empowerment is so difficult to disentangle from the heightened expectations and scrutiny of commodified body culture, social nakedness makes sense as a practice that promises to do just that: empower the self by severing ties to the social and sexual signifiers of clothing. The body, at its most vulnerable, can also be its most potent, self-actualized state.

But, however personally empowering the naked body might be, its public exposure prompts deep feelings of ambivalence that are exacerbated by the physical space in which the nudity occurs. Is it natural or unnatural? Is it beautiful or repellent? Is it dangerous or vulnerable? Is it legal or is it not? Is it lewd or simply nude? While so much of the effort behind organized nudism and private experiments in naked living has been about undoing anxieties around health, sex, and social norms, ultimately the same ambivalence about the body remains despite enormous socioeconomic, political, and cultural shifts over the past hundred years. Under late capitalism, this ambivalence makes the body the perfect commodity. It focuses attention on individual needs and deflects attention away from collectivity; it constantly changes and thus demands never-ending care and upkeep; it is ever-present and inescapable; and it generates enough unease to fuel the purchase of an infinite number of products and services. The more unsteady the economy and world feels, the more we try to mold our bodies into shapes and states of being that will bring us a sense of grounded stability; yet, our body's fundamental impermanence is one of the only absolute truths that we, as human beings, have.

It is not a coincidence, then, that the free and natural lifestyle's emphasis on alternative health pursuits and detoxifying the body, for example, has grown vastly in popularity as public debate over healthcare access has become sharper and, frankly, more panicked. On the one hand, free and natural living has become a luxury for those who can afford it. On the other, it has evolved into a poignant mantra for those who are economically shut out of the medical system and hope, desperately, that living more naturally might make them well. Indeed, the free and natural lifestyle's origins are partly found in early twentieth-century efforts to democratize public health. Today, even if they can afford it, many patients do not trust the American for-profit medical system; others, while not ideologically opposed to privatized healthcare, are uncomfortable with Western medicine's surgical and pharmaceutical intrusions into their bodies. Free and natural living, under the auspices of wellness, provides a route by which to circumvent contemporary medical treatment and the maw of inefficient health insurance bureaucracies.

While we may personally always feel anxious and ambivalent about our own bodies, as cultural theorist Ruth Barcan notes, "the regulation of nudity often occurs in the shadow of hidden ambivalence about what it is to be human."[29] This is a trenchant point given that so much of the effort to legislate nudity in the United States has been about shoring up social norms in the face of enormous cultural change. To assert that nude bodies have specific and appropriate contexts and are thereby degenerate and immoral in others is to assert, perhaps, that humanness is in flux. The anxiety and ambivalence about where our humanness lies between the boundaries of modern society and nature is underscored by the persistent claims to a natural state by both advocates of naked living and those repelled by it. The ambivalence, then, is also about what renders one a natural being, an immense judgment which carries with it the power and prejudices of a society at any given time. In the name of upholding the "nature of things," women have been denied the vote, interracial sex outlawed, homosexuals and transsexuals arrested, beaten, or killed, and exploitative class hierarchies upheld, allowing poverty to flourish and immigrants to be exiled. Thus, the very fact that the natural body remains an unresolved site upon which contemporary sexual politics, medical policy, and civil rights are debated makes clear that any empowerment derived from it must move beyond individual desires for expressive freedom to collective efforts for social equality. Perhaps neither nudism nor naked protest movements have managed to pull it off, so to speak, but they have forced a sustained, tenacious, and fearless rethinking of the naturalness of the human body that might ultimately free us to live more equitable, gentle, and less anxious lives.

NOTES

INTRODUCTION

1. George Wharton James, *Living the Radiant Life: A Personal Narrative* (Pasadena, CA: Radiant Life Press, 1916), 1.

2. George Wharton James, *The Indians' Secrets of Health, or What the White Race May Learn from the Indian* (Chicago: Forbes, 1908; new and enl. ed., Pasadena, CA: Radiant Life Press, 1917), 201. Citations refer to the later edition.

3. James, *Living the Radiant Life*, 8.

4. Ibid.

5. Ibid., 21.

6. Ibid., 101.

7. Ibid., 106–107.

8. Ibid., 108.

9. Ibid., 103.

10. Ibid.

11. Ibid., 39.

12. For more on the relationship between Christian thought and American body culture in the early twentieth century, see R. Marie Griffith, *Born Again Bodies: Flesh and Spirit in American Christianity* (Berkeley: University of California Press, 2004).

13. *Los Angeles Times*, July 2, 1889, and April 24, 1889, cited in Peter Wild, *George Wharton James* (Boise, ID: Boise State University Western Writers Series, 1990), 16.

14. See Griffith, *Born Again Bodies*; and also Mark Adams, *Mr. America: How Muscular Millionaire Bernarr Macfadden Transformed the Nation Through Sex, Salad, and the Ultimate Starvation Diet* (New York: Harper, 2009).

15. James, *Living the Radiant Life*, xiii. Historian James C. Whorton has noted that there was overlap between Macfadden's philosophies of physical fitness and emergent ideas about "nature cures," and what we would now consider "alternative" health practices. Macfadden "called for sunshine, pure air, dietary restraint as supplements to exercise and tirelessly attacked the allopathic profession." James C. Whorton, *Nature Cures: The History of Alternative Medicine in America* (Oxford: Oxford University Press, 2002), 205.

16. There is a large literature on the transformation of American culture in the late nineteenth and early twentieth centuries, and its role in the reshaping of body norms and rituals. See, for example, T. J. Jackson Lears, *No Place of Grace: Antimodernism and the Transformation of American Culture, 1880–1920* (1981; repr., Chicago: University of Chicago Press, 1994); John Kasson, *Houdini, Tarzan, and the Perfect Man: The White Male Body*

and the Challenge of Modernity in America (New York: Hill and Wang, 2002); Heather Addison, *Hollywood and the Rise of Physical Culture* (New York: Routledge, 2003); Joan Jacobs Brumberg, *Fasting Girls: The Emergence of Anorexia Nervosa as a Modern Disease* (Cambridge, MA: Harvard University Press, 1988); Harvey Green, *Fit for America: Health, Fitness, Sport and American Society* (New York: Pantheon, 1986); Margaret A. Lowe, *Looking Good: College Women and Body Image, 1875–1930* (Baltimore: Johns Hopkins University Press, 2003); Hillel Schwarz, *Never Satisfied: A Cultural History of Diets, Fantasies, and Fat* (New York: Free Press, 1986); Peter Stearns, *Fat History: Bodies and Beauty in the Modern West* (New York: New York University Press, 1997; repr., with a new preface, 2002).

17. *Physical Culture*, December 1924, 1 and 6.

18. Carolyn Thomas de la Peña, *The Body Electric: How Strange Machines Built the Modern American* (New York: New York University Press, 2003).

19. See Hazel Carby, "Policing the Black Woman's Body in an Urban Context," *Critical Inquiry* 18, no. 4 (Summer 1992), 738–755; Cheryl D. Hicks, "'Bright and Good Looking Colored Girl': Black Women's Sexuality and 'Harmful Intimacy' in Early-Twentieth-Century New York," *Journal of the History of Sexuality* 18, no. 3 (September 2009), 418–456.

20. Kathy Peiss, *Cheap Amusements: Working Women and Leisure in Turn-of-the-Century New York* (Philadelphia: Temple University Press, 1986).

21. For more on turn-of-the-century middle-class camping practices, and the relationship between outdoor experience and class reification, see Phoebe Kropp, "Wilderness Wives and Dishwashing Husbands: Comfort and the Domestic Arts of Camping in America, 1880–1910," *Journal of Social History* 43, no. 1 (Fall 2009), 5–30.

22. See Robert Love, *The Great Oom: The Improbable Birth of Yoga in America* (New York: Viking, 2010).

23. *The Nudist: Sunshine and Health* 6, no. 1 (January 1937), 22. Robert J. Young Collection, Wolfsonian-Florida International University Rare Book and Special Collections Library, Miami Beach, Florida.

24. Marshall Berman, *The Politics of Authenticity: Radical Individualism and the Emergence of Modern Society* (New York: Atheneum, 1970; new, updated ed., London: Verso, 2009), xvii. Citation refers to the more recent edition.

25. For more on the relationship between modernity and authenticity, see Anthony Giddens, *Modernity and Self-Identity: Self and Society in the Late Modern Age* (Stanford, CA: Stanford University Press, 1991); Miles Orvell, *The Real Thing: Imitation and Authenticity in American Culture, 1880–1940* (Chapel Hill: University of North Carolina Press, 1989); Doug Rossinow, *The Politics of Authenticity: Liberalism, Christianity and the New Left in America* (New York: Columbia University Press, 1998).

26. Garner P. Roney, "Bathe Your Body in the Sun," *Physical Culture* 56, no. 1 (July 1926), 104.

27. Morris Fishbein, *Fads and Quackery in Healing: An Analysis of the Foibles of the Healing Cults, with Essays on Various Other Peculiar Notions in the Health Field* (New York: Covici, Friede, 1932), 161–162.

28. In the past decade and a half, there has been a revitalized interest in theorizing the body, and a concomitant flurry of recent scholarship on nudity and nakedness. The majority of these works hail from European and Commonwealth history, including works by Michael Hau, *The Cult of Health and Beauty in Germany: A Social History, 1890–1930*

(Chicago: University of Chicago Press, 2003); Caroline Daley, *Leisure and Pleasure: Reshaping and Revealing the New Zealand Body, 1900–1960* (Auckland: Auckland University Press, 2003); Ruth Barcan, *Nudity: A Cultural Anatomy* (Oxford: Berg, 2004); Chad Ross, *Naked Germany: Health, Race, and the Nation* (Oxford: Berg, 2005); John Alexander Williams, *Turning to Nature in Germany: Hiking, Nudism, and Conservation, 1900–1940* (Stanford, CA: Stanford University Press, 2007); Philip Carr-Gomm, *A Brief History of Nakedness* (London: Reaktion Books, 2010); Stephen Harp, *Au Naturel: Naturism, Nudism, and Tourism in Twentieth-Century France* (Baton Rouge: Louisiana State University Press, 2014); Davina Cooper, *Everyday Utopias: The Conceptual Life of Promising Spaces* (Durham, NC: Duke University Press, 2014). This literature is largely concerned with the layered cultural meanings of nudity, the sexualized appropriation of nudity in the West, rescuing nudism from the annals of Aryan fascism, and reconnecting modern body politics to nation building. United States nudist practice, while a source of sociological interest in the 1960s and 1970s, has only recently produced a major monograph, Brian Hoffman's excellent *Naked: A Cultural History of American Nudism* (New York: New York University Press, 2015). Hoffman's meticulous study of organized nudism in the United States helps us understand the modern meanings of nudity within the context of changing sexual mores, mid-century obscenity trials, and an emergent gay rights movement.

29. For more on the integrated experience of body, region, and image in Los Angeles, see Jennifer A. Watts and Claudia Bohn-Spector, *This Side of Paradise: Body and Landscape in Los Angeles Photographs* (London: Merrell, 2008).

30. Eve Babitz, "Bodies and Souls," in *Sex, Death, and God in LA*, ed. David Reid (Berkeley: University of California Press, 1992), 108.

31. Peggy Orenstein, *Girls and Sex: Navigating the Complicated New Landscape* (New York: Harper Collins, 2016).

32. For excellent critiques of contemporary wellness culture, see Carl Cederström and André Spicer, *The Wellness Syndrome* (Cambridge: Polity, 2015) and Barbara Ehrenreich, *Natural Causes: An Epidemic of Wellness, the Certainty of Dying, and Killing Ourselves to Live Longer* (New York: Hachette Book Group, 2018).

CHAPTER 1

1. "Girl Wife Suicide Inquiry Closed," *Los Angeles Times*, July 20, 1939, A18.

2. "Gay Party at Nudist Camp Ends in Girl's Tragic Death," *Los Angeles Times*, July 19, 1939, A1; Jon Hunter, "The Day Nudism Died in Los Angeles," *The Sundial* (July 1967), Elysium Papers, Private Collection, Southern California Naturist Association, Moorpark, California; Dick Washburne, clipping, *Los Angeles Herald-Express*, July 25, 1939, A1; John H. Burnett, "The Fallen Fathers of the Angel City," *Sunshine and Health* 9 (February 1940), Robert J. Young Collection, Wolfsonian-Florida International University Rare Book and Special Collections Library; Jayne Bernard, "Sunbathing in Southern California: An Historical Overview," in *The Westerners Brand Book, 16*, ed. Raymund F. Wood (Los Angeles: Westerners Los Angeles Corral, 1982), 24; William E. Hartman, Marilyn Fithian, and Donald Johnson, *Nudist Society: The Controversial Study of the Clothes-Free Naturist Movement in America* (Los Angeles: Elysium Growth Press, 1970; rev. and updated by Iris Bancroft, 1991), 26. All citations refer to the recent edition.

3. John Alexander Williams, *Turning to Nature in Germany: Hiking, Nudism, and*

Conservation, 1900–1940 (Stanford, CA: Stanford University Press, 2007), 11–12. There is a significant literature on the origins of nudist practice outside the United States. In addition to Williams, also see Michael Hau, *The Cult of Health and Beauty in Germany: A Social History, 1890–1930* (Chicago: University of Chicago Press, 2003); Caroline Daley, *Leisure and Pleasure: Reshaping and Revealing the New Zealand Body, 1900–1960* (Auckland: Auckland University Press, 2003); James Woycke, *Au Naturel: The History of Nudism in Canada* (Etobicoke, Ontario: Federation of Canadian Naturists, 2003); Chad Ross, *Naked Germany: Health, Race, and the Nation* (Oxford: Berg, 2005); Evert Peeters, "Authenticity and Asceticism: Discourse and Performance in Nude Culture and Health Reform in Belgium, 1920–1940," *Journal of the History of Sexuality* 15 (September 2006): 432–461; Nina J. Morris, "Naked in Nature: Naturism, Nature, and the Senses in Early Twentieth Century Britain," *Cultural Geographies* 16 (2009): 283–308; Stephen Harp, *Au Naturel: Naturism, Nudism, and Tourism in Twentieth-Century France* (Baton Rouge: Louisiana State University Press, 2014).

4. Howard C. Warren, "Social Nudism and the Body Taboo," *Psychological Review*, March 1933. Reprinted in Hartman, Fithian, and Johnson, *Nudist Society: The Controversial Study of the Clothes-Free Naturist Movement in America*, appendix 1, 395–410. Warren's essay was also reprinted in *The Nudist* 11, no. 5 (July 1933).

5. Frances Merrill and Mason Merrill, *Among the Nudists* (London: Noel Douglas, 1931), 234–235.

6. Ibid., 241.

7. Frances Merrill and Mason Merrill, *Nudism Comes to America* (Garden City, NY: Garden City Publishing, 1932), 41.

8. Kurt Barthel, "The Beginning of a National Organization," clipping from *Sunshine and Health* 1956, 3–4, Pomona Public Library Free Beach Collection; "24 Seized in Raid on Nudist Cult Here," *New York Times*, December 8, 1931, 3; *American Sunbathing Association Bulletin* 50 (November 2001): 26–27, Robert J. Young Collection, Wolfsonian-Florida International University Rare Book and Special Collections Library, Miami Beach, Florida.

9. "24 Seized in Raid on Nudist Cult Here," *New York Times*, December 8, 1931, 3; Barthel, "Beginning of a National Organization," 4; "The Saga of Elysium, 1967–1984," *Journal of the Senses* 67 (Spring 1984): 2, Pomona Public Library Free Beach Collection; *American Sunbathing Association Bulletin* 50 (November 2001): 26–27.

10. In 1933, *Time* magazine reported that *The Nudist* had 2000 subscribers with a monthly newsstand circulation of 110,000. "The Press: Sunshine," *Time*, November 27, 1933.

11. "America's First and Finest Naturist Community," accessed February 1, 2016, http://www.skyfarm.com/history.html.

12. *The Nudist: Official Publication of the International Nudist Conference* 1 (July 1933): 5, Robert J. Young Collection, Wolfsonian-Florida International University Rare Book and Special Collections Library, Miami Beach, Florida.

13. Barthel, "Beginning of a National Organization," 4.

14. Ilsley Boone, "Principles and Standards," *The Nudist: Official Publication of the International Nudist Conference* 11, no. 5 (July 1933), Robert J. Young Collection, Wolfsonian-Florida International University Rare Book and Special Collections Library, Miami Beach, Florida.

15. "Definition of a Nudist," *Sunshine and Health* 12 (November 1943): 26, Robert J. Young Collection, Wolfsonian-Florida International University Rare Book and Special Collections Library, Miami Beach, Florida.

16. Brian Hoffman makes the point that the move of nudists into the countryside came after unsuccessful bids in the early 1930s to establish designated nude beaches in Chicago and nude exercise clubs in New York City. For an account of the difficulties of instituting nudism in cities, see Brian Hoffman, "Indecent Exposure: The Battle for Nudism in the American Metropolis," in *Naked: A Cultural History of American Nudism* (New York: New York University Press, 2015), 17–47.

17. Marguerite S. Shaffer, "On the Environmental Nude," *Environmental History* 13 (January 2008): 127.

18. Early nudist photography did not only carefully wed nakedness and nature in order to establish the wholesomeness of nudist practice, it also contributed to new ways of seeing nude bodies in art. In the wake of nudist photography's insistence on group shots, its celebration of nudity for its nudity (not as a metaphoric allusion or mythical ideal), and its modern context, fine art photography began to incorporate more realistic, and informally posed, nude bodies. This stylistic change began in the mid-1930s and became widespread in the 1970s. See Philip Gleason Stewart, "The New-Genre Nude: A New Fine Art Motif Derived from Nudist Magazine Photography" (PhD diss., Ohio State University, 1986).

19. For an analysis of the trope of the artful nude in nature, see Bram Dijkstra, *Naked: The Nude in America* (New York: Rizzoli, 2010), 82–85.

20. *The Nudist: Sunshine and Health* 5, no. 11 (November 1936): 9.

21. See Chad Ross, *Naked Germany: Health, Race, and the Nation* (Oxford: Berg, 2005); and Williams, *Turning to Nature in Germany*.

22. "The Restoration of German Nudism," *The Nudist: Sunshine and Health* 5, no. 8 (August 1936): 7, Robert J. Young Collection, Wolfsonian-Florida International University Rare Book and Special Collections Library, Miami Beach, Florida.

23. For other references to German nudism, as well as discussions of the fate of naturism in Europe, see *The Nudist* 1 (July 1933): 5, 26, Robert J. Young Collection, Wolfsonian-Florida International University Rare Book and Special Collections Library, Miami Beach, Florida.

24. Barthel, "Beginning of a National Organization," 3.

25. See, for example, *The Nudist* 4, no. 12 (December 1935): 64; and *The Nudist* 5, no. 2 (February 1936), Robert J. Young Collection, Wolfsonian-Florida International University Rare Book and Special Collections Library, Miami Beach, Florida.

26. Maurice Parmelee, *Nudism in Modern Life* (New York: Garden City Publishing, 1931), 154.

27. Ibid., 236.

28. Ibid., 237.

29. Ibid.

30. Ibid.

31. Ibid., 235.

32. Ibid., 158.

33. There is a large literature on colonial racism, which covers much of the world, but nudists and health advocates in the early twentieth century were especially taken with

the native inhabitants of tropical regions, largely because of new interest in the sun as a healing agent, a central tenet of nudism. Treatises from health manuals, tourist brochures, and nudist magazines reflected a deeply conflicted fascination with the natural health and "primordial nudity" of indigenous people, who were often simultaneously described as "barbarous" or "savage." For an especially rich analysis, see Catherine Cocks, *Tropical Whites: The Rise of the Tourist South in the Americas*, Nature and Culture in America (Philadelphia: University of Pennsylvania Press, 2013).

34. Boone, "Principles and Standards," *The Nudist* 11, no. 5 (July 1933): 5.

35. For a discussion of the issue of nudist racial integration in the 1960s, see Hal Collins, "Nudism and the Negro," *Sunshine and Health* 33, no. 2 (March–June 1966): 26–29.

36. E. J. Samuels, "Light Out of Darkness," *Sunshine and Health* 13, no. 11 (November 1944): 19, Robert J. Young Collection, Wolfsonian-Florida International University Rare Book and Special Collections Library, Miami Beach, Florida.

37. Steve Brenton, "A Plan for Colored Nudists," *Sunshine and Health* 14, no. 6 (June 1945): 7, Robert J. Young Collection, Wolfsonian-Florida International University Rare Book and Special Collections Library, Miami Beach, Florida. Also see Hoffman, *Naked: A Cultural History of American Nudism*, 144–149, for a detailed discussion of the American Sunbathing Association's stance on racial integration.

38. E. J. Samuels, "On Negro Nudism," *Sunshine and Health* 14, no. 8 (August 1945): 21, Robert J. Young Collection, Wolfsonian-Florida International University Rare Book and Special Collections Library, Miami Beach, Florida.

39. Ibid., 22.

40. Ibid.

41. "Organized Negro Nudism," *Sunshine and Health* 14, no. 9 (September 1945): 11, Robert J. Young Collection, Wolfsonian-Florida International University Rare Book and Special Collections Library, Miami Beach, Florida.

42. "The Readers Forum," *Sunshine and Health* 15, no. 2 (February 1946), Robert J. Young Collection, Wolfsonian-Florida International University Rare Book and Special Collections Library, Miami Beach, Florida.

43. Fred Ilfeld Jr. and Roger Lauer, *Social Nudism in America* (New Haven, CT: College and University Press, 1964), 47.

44. Ibid.

45. Hartman, Fithian, and Johnson, *Nudist Society: The Controversial Study of the Clothes-Free Naturist Movement in America*, 55, 1991 edition.

46. Ibid., 57.

47. For more on California's place in the health movements of the nineteenth century, see John Baur's classic *The Health Seekers of Southern California, 1870–1900* (San Marino, CA: Huntington Library, 1959). For a brilliant study of the relationship of California's nineteenth-century health seekers and the political economy of the environment, see Linda Nash, *Inescapable Ecologies: A History of Environment, Disease, and Knowledge* (Berkeley: University of California Press, 2006).

48. Carey McWilliams, *Southern California Country: An Island on the Land* (New York: Duell, Sloan and Pearce, 1946; Salt Lake City: Gibbs-Smith, 1973), 96–99.

49. Ibid., 110–111.

50. Catherine Cocks, "The Pleasures of Degeneration: Climate, Race, and the Origins of the Global Tourist South in the Americas," *Discourse* 29 (Spring and Fall 2007): 228; Kerry Segrave, *Suntanning in 20th Century America* (Jefferson, NC: McFarland, 2005).

51. Ernestine H. Middleton, "The Wealth of Health and Happiness," *The Nudist* 3, no. 10 (November 1934): 22, Robert J. Young Collection, Wolfsonian-Florida International University Rare Book and Special Collections Library, Miami Beach, Florida.

52. C. W. Saleeby, foreword to *Man and Sunlight*, by Hans Surén (Slough: Sollux, 1927), v., quoted in Ken Worpole, *Here Comes the Sun: Architecture and Public Space in Twentieth-Century European Culture* (London: Reaktion Books, 2000), 44.

53. "Nudist Colony Members Quit: High Winds and Prosecutor Cool Enthusiasm," *Los Angeles Times*, May 23, 1933, A1.

54. "Nudist Defies Ouster Move," *Los Angeles Times*, May 24, 1933, 10.

55. "Nudists Will Dress Up," *Los Angeles Times*, May 28, 1933, E6.

56. "Clothes 'Restraint' Hit: 'Why We Want to Go Naked,' Told Riverside Lions by Nudist Colony Leader," *Los Angeles Times*, July 19, 1933, 10.

57. Eric Schaefer, *"Bold! Daring! Shocking! True!": A History of Exploitation Films, 1919–1959* (Durham, NC: Duke University Press, 1999), 294–295.

58. Ibid., 131.

59. Robert M. Payne, "Beyond the Pale: Nudism, Race, and Resistance in 'The Unashamed,'" *Film Quarterly* 54, no. 2 (Winter 2000–2001): 29.

60. Robert V. Hine, *California's Utopian Colonies* (San Marino, CA: Huntington Library, 1953; repr., with a new preface, Berkeley: University of California Press, 1983), 177.

61. "Four Hundred Nudists Frolic," *Los Angeles Times*, September 11, 1933, A3.

62. Ibid.

63. "Nudists Seek Solitude at Bohemian Carmel," *Los Angeles Times*, November 6, 1931, 8; "Nudist Colony Prospers Under Mexican Sanction," *Los Angeles Times*, January 24, 1932, 4.

64. "Our Unfeathered Friends," *New Outlook*, June 1934, 64, cited in Schaefer, *"Bold! Daring! Shocking! True!": A History of Exploitation Films*, 295.

65. See Diana Lindsay, ed., *Marshal South and the Ghost Mountain Chronicles: An Experiment in Primitive Living* (San Diego, CA: Sunbelt Publications, 2005).

66. Roger Showley, "Balboa Park: Nudists Haven in 1935-6," *San Diego Union-Tribune*, May 20, 2015, accessed August 9, 2017.

67. *The Nudist* 5, no. 6 (June 1936): 20, Robert J. Young Collection, Wolfsonian-Florida International University Rare Book and Special Collections Library, Miami Beach, Florida.

68. Cec Cinder, *The Nudist Idea* (Riverside, CA: Ultraviolet Press, 1998), 538.

69. Ibid., 537–538.

70. Hobart Glassey, "Building at Elysian Fields," *The Nudist* 3, no. 10 (November 1934): 19, Robert J. Young Collection, Wolfsonian-Florida International University Rare Book and Special Collections Library, Miami Beach, Florida.

71. "Nudists and Officers Set for Hide and Seek," *Los Angeles Times*, January 18, 1934, 8.

72. "Nudist Leaders Given Freedom," *Los Angeles Times*, January 23, 1934; Glassey, "Building at Elysian Fields."

73. "Elysia Nudist Colony near Elsinore Threatened by Financial Rift," *Los Angeles Times*, February 5, 1935, pt. 2, 5; "President Denies Rift Perils Nudist Colony," *Los Angeles Times*, February 10, 1935, 20.

74. John Richard Finch, "Nudism: The Modern Miracle," *The Nudist: Sunshine and Health* 6, no. 7 (July 1937): 19–20, Robert J. Young Collection, Wolfsonian-Florida International University Rare Book and Special Collections Library, Miami Beach, Florida.

75. See Payne, "Beyond the Pale: Nudism, Race, and Resistance in 'The Unashamed'"; *The Unashamed*, dir. Allen Stuart (USA, Cine-Grand Films Inc., 1938).

76. Bernard, "Sunbathing in Southern California," 21–22.

77. Cinder, *The Nudist Idea*, 538–539; Cecilia Rasmussen, "It's a Wrap for a Rustic, Remote Nudist Refuge," *Los Angeles Times*, March 4, 2007.

78. Bernard, "Sunbathing in Southern California," 24; "Nudist Child Hit by Bullet," *Los Angeles Times*, April 1, 1939.

79. Hunter, "The Day Nudism Died in Los Angeles"; Burnett, "The Fallen Fathers of the Angel City," 20.

80. Burnett, "The Fallen Fathers of the Angel City," 19.

81. "Sheriff Plans Nudist Survey," *Los Angeles Times*, July 26, 1939, A3.

82. Hunter, "The Day Nudism Died in Los Angeles"; "Legislation on Nudist Camps Sought by County Supervisors," *Los Angeles Times*, August 2, 1939, A1.

83. "Ban on Nudist Camps Blocked: Supervisors Divided but Question Revived for Further Study," *Los Angeles Times*, August 18, 1939.

84. Burnett, "The Fallen Fathers of the Angel City," 21.

85. "Nudity Topic of Police Board," *Los Angeles Times*, August 9, 1939, 18.

86. "Nudist Camps Regulated," *Los Angeles Times*, September 6, 1939, A1.

87. Ibid., A2.

88. "Nudist Camps Regulated."

89. Los Angeles County Ordinance #3428, reprinted "The Saga of Elysium: 1967–1984," *Journal of the Senses* 67 (Spring 1984): 2.

90. Burnett, "The Fallen Fathers of the Angel City," 21; "Nudist Control Measure Ready," *Los Angeles Times*, October 11, 1939, 8; "Council Votes Curb on Nudists," *Los Angeles Times*, November 10, 1939, A1; "Nudist Camp Curb Signed by Mayor," *Los Angeles Times*, November 15, 1939, 13.

91. Carl Easton Williams, "The President's Message," *Sunshine and Health*, November 1941, 27, Robert J. Young Collection, Wolfsonian-Florida International University Rare Book and Special Collections Library, Miami Beach, Florida.

92. "Nudist Camp Pair Arrested," *Los Angeles Times*, May 27, 1940, A1.

93. "Nudist Camp Case Ends in Conviction: San Fernando Valley Woman Found Guilty," *Los Angeles Times*, July 19, 1940, A1.

94. "Bible Quoted in Battle over Girls' Showers," *Los Angeles Times*, March 9, 1940, 3.

95. "Boys and Girls, All in Nude, to Attend Classes Together," *Los Angeles Times*, July 22, 1939, 1.

96. "Justice Indicates He May Bar Russell from College Position," *Los Angeles Times*, March 28, 1940, 1; "Bertrand Russell and Wife Deny Nudist Camp Charge," *Los Angeles Times*, March 29, 1940, A1.

97. Robert A. Heinlein, "The Year of the Jackpot," *Galaxy Science Fiction*, March 1952.

CHAPTER 2

1. Philip M. Lovell, "Care of the Body: The Home Built for Health," *Los Angeles Times*, December 15, 1929, F26.

2. Gary Marmorstein, "Steel and Slurry: Dr. Philip M. Lovell, Architectural Patron," *Southern California Quarterly* 84 (Fall 2002): 241–244; Ehrhard Bahr, *Weimar on the Pacific: German Exile Culture in Los Angeles and the Crisis of Modernism* (Berkeley: University of California Press, 2007), 157. For more on Lovell's enthusiasm for naturopathic health food, and the popularity of raw food diets in 1920s Los Angeles, see Jonathan Kauffman, *Hippie Food: How Back-to-the-Landers, Longhairs, and Revolutionaries Changed the Way We Eat* (New York: William Morrow, 2018), 23–27.

3. See Thomas Hines, *Architecture of the Sun: Los Angeles Modernism, 1900–1970* (New York: Rizzoli, 2010); August E. Sarnitz, "Proportion and Beauty—the Lovell Beach House by Rudolph Michael Schindler, Newport Beach, 1922–1926," *Journal of the Society of Architectural Historians* 45, no. 4 (December 1986): 374–388.

4. Lovell, "Care of the Body: The Home Built for Health."

5. Hines, *Architecture of the Sun*, 303–315; Merry Ovnick, *Los Angeles: The End of the Rainbow* (Los Angeles: Balcony Press, 1994), 219. For more on the corporeality and sexual psychology of Neutra's architectural modernism, see Barbara Lamprecht, *Richard Neutra: Furniture; The Body and the Senses* (New York: Wasmuth, 2015); Sylvia Lavin, "Open the Box: Richard Neutra and the Psychology of the Domestic Environment," *Assemblage* 40 (December 1999): 6–25.

6. Lovell, "Care of the Body: The Home Built for Health."

7. Esther McCoy, "Neutra: An Appreciation," *LA Architect* (June 1977), reprinted in *Piecing Together Los Angeles: An Esther McCoy Reader*, ed. Susan Morgan (Valencia, CA: East of Borneo Books, 2012), 131.

8. Lovell, "Care of the Body: The Home Built for Health"; Hines, *Architecture of the Sun*, 315; Marmorstein, "Steel and Slurry," 255.

9. Richard J. Neutra, "Some Notes on the Complex of Nudism," *Nude Living* 1 (April 1962): 7–10, Richard and Dion Neutra Papers, Collection 1179, Box 1476, folder 14, Department of Special Collections, Charles E. Young Research Library, University of California, Los Angeles. Many thanks to Barbara Lamprecht for alerting me to this document.

10. Philip M. Lovell, "Care of the Body," *Los Angeles Times*, June 29, 1924, J24. Lovell's desire for a flat roof as a health cure was inspired by the tuberculosis architecture of the late nineteenth century. See Margaret Campbell, "What Tuberculosis Did for Modernism: The Influence of a Curative Environment on Modernist Design and Architecture," *Medical History* 49 (2005): 463–488.

11. R. M. Schindler, "Care of the Body," *Los Angeles Times*, May 2, 1926, K28.

12. Janice Sterne, "Our Furniture and Our Health," *Physical Culture* (October 1912): 430.

13. For more on the display of the body in modernist architecture, see Alice T. Friedman, *American Glamour and the Evolution of Modern Architecture* (New Haven, CT: Yale University Press, 2010).

14. *All About Santa Barbara, California: The Sanitarium of the Pacific Coast* (Santa Barbara, CA: Daily Advertizer Printing House, 1878), 30, rare books file #246941, Department of Special Collections, Huntington Library, San Marino, California.

15. "Life in the Open Air," *Los Angeles Times*, January 1, 1899, 2.

16. John Stanislav Sadar, "Material Heliotechnics: A Tale of Two Bodies," in *Healing Spaces, Modern Architecture, and the Body*, ed. Sarah Schrank and Didem Ekici, Ashgate Studies in Architecture Series (London: Routledge, 2017), 67.

17. Auguste Rollier, "Heliotherapy: Its Therapeutic, Prophylactic and Social Value," *American Journal of Nursing* 27, no. 10 (October 1927): 815.

18. A. J. Scott Pinchin, "Sunbathing and Tuberculosis," *British Medical Journal* 2 (July 14, 1934): 85; Kerry Segrave, *Suntanning in 20th Century America* (Jefferson, NC: McFarland, 2005).

19. Edgar Mayer, "Sun-Bathing and Sun-Lamps," *American Journal of Nursing* 33 (August 1933): 739–746; "Sunbathing and You," *Sun Magazine* 11 (January 1961): 7, Robert J. Young Collection, Wolfsonian-Florida International University Rare Book and Special Collections Library, Miami Beach, Florida; Philip M. Lovell, "Health Makes the Home," *Los Angeles Times*, December 22, 1940, G17.

20. Lewis E. Hertslet, "Skin and Sun," *British Medical Journal* 2 (August 11, 1928): 275–276; G. Gregory Kayne and J. E. Wood, "Sunbathing and Tuberculosis," *British Medical Journal* 2 (July 21, 1934): 138.

21. Segrave, *Suntanning in 20th Century America*, 53; "Glass Houses for Health," *New York Times*, July 1, 1927, 20. For more examples of the relationship between architectural modernism and the body, see Sarah Schrank and Didem Ekici, eds., *Healing Spaces, Modern Architecture, and the Body*, Ashgate Studies in Architecture Series (London: Routledge, 2017).

22. "Physicians Design Home of Health," *New York Times*, May 25, 1930, 171.

23. Leicester B. Holland, "Nudism and Modern Architecture," *Architect and Engineer*, March 1937, 41–42, California Historical Society Collection, San Francisco, California.

24. Maurice Farr Parmelee, *Nudism in Modern Life* (Garden City, NY: Garden City Publishing, 1931), 258.

25. Ibid., 6.

26. Parmelee, *Nudism in Modern Life*, 213.

27. Ibid., 216.

28. Ruth Barcan, "'The Moral Bath of Bodily Unconsciousness': Female Nudism, Bodily Exposure, and the Gaze," *Continuum: Journal of Media and Cultural Studies* 15 (November 2001): 309.

29. Ebenezer Howard, *Garden Cities of To-Morrow* (London, 1902; repr., ed. with a preface by F. J. Osborn and an introductory essay by Lewis Mumford, London: Faber and Faber, 1946); John Alexander Williams, *Turning to Nature in Germany: Hiking, Nudism, and Conservation, 1900–1940* (Stanford, CA: Stanford University Press, 2007), 12.

30. Parmelee, *Nudism in Modern Life*, 222–223.

31. *The Nudist: Sunshine and Health* 6 (January 1937): 22, Robert J. Young Collection, Wolfsonian-Florida International University Rare Book and Special Collections Library, Miami Beach, Florida.

32. *The Nudist: Sunshine and Health* 7 (June 1938): 12, Robert J. Young Collection, Wolfsonian-Florida International University Rare Book and Special Collections Library, Miami Beach, Florida. The innovators of the sun tub may have been inspired by the revolving summer houses constructed in the United Kingdom in the early twentieth century. See Campbell, "What Tuberculosis Did for Modernism," 478–482.

33. Alois S. Knapp, "We, the War, and the Present Emergency," *Sunshine and Health*, May 1942, 13, Robert J. Young Collection, Wolfsonian-Florida International University Rare Book and Special Collections Library, Miami Beach, Florida.

34. In the first broad sociological study of nudism in the United States, published by William E. Hartman, Marilyn Fithian, and Donald Johnson in 1970, the authors concluded that, of their sample, close to 90 percent of those who visited nudist camps also practiced "home nudism." William E. Hartman, Marilyn Fithian, and Donald Johnson, *Nudist Society: The Controversial Study of the Clothes-Free Naturist Movement in America* (Los Angeles: Elysium Growth Press, 1970; rev. and updated by Iris Bancroft, 1991), 187, 428. Citations refer to the more recent edition.

35. "A Small House for the Sunshine," *Sunshine and Health* 18, no. 1 (January 1949), Robert J. Young Collection, Wolfsonian-Florida International University Rare Book and Special Collections Library, Miami Beach, Florida.

36. Evidence of the flurry of new interest in social nudism can be found in the *Los Angeles Times*, which in 1953 reported on a surge of new American Sunbathing Association members. See "Nudists Gathering for Convention: 1500 Sunbathers Will Open National Meeting at Cajon Ranch," *Los Angeles Times*, August 6, 1953, 2; Art Ryon, "Nudists Show Healthy Gains in Numbers and Finances," *Los Angeles Times*, August 7, 1953, 2; Art Ryon, "Attendance Soars Over 400 at Nudists' Camp," *Los Angeles Times*, August 8, 1953, 2.

37. Ken Price, "Let's Visit the Smiths," *Sunshine and Health* 25 (June 1956): 6–11, Robert J. Young Collection, Wolfsonian-Florida International University Rare Book and Special Collections Library, Miami Beach, Florida.

38. "The Sun Shines in Your Own Backyard," *Sunshine and Health*, February 1954, 6, Robert J. Young Collection, Wolfsonian-Florida International University Rare Book and Special Collections Library, Miami Beach, Florida.

39. *Sunshine and Health* 25 (December 1946), cover, Robert J. Young Collection, Wolfsonian-Florida International University Rare Book and Special Collections Library, Miami Beach, Florida.

40. No one captured the cultural value of staging American middle-class family life within the private home better than the photographer, Maynard L. Parker. For more, see Jennifer A. Watts, ed., *Maynard L. Parker: Modern Photography and the American Dream* (New Haven, CT: Yale University Press, 2012).

41. Kenn Trumble, as told to Stan Sohler, "Sun-Fan House," *Sunshine and Health* 29, no. 4 (April 1960): 4, Robert J. Young Collection, Wolfsonian-Florida International University Rare Book and Special Collections Library, Miami Beach, Florida.

42. Ibid., 6.

43. Ibid., 8. I would like to thank Ron Rarick, PhD, of the School of Art, Ball State University, for correcting my previous interpretation of this architectural feature.

44. Barbara Miller Lane, *Houses for a New World: Builders and Buyers in American Suburbs, 1945–1965* (Princeton, NJ: Princeton University Press, 2015), 24–25. Thank you to Leslie Topp for bringing this book to my attention.

45. See Carl Abbott, *New Urban History: Growth and Politics in Sunbelt Cities* (Chapel Hill: University of North Carolina Press, 1981); Carl Abbott, *How Cities Won the West: Four Centuries of Urban Change in Western North America* (Albuquerque: University of New Mexico Press, 2008); Raymond Mohl, ed., *Searching for the Sunbelt: Historical Perspec-*

tives on a Region (Knoxville: University of Tennessee Press, 1990); Gary Mormino, *Land of Sunshine, State of Dreams: A Social History of Modern Florida* (Gainesville: University Press of Florida, 2008); Michelle Nickerson and Darren Dochuk, eds., *Sunbelt Rising: The Politics of Place, Space, and Region* (Philadelphia: University of Pennsylvania Press, 2011).

46. Trumble, "Sun-Fan House," 8; Angie de Angeles, "The Naked Truth," *Orange and Blue Magazine* (College of Journalism and Communications, University of Florida), Spring 2007.

47. Phillip Edward Buchy, "A Nudist Resort" (master of architecture thesis, Miami University, 2005). Perusing the real estate listings for Pasco County and especially the broader Tampa area reveals hundreds of clothing-optional condominiums for sale in the Caliente and Paradise Lakes developments. See, for example, *Pasco Naturally Magazine*, January 2011, 20–21.

48. De Angeles, "The Naked Truth"; "Modern Naturism," November 7, 2009.

49. Sean Mussenden, "Man Envisions Christian Nudist Colony for Families," *Orlando Sentinel*, January 6, 2004; Lisa San Pascual, "Bare Naked Christians," *Religion in the News* 7 (Spring 2004); David Usborne, "Call to Bare at Nudist Camp for Christians," *Independent*, January 8, 2004.

50. Phil Davis, "Florida County Is Nudist Mecca," Associated Press, June 12, 2006.

51. Trumble, "Sun-Fan House," 8, 28.

52. Ibid.

53. For more on Cliff May and the development of the California ranch house, see Jocelyn Gibbs and Nicholas Olsberg, eds., *Carefree California: Cliff May and the Romance of the Ranch House* (New York: Rizzoli, 2012).

54. See Lawrence Culver, "From Resorts to the Ranch House," chapter 7 in *The Frontier of Leisure: Southern California and the Shaping of Modern America* (Oxford: Oxford University Press, 2010).

55. Culver, "From Resorts to the Ranch House," 160.

56. See Adele Cygelman, David Glomb, and Joseph Rosa, *Palm Springs Modern: Houses in the California Desert* (New York: Rizzoli, 1999); Alan Hess and Andrew Danish, *Palm Springs Weekend: The Architecture and Design of a Midcentury Oasis* (San Francisco: Chronicle Books, 2001).

57. Lee Edmunds, "Build a Backyard Retreat," *Sunshine and Health* 29 (December 1960): 25, Robert J. Young Collection, Wolfsonian-Florida International University Rare Book and Special Collections Library, Miami Beach, Florida.

58. Culver, "From Resorts to the Ranch House," 187.

59. For more on the corporeal aesthetics of the private pool, see Daniell Cornell, *Backyard Oasis: The Swimming Pool in Southern California Photography, 1945–1982* (Munich: Delmonico Books, 2012).

60. "The Sun Shines in Your Own Backyard," *Sunshine and Health*, February 1954, 6, Robert J. Young Collection, Wolfsonian-Florida International University Rare Book and Special Collections Library, Miami Beach, Florida.

61. Curtis Besinger, "Why This House Is a Pace Setter," *House Beautiful*, February 1959, 73.

62. Ibid., 91.

63. Guy Henle, "The Pros and Cons of Swimming Pools," *House Beautiful*, April 1959, 138.

64. Sadar, "Material Heliotechnics: A Tale of Two Bodies," 69.

65. Alsynite Company of America advertisement, *House Beautiful*, May 1960, 149.

66. Sunbrella advertisement, *Sunset: The Magazine of Western Living*, May 1967, 118.

67. "For the Do It Yourself Addict," *Sunshine and Health* 27 (February 1958): 14, Robert J. Young Collection, Wolfsonian-Florida International University Rare Book and Special Collections Library, Miami Beach, Florida.

68. Kent Keegan and Pamela Jacobs Keegan, *Swimming Pools: Projects for Hot Tubs, Spas, Lanais, Cabanas, Gazebos, Fountains, Ornamental Pools, Fences* (Passaic, NJ: Creative Homeowner Press, 1981), 10.

69. Wolfgang Langewiesche, "Your House in Florida," *House Beautiful*, January 1950, 70–76.

70. Wolfgang Langewiesche, "How to Live Comfortably in the Southwest Desert," *House Beautiful*, April 1950, 151–160.

71. "Six Other Ways to Have an Inner Garden in Six Other Climates," *House Beautiful*, February 1959, 122.

72. Langewiesche, "How to Live Comfortably in the Southwest Desert," 160.

73. Living in the Buff Recreational Associations, Promotional Flyer, n.d., Pomona Public Library Free Beach Collection. See also Dale Fetherling, "Nudists Shed Stigma Along with Their Clothes," *Los Angeles Times*, August 14, 1977, A1.

74. "Clothing Optional Apartments Seen," *Arcadia Tribune*, June 1, 1978, Pomona Public Library Free Beach Collection.

75. Claudia Suppe, "Living Nude in LA: Successful Nudist Apartment Building," *Bare in Mind: A Nudist News Service* 11, no. 6 (July 1983): 1, Pomona Public Library Free Beach Collection.

76. John R. Stilgoe, "Privacy and Energy-Efficient Residential Site Design: An Example of Context," *Journal of Architectural Education* 37 (Spring–Summer 1984): 24.

77. Besinger, "Why This House Is a Pace Setter," 88.

78. Ibid., 85; Elizabeth Gordon, "It Provides Space for Mental Expansion," *House Beautiful*, February 1959, 106. For more on the influence of *House Beautiful*, and especially editor-in-chief, Elizabeth Gordon, on middle-class domestic taste, see Monica Penick, *Tastemaker: Elizabeth Gordon, House Beautiful, and the Postwar American Home* (New Haven: Yale University Press, 2017).

79. "Replacing Their Shade Tree . . . A New Patio Roof," *Sunset: The Magazine of Western Living*, June 1967, 184.

80. "How to Manipulate Sun and Shade," *House Beautiful*, July 1950, 44.

81. "Americans Have a Talent for Making a Little Go a Long Way," *House Beautiful*, November 1950, 210–211.

82. There is extensive literature tracing the racialized implications of postwar urban policy and the processes of suburbanization. See, for example, Eric Avila, *Popular Culture in the Age of White Flight: Fear and Fantasy in Suburban Los Angeles* (Berkeley: University of California Press, 2004); George Lipsitz, *The Possessive Investment in Whiteness: How White People Profit from Identity Politics* (Philadelphia: Temple University Press, 1998); Thomas Sugrue, *The Origins of the Urban Crisis: Race and Inequality in Postwar Detroit* (Princeton, NJ: Princeton University Press, 2005).

83. There is important scholarship examining the "tropical" and its relationship to

race, transnationalism, and imperialism in the twentieth century. See Catherine Cocks, *Tropical Whites: The Rise of the Tourist South in the Americas*, Nature and Culture in America (Philadelphia: University of Pennsylvania Press, 2013); Catherine Cocks, "The Pleasures of Degeneration: Climate, Race, and the Origins of the Global Tourist South in the Americas," *Discourse* 29 (Spring and Fall 2007): 215–235; Caroline Daley, *Leisure and Pleasure: Reshaping and Revealing the New Zealand Body, 1900–1960* (Auckland: Auckland University Press, 2003); Ryan Johnson, "European Cloth and 'Tropical' Skin: Clothing, Material and British Ideas of Health and Hygiene in Tropical Climates," *Bulletin of the History of Medicine* 83 (Fall 2009): 530–560.

CHAPTER 3

1. Aileen Goodson, *Experiment in Nude Psychotherapy* (Los Angeles: Elysium Institute, 1967), 4–13, Pomona Public Library Free Beach Collection, Pomona, California.

2. Ian Nicholson, "Baring the Soul: Paul Bindrim, Abraham Maslow and 'Nude Psychotherapy,'" *Journal of the History of the Behavioral Sciences* 43, no. 4 (Fall 2007): 353.

3. Ibid., 347; *Life* magazine, July 12, 1968, clipping, Elysium Papers, Private Collection, Southern California Naturist Association Archives, Moorpark, California.

4. "A 24-hour marathon with group nudity," *Life* magazine, July 12, 1968.

5. Nicholson, "Baring the Soul," 345.

6. Ibid., 338; Myrna Oliver, "E. Paul Bindrim; Father of Nude Psychotherapy," *Los Angeles Times*, January 8, 1998.

7. Nicholson, "Baring the Soul," 340.

8. Ibid., 341.

9. Ibid.

10. Ibid., 352.

11. There is an enormous Wilhelm Reich literature, both by, and about, him, and an updated historiographical study is in order, but for works that offer a general survey of his life and study see Myron Sharaf, *Fury on Earth: A Biography of Wilhelm Reich* (New York: Da Capo Press, 1994); Christopher Turner, *Adventures in the Orgasmatron: How the Sexual Revolution Came to America* (New York: Farrar, Straus, and Giroux, 2011). For a wonderful account of how Reich's ideas influenced modern architecture and domestic space in the United States, making a case for the sexuality of modernism and the relationship between the body and architecture, see Sylvia Lavin, "Open the Box: Richard Neutra and the Psychology of the Domestic Environment," *Assemblage* 40 (December 1999): 6–25.

12. Oliver, "E. Paul Bindrim; Father of Nude Psychotherapy"; *Bindrim v. Mitchell* 92 Cal. App. 3d 61 (Cal. Ct. App. 1979), 2.

13. The early study of the relationship between mind and body, of which nude psychotherapy was a part, has evolved into a range of innovative treatments for physical and psychological trauma. For examples of these therapies, see Bessel van der Kolk, *The Body Keeps the Score: Brain, Mind, and Body in the Healing of Trauma* (New York: Viking, 2014).

14. William E. Hartman and Marilyn A. Fithian, "Additional Comment on the Sexological Examination: A Reply to Hoch," *Journal of Sex Research* 18, no. 1 (February 1982): 68.

15. Charles Figley, "Review of Treatment of Sexual Dysfunction," *Journal of Family Counseling* 2, no. 1 (1974): 68–80.

16. Figley, "Review of Treatment of Sexual Dysfunction"; "William Hartman, 78, Influenced Sex Research," *New York Times*, October 13, 1997; Elaine Woo, "Influential Sex Therapist and Researcher," *Los Angeles Times*, September 19, 2008.

17. Woo, "Influential Sex Therapist and Researcher."

18. Ibid.

19. Hartman and Fithian, "Additional Comment on the Sexological Examination: A Reply to Hoch," 64–71.

20. Ibid., 65.

21. William E. Hartman, Marilyn Fithian, and Donald Johnson, *Nudist Society: The Controversial Study of the Clothes-Free Naturist Movement in America* (Los Angeles: Elysium Growth Press, 1970; rev. and updated by Iris Bancroft, 1991).

22. Ibid., appendices 4–6, 423–441. Citations refer to revised edition.

23. Ibid., appendix 6, 433.

24. Ibid., 187, 428.

25. Ibid., 187, 429.

26. Ibid., appendix 2, 412–413; appendix 6, 433–438.

27. Ibid., 285–304.

28. Abraham H. Maslow, *Eupsychian Management* (Homewood, IL: Irwin-Dorsey Press, 1965), 160, cited in Hartman, Fithian, and Johnson, 286.

29. Hartman, Fithian, and Johnson, 287.

30. Ibid., 301–302.

31. Ibid., 313.

32. Ibid., 312.

33. Howard C. Warren, "Social Nudism and the Body Taboo," academic paper, Department of Psychology, Princeton University, reprinted in Hartman, Fithian, and Johnson, 405.

34. Manfred F. DeMartino, *The New Female Sexuality: The Sexual Practices and Experiences of Social Nudists, "Potential" Nudists, and Lesbians* (New York: Julian Press, 1969); Manfred F. DeMartino Collection of CBS Radio Scripts, 1943–1945, File Number, RPA 00189, Library of Congress, Washington, DC.

35. Iris Bancroft, "Introduction," Hartman, Fithian, and Johnson, *Nudist Society: The Controversial Study of the Clothes-Free Naturist Movement in America*, v–viii. Citations refer to the 1991 edition.

36. Hartman, Fithian, and Johnson, ix.

37. Academic interest in the sexuality of nudism continued well into the 1980s concluding, overwhelmingly, that while nudists might be understood by the public as being more sexually active than average Americans, there was "no direct relationship between nudity and sexually permissive behaviors," as reported by Marilyn D. Story, "A Comparison of Social Nudists and Non-Nudists on Experience with Various Sexual Outlets," *Journal of Sex Research* 23, no. 2 (May 1987): 197.

38. "The Saga of Elysium: 1967–1984," *Journal of the Senses* 67 (Spring 1984): 3.

39. Golda Sirota, "Ed Lange the Man: Sinner or Saint?" *Topanga Messenger*, October 5, 1979, 1.

40. Sirota, "Ed Lange the Man: Sinner or Saint?" 2.

41. "Ed Lange, Biographical Information," Elysium Papers, Private Collection, Southern California Naturist Association Archives, Moorpark, California.

42. Ed Lange, interview by Art Kunkin, Society of Magazine Publishers, unpublished transcription, May 10, 1989, 7–8, Elysium Papers, Private Collection, Southern California Naturist Association Archives, Moorpark, California.

43. Brian Hoffman, "'A Certain Amount of Prudishness': Nudist Magazines and the Liberalization of American Obscenity Law, 1947–1958," *Gender and History* 22, no. 3 (November 2010): 719. Until quite recently, in American culture, female pubic hair was considered sexually appealing and a mark of sexual maturity. For the courts, in the 1940s and 1950s, to single out exposed female pubic hair as especially obscene speaks as much to the courts' misogyny as it does to female pubic hair's sex appeal. For more on the aesthetics of pubic hair, see Rebecca M. Herzig, *Plucked: A History of Hair Removal* (New York: New York University Press, 2015), 136.

44. Hoffman, "'A Certain Amount of Prudishness,'" 719–720.

45. Whitney Strub, *Obscenity Rules: Roth v. United States and the Long Struggle over Sexual Expression* (Lawrence: University Press of Kansas, 2013), 129–130.

46. Hoffman, "'A Certain Amount of Prudishness,'" 725.

47. Strub, *Obscenity Rules*, 1.

48. *Roth v. United States*, 354 U.S. 476 (1957).

49. Strub, *Obscenity Rules*, 183.

50. Hoffman, "'A Certain Amount of Prudishness,'" 728.

51. Boone's big win was not just celebrated by nudists but also by the emergent gay rights movement. The Mattachine Society immediately saw the decision as significant for the publishing of gay magazines and literature and a potential tool for fighting homophobia in the courts. See John Logan, "Victory for *One*," *Mattachine Review*, February 1958.

52. Hoffman, "'A Certain Amount of Prudishness,'" 711.

53. *Sunshine Book Company and Solair Union Naturisme, Inc., Appellants, v. Arthur E. Summerfield, Individually and as Postmaster General of the United States, Appellee*, 249 F.2d 114 (D.C. Cir. 1957), cited in Edward De Grazia, *Censorship Landmarks* (New York: R. R. Bowker, 1969), 248. The 1956 circulation figures of forty thousand (ten thousand to subscribers) were cited in conservative columnist, James Jackson Kilpatrick's 1960 anti-obscenity treatise, *The Smut Peddlers*, as greater than the circulation of either *The Reporter*, *New Republic*, *The Nation*, or *National Review*. James Jackson Kilpatrick, *The Smut Peddlers* (Garden City, NY: Doubleday, 1960), 15.

54. Hoffman, "'A Certain Amount of Prudishness,'" 714–716.

55. Fred Ilfeld Jr. and Roger Lauer, *Social Nudism in America* (New Haven, CT: College and University Press, 1964), 143.

56. See Sarah Schrank, *Art and the City: Civic Imagination and Cultural Authority in Los Angeles* (Philadelphia: University of Pennsylvania Press, 2009).

57. Ken Price, "Nudist Photo Workshop #6," *Sunshine and Health*, September 1956, 21, Robert J. Young Collection, Wolfsonian-Florida International University Rare Book and Special Collections Library, Miami Beach, Florida.

58. Ken Price, "Two Round Patches," *Sunshine and Health*, June 1961, 9, Robert J. Young Collection, Wolfsonian-Florida International University Rare Book and Special Collections Library, Miami Beach, Florida.

59. "Contractor Named Head of US Nudists," *Washington Post*, August 15, 1952, 16; Anthony Lewis, "US Seeks to Void Obscenity Ruling: Ban on Nudist Publications Called

Misinterpretation of High Court Finding," *New York Times*, November 20, 1957, 30; "Supreme Court Decisions," *New York Times*, December 9, 1957; *Mervin Mounce, petitioner v. United States of America*, 355 U.S. 180 (78 S.Ct. 267, 2 L.Ed.2d 187).

60. Lange, interview by Kunkin, 23.

61. June Lange, "Nudism Needn't Be Neolithic," *Sunbathing Review*, Spring 1959, 37–38, Robert J. Young Collection, Wolfsonian-Florida International University Rare Book and Special Collections Library, Miami Beach, Florida.

62. What is especially interesting about June Lange's essay about these Californians and their depilated pubic hair is how *early* in American body history they were removing it, and how confused nudists were about interpreting it. Since female pubic hair was considered obscene by the courts, one might infer that removing it would mark the pubic area asexual. But, clearly, the negative nudist reaction to pubic hair removal, and the general nudist protocol to leave one's pubic hair alone, just by admitting that it was there at all seemed to oversexualize female genitalia. In the twenty-first century, female pubic hair has undergone a marked change in that the widespread cultural preference, particularly among younger women, is not to have any at all. Critics often point out that this is a by-product of a cultural desire to infantilize adult women's bodies and the mainstreaming of pornography, where there isn't a female pubic hair to be found (except in extra-hairy fetish porn). Ironically, what distinguished raunchy triple-X pornography in the 1970s from what came before was its preponderance of visual female pubic hair. In 1959, by shaving off their pubic hair, these female nudists were provocatively fifty years ahead of their time. For more on the topic of female pubic hair removal, see Herzig, *Plucked: A History of Hair Removal*, 135–151.

63. Stephen J. Gertz, "Everybody Loves Milton," *eI17* 3, no. 6 (December 2004). For more on Milton Luros's soft-core publishing empire, see Stephen J. Gertz, "West Coast Blue," in *Sin-A-Rama: Sleaze Paperbacks of the Sixties*, ed. Brittany A. Daley and Stephen J. Gertz (Los Angeles: Feral House, 2005), 28–29.

64. Cec Cinder, *The Nudist Idea* (Riverside, CA: Ultraviolet Press, 1998), 574, 576; Lange, interview by Kunkin, 22–23; Hoffman, "'A Certain Amount of Prudishness,'" 729.

65. Dian Hanson, *Naked as a Jaybird and Loving It* (Los Angeles: Taschen, 2003), 24–29.

66. Ibid., 37.

67. "The Saga of Elysium, 1967–1984," 3; Gary Mussell, "Remembering Elysium," 2011, 3, Elysium Papers, Private Collection, Southern California Naturist Association Archives, Moorpark, California.

68. Mussell, "Remembering Elysium," 3.

69. Elysium Growth Press Catalog, n.d., Elysium Papers, Private Collection, Southern California Naturist Association Archives, Moorpark, California.

70. Ibid.

71. "Lange, Biographical Information."

72. Elysium Growth Press Catalog.

73. Ibid.

74. *American Sunbathing Association Bulletin* 50 (November 2001): 26–27, Robert J. Young Collection, Wolfsonian-Florida International University Rare Book and Special Collections Library, Miami Beach, Florida.

75. Jeffrey J. Kripal, *Esalen: America and the Religion of No Religion* (Chicago: University of Chicago Press, 2007), 86.

76. Ibid., 87.

77. Ibid., 138.

78. "The Saga of Elysium, 1967–1984," 3.

79. "The Group Leader's Workshop," VII-2/33, 1970, 2, Elysium Papers, Private Collection, Southern California Naturist Association Archives, Moorpark, California; Elysium Press Release, August 1, 1978, Elysium Papers, Private Collection, Southern California Naturist Association Archives, Moorpark, California.

80. "The Saga of Elysium, 1967–1984," 2–4.

81. "Lange, Biographical Information."

82. Mussell, "Remembering Elysium," 4.

83. "The Group Leader's Workshop," VII-2/33, 1970, 3.

84. Ibid., 2.

85. Ibid., 3.

86. Lange, interview by Kunkin, 24.

87. Ed Lange, "The Elysium Creed," quoted in Mussell, "Remembering Elysium," 4.

88. "The Group Leader's Workshop," VII-2/33, 1970, 2.

89. Mussell, "Remembering Elysium," 5.

90. Mussell, "Remembering Elysium," 11.

91. Ken Hansen, "Raid Repeated as Nudists Seek Ban," *Los Angeles Times*, July 2, 1968, pt. 2-F, 8.

92. Ken Hansen, "Proponents of Nudism Attack '39 County Ban," *Los Angeles Times*, July 7, 1968, 3.

93. Ibid.

94. Ken Hansen, "County Ban on Nudism Upheld by US Judge; State Test Set," *Los Angeles Times*, July 12, 1968, pt. 2-F, 1; Stanley Fleishman Papers Finding Aid, 1955–1975, UCLA Library Special Collections, Charles E. Young Research Library.

95. Ken Hansen, "Judge Backs Topanga Canyon: Nudism Law Struck Down," *Los Angeles Times*, July 19, 1968, pt. 2, 7.

96. Ray Zeman, "Abolition of Obscenity Commission Proposed," *Los Angeles Times*, October 30, 1968, pt. 2, 1.

97. "DA's Office Seeks Nude Law Hearing," *Santa Monica Evening Outlook*, December 12, 1968, 13.

98. Letter from John Maharg, county counsel, and Edward Gaylord, assistant county counsel, to Los Angeles County Board of Supervisors, Re: License for Nudist Camps, July 21, 1970, Elysium Papers, Private Collection, Southern California Naturist Association Archives, Moorpark, California.

99. Ordinance No. 10,600 adding Chapter XX to Ordinance No. 5860, July 22, 1970, Elysium Papers, Private Collection, Southern California Naturist Association Archives, Moorpark, California.

100. "Nudist Camps Told to Apply for Licenses," *Los Angeles Times*, September 1, 1970, pt. 2, 6.

101. Louise Larson, "Lange Yet to File for Nudity License," *Santa Monica Evening Outlook*, August 29, 1970, 3.

102. Louise Larson, "Prejudice Seen in Nude Law," *Santa Monica Evening Outlook*, July 24, 1970, 18.

103. Louise Larson, "Nudist Camp Curb Backed by Chamber of Commerce," *Santa Monica Evening Outlook*, August 7, 1970, 1.

104. Ibid.

105. Barney Berkey, "Elysium Bares Much, But Can't Bear Scrutiny," *North Shore Shopper*, September 3, 1970, 2.

106. "Anti-Nude Law Is Ruled Constitutional by Judge," *Los Angeles Herald-Examiner*, August 21, 1970.

107. Robert G. Johnston, letter to the Los Angeles County Board of Supervisors, October 17, 1970, Elysium Papers, Private Collection, Southern California Naturist Association Archives, Moorpark, California.

108. Howard Kennedy, "Psychologists Urge Repeal of Law Requiring Nudist Camp Licensing," *Los Angeles Times*, October 4, 1970.

109. Mrs. J. E. Dryer, "Topanga 'Perfect' for Elysium Field," *Topanga Shopper*, June 25, 1970.

110. Elizabeth Putnam, "Freedom to Grow," *North Shore Shopper*, November 5, 1970, 9.

111. Stanley E. Russell, letter to Robert Myers, assistant chief deputy, Los Angeles County Board of Supervisors, August 3, 1970, Elysium Papers, Private Collection, Southern California Naturist Association Archives, Moorpark, California.

112. "Court Tests Nudity Validity," *Topanga Shopper*, November 19, 1970; "Merrick Upholds Nudist Ordinance," *Santa Monica Evening Outlook*, November 25, 1970, 8; "Topangans Bare Happy Thoughts," *Topanga Shopper*, December 3, 1970.

113. "Topangan Facing Smut Mail Trial," *Santa Monica Evening Outlook*, July 24, 1970, 4; "Nudist Colonies May Be Stripped," *Topanga Shopper*, July 30, 1970.

114. "Nudists Peril Values," *Malibu News*, July 9, 1970; Mary Ann Coblentz, "'Wholesome' Attitudes Seem Unwholesome," letter to the editor, clipping service, n.d., Elysium Papers, Private Collection, Southern California Naturist Association Archives, Moorpark, California.

115. "Nudist Colony Attempts to Topple License Law," *Los Angeles Times*, October 28, 1970, pt. 2-F, 6; "A Peel Leads to Appeal," *Topanga Shopper*, December 10, 1970.

116. "Court Supports Topanga Nudists," *Santa Monica Evening Outlook*, March 29, 1972, 1; Gene Blake, "Right to Assemble in Nude Upheld by Court," *Los Angeles Times*, March 31, 1972, pt. 2-F, 3; "Nudists Win Freedom in Topanga Canyon," *Topanga Mail*, April 6, 1972, 1.

117. Charles R. Donaldson, "County Will Appeal Nudist Camp Ruling," *Los Angeles Times*, March 30, 1972, pt. 7.

118. Elysium Institute Press Release, March 31, 1972, Elysium Papers, Private Collection, Southern California Naturist Association Archives, Moorpark, California.

119. For more on shifting conservative tactics in controlling urban sex districts, and especially pornographic movie theaters, see Whitney Strub, "The Clearly Obscene and the Queerly Obscene: Heteronormativity and Obscenity in Cold War Los Angeles," *American Quarterly* 60, no. 2 (June 2008): 373–398; Eric Schaefer and Eithne Johnson, "Quarantined! A Case Study of Boston's Combat Zone," in *Hop on Pop: The Politics and Pleasures of Popular Culture*, ed. Henry Jenkins, Tara McPherson, and Jane Shattuc (Durham, NC: Duke University Press, 2002), 430–453.

120. Charles R. Donaldson, "Supervisors Declare War on Nudists," *Los Angeles Times*, June 8, 1972, WS1; Skip Ferderber, "Nudist Camp Foes Seeking County's Help," *Los Angeles Times*, December 5, 1974, WS1; Gerald Faris, "County Planning Board Checking Zone Status of Elysium Nudist Camp," *Los Angeles Times*, September 21, 1975, A2.

121. Ed Lange, "Topanga's Elysium Fight for Survival," *The Messenger* 9, no. 3 (February 14-27, 1985): 6, Elysium Papers, Private Collection, Southern California Naturist Association Archives, Moorpark, California.

122. "Nudist Camp Trying to Gain Legal Status Again," *Los Angeles Daily News*, April 28, 1983, 8; "The Naked Truth, at Last," *LA Weekly*, May 3-9, 1985; Anne Morgenthaler, "County Blocked from Closing Topanga Nudist Camp," *Santa Monica Evening Outlook*, May 8, 1986; Aaron Curtiss, "Proper Permit Is in Sight for Nudist Camp," *Los Angeles Times*, September 22, 1992, B3; Curtiss, "Nudist Camp Bears Burden of Ongoing Zoning, Land Issues," *Los Angeles Times*, October 5, 1992, B3; "Elysium Wins Approval for Five Year Conditional Use Permit," Elysium Press Release, December 3, 1992, Elysium Papers, Private Collection, Southern California Naturist Association Archives, Moorpark, California; Pam Linn, "Nudist Colony Gets Five More Years in Topanga," *Malibu Times*, December 10, 1992.

123. Sirota, "Ed Lange the Man: Sinner or Saint?" 2.

124. Bob Pool, "County's Last Nudist Resort Closes," *Los Angeles Times*, November 21, 2001.

CHAPTER 4

1. The term "sexual revolution" was coined by Wilhelm Reich, whose 1920s book, *The Sexual Struggle of Youth*, was reprinted in the United States in 1945 as *The Sexual Revolution*. Reich's hope for sweeping reforms and his controversial ideas about sex did not take hold beyond the therapeutic settings of the 1960s and 1970s, but early twentieth-century urban industrial life did usher in a new openness about sex. Dating, or "treating," replaced traditional courtship, and birth control, while not legal in the United States until 1936, brought down American birth rates. In the early 1960s, the sexual revolution referred to the medical and technological advances made by the birth control pill and the disentangling of sex from procreation. By the 1970s, the sexual revolution loosely referred to the increase in nudity in film, the rise of the adult bookstore and hard-core pornography theaters, but also to the swirl of sexual liberationist ideas emerging from the gay rights movement, feminism, and the counterculture, which challenged traditional ideas about marriage, family, and gender. Sex education in schools, the abortion rights struggle, and the growing ease of accessing birth control were all part of the postwar "revolution." For more, see David Allyn, *Make Love, Not War: The Sexual Revolution; An Unfettered History* (New York: Routledge, 2001).

2. Gay Talese, *Thy Neighbor's Wife* (Garden City, NY: Doubleday, 1980; newly updated, New York: Harper Perennial, 2009), 45. Citations refer to the most recent edition.

3. Ibid., 527.

4. Anatole Broyard, "Books of the Times: Pontifications a Shared Responsibility," *New York Times*, April 30, 1980, C27; Wayne Warga, "Boswell of the Sexual Revolution," *Los Angeles Times*, May 23, 1980, G21; Susan Jacoby, "Hers," *New York Times*, August 14, 1980, C2.

5. Jacoby, "Hers."

6. Tony Schwartz, "U.A. Pays $2.5 Million for Book by Gay Talese," *New York Times*, October 9, 1979, C9.

7. Claudia Eller, "Big-Bucks Book Biz," *Los Angeles Times*, June 16, 1993, WB5.

8. Schwarz, "U.A. Pays $2.5 Million for Book by Gay Talese."

9. For a marvelous treatment of the fetishism of domesticity in suburban fiction, see Christopher Kocela, *Fetishism and Its Discontents in Post-1960s American Fiction* (New York: Palgrave Macmillan, 2010), 170-178.

10. For the effects of suburbia on gender relations and social norms see Betty Friedan, *The Feminine Mystique* (New York: Norton, 1963); Daniel Horowitz, *Betty Friedan and the Making of "The Feminine Mystique": The American Left, the Cold War, and Modern Feminism* (Amherst: University of Massachusetts Press, 2000); Elaine Tyler May, *Homeward Bound: American Families in the Cold War Era* (New York: Basic Books, 1988; rev. and updated ed., 2008); Dolores Hayden, *Redesigning the American Dream: Gender, Housing, and Family Life* (New York: Norton, 2002). For suburban consumer culture see Karal Ann Marling, *As Seen on TV: The Visual Culture of Everyday Life in the 1950s* (Cambridge, MA: Harvard University Press, 1996); Lynn Spigel, *Make Room for TV: Television and the Family Ideal in Postwar America* (Chicago: University of Chicago Press, 1992); Lizabeth Cohen, *A Consumer's Republic: The Politics of Mass Consumption in Postwar America* (New York: Vintage, 2003).

11. Joseph C. Ingraham, "Housing Delays Laid to Politics," *New York Times*, September 29, 1955, 55.

12. Ibid.

13. Elizabeth Fraterrigo, "The Answer to Suburbia: *Playboy*'s Urban Lifestyle," *Journal of Urban History* 34 (July 2008): 751.

14. May, *Homeward Bound*.

15. For more on swinging in the suburbs, see Allyn, *Make Love, Not War*, 206-227.

16. Adam Parfrey, "The Smut Peddlers," in *Sin-A-Rama: Sleaze Sex Paperbacks of the 1960s*, ed. Brittany A. Daley and Stephen J. Gertz (Los Angeles: Feral House, 2005), 8.

17. Irving Wallace, *The Chapman Report* (New York: Simon and Schuster, 1960).

18. Daniel Talbot, "In a Swamp of Erotica," *New York Times*, May 29, 1960, BR18.

19. Oren A. Lang, *Shopping Center Sex* (New York: Universal, 1964), 132.

20. Greg Caldwell, *Suburban Sex* (New York: Original Bedside Books, 1963), 13.

21. Ibid., 190.

22. Edward Ronns, *The Big Bedroom* (New York: Pyramid Books, 1959), 8-9.

23. Ibid., 103.

24. Brian Greene, "Orrie Hitt, the Shakespeare of Shabby Street," CriminalElement.com, June 25, 2013.

25. Ibid.

26. Orrie Hitt, *Suburban Wife* (New York: Beacon Books, 1958), 33.

27. Ibid.

28. Ken Price, "Nudism Moves Uptown," *Sunshine and Health*, September 1959, 5, Robert J. Young Collection, Wolfsonian-Florida International University Rare Book and Special Collections Library, Miami Beach, Florida.

29. Ibid., 28.

30. Ibid.

31. "Victory," *Sunshine and Health*, October 1959, 14, Robert J. Young Collection, Wolfsonian-Florida International University Rare Book and Special Collections Library, Miami Beach, Florida.

32. Ken Price, "So Far, So Bad," *Sunshine and Health*, October 1960, 23–30, Robert J. Young Collection, Wolfsonian-Florida International University Rare Book and Special Collections Library, Miami Beach, Florida.

33. See Brian Hoffman, *Naked: A Cultural History of American Nudism* (New York: New York University Press, 2015), 195–196.

34. "Nudist Film Approved," *New York Times*, November 15, 1956, 43; "Nudist Film Gains in Censor Battle," *New York Times*, July 4, 1957, 16.

35. Eric Schaefer, *"Bold! Daring! Shocking! True!": A History of Exploitation Films, 1919–1959* (Durham, NC: Duke University Press, 1999), 300.

36. Michael J. Bowen, "Embodiment and Realization: The Many Film-Bodies of Doris Wishman," *Wide Angle* 19, no. 3 (1997): 64–90.

37. Douglas Martin, "Doris Wishman, 'B' Film Director, Dies," *New York Times*, August 19, 2002, A13.

38. Ibid.

39. Whitney Strub, "The Clearly Obscene and the Queerly Obscene: Heteronormativity and Obscenity in Cold War Los Angeles," *American Quarterly* 60, no. 2 (June 2008): 389–390.

40. Sandstone Brochure cited in Gay Talese, *Thy Neighbor's Wife*, 332.

41. Sandstone Workshop Calendar, Elysium Papers, Private Collection, Southern California Naturist Association, Moorpark, California.

42. Alex Mar, "What Happened to the 'Most Liberated Woman in America'?" *Atlas Obscura*, June 7, 2016.

43. Jonathan Dana and Bunny Dana, dir., *Sandstone*, 1975, 85 min.

44. Ibid.

45. Ibid.

46. Tom Hatfield, *Sandstone Experience* (New York: Crown, 1975); Howard Kennedy, "Group Asks County for Nudist Permit," *Los Angeles Times*, August 26, 1970, pt. 2-F, 6.

47. "Nudist Camps Told to Apply for Licensing," *Los Angeles Times*, September 1, 1970, pt. 2-F, 6.

48. "Test of New Growth Center Law Begins," *Santa Monica Evening Outlook*, October 27, 1970, 12; "Sheriff Cites Nudist Colony: No License," *Los Angeles Times*, October 27, 1970, pt. 2-F, 6.

49. Howard Kennedy, "'Growth Centers' Find Nudity Controversial," *Los Angeles Times*, October 10, 1970, pt. 2, 2.

50. Ibid.

51. Charles Hillinger, "Sexual Revolution in US Puts Chill on Nudist Camps," *Los Angeles Times*, December 28, 1970.

52. Ibid.

53. Rod Swenson, "Duo in the Sun," *Penthouse*, September 1975, 66.

54. See Eric Schaefer and Eithne Johnson, "Quarantined! A Case Study of Boston's Combat Zone," in *Hop on Pop: The Politics and Pleasures of Popular Culture*, ed. Henry Jenkins, Tara McPherson, and Jane Shattuc (Durham, NC: Duke University Press, 2002),

430–453; Whitney Strub, *Perversion for Profit: The Politics of Pornography and the Rise of the New Right* (New York: Columbia University Press, 2011), 170–172; Dian Hanson, *Naked as a Jaybird and Loving It* (Los Angeles: Taschen, 2003), 44.

55. For a discussion of the Miller decision, see Whitney Strub, *Obscenity Rules: Roth v. United States and the Long Struggle over Sexual Expression* (Lawrence: University Press of Kansas, 2013), 208–217.

56. Charles Winick, "A Content Analysis of Sexually Explicit Magazines Sold in an Adult Bookstore," *Journal of Sex Research* 21 (May 1985): 208.

57. See Talese, *Thy Neighbor's Wife*; Hatfield, *Sandstone Experience*; William Yardley, "John Williamson, 80, Co-Founder of Retreat Known For Sex," *New York Times*, May 5, 2013, 24.

58. *Local Swingers: Adult Contact Magazine*, 51st ed., Summer 1982.

59. Barbara Penner, *Bathroom* (London: Reaktion Books, 2013), 183.

60. Joan Campbell and George Campbell, "Build a Hot Tub!" *Mother Earth News* (March–April 1980).

61. See Laura Kipnis, *Bound and Gagged: Pornography and the Politics of Fantasy in America* (Durham, NC: Duke University Press, 1998).

62. Larry Sultan, *Here and Home* (Los Angeles County Museum of Art; Munich: Delmonico Books, 2014), 38.

CHAPTER 5

1. Steven Yaccino, "On the Beach, in the Buff. In Wisconsin?" *New York Times*, July 10, 2012, A10.

2. Whitney Strub, *Perversion for Profit: The Politics of Pornography and the Rise of the New Right* (New York: Columbia University Press, 2011), 5–6.

3. For more on the instability of nudity for building a social movement, see Ruth Barcan, *Nudity: A Cultural Anatomy* (Oxford: Berg, 2004), 166.

4. Leon Elder, *Free Beaches: A Phenomenon of the California Coast* (Santa Barbara, CA: Capra Press, 1974), 15.

5. Jack D. Douglas, Paul K. Rasmussen, and Carol Ann Flanagan, *The Nude Beach* (Beverly Hills, CA: Sage, 1977), 223.

6. Elder, *Free Beaches*, 15.

7. Tom Caldwell, "Slight Setback at California Free Beach," *American Sunbathing Bulletin*, Spring 1972, 6.

8. Catherine Cocks, "The Pleasures of Degeneration: Climate, Race, and the Origins of the Global Tourist South in the Americas," *Discourse* 29 (Spring and Fall 2007).

9. Andrew W. Kahrl, *Free the Beach: The Story of Ned Coll and the Battle for America's Most Exclusive Shoreline* (New Haven, CT: Yale University Press, 2018), 6.

10. Ibid., 13.

11. Barcan, *Nudity: A Cultural Anatomy*, 9. Here, Barcan explains "the power and instability of the clothing/nudity opposition," the point being that much clothing is meant to allow the body to appear naked or at least emphasize sexualized parts. At the same time, bare flesh isn't always nude—for example, one's exposed arm or leg. Furthermore, men's and women's experiences of nakedness can be very different, and also read very differently.

12. Peggy Heinrich and Ray J. Worssam, "Bathing Machines Brought Elegance to Skinny Dipping," *Smithsonian* 5, no. 4 (July 1974): 57.

13. Lena Lenček and Gideon Bosker, *The Beach: The History of Paradise on Earth* (New York: Viking, 1998), 83–85.

14. "Long Beach: Nude Japs Take a Dip," *Los Angeles Times*, June 27, 1904, 15.

15. "Nude Bathers Stir Residents of Coast Line," *Los Angeles Times*, February 3, 1931, A6; "Court Disapproves Bathers in Nude," *Los Angeles Times*, August 19, 1930.

16. Walter H. Case, *History of Long Beach and Vicinity*, vol. 1 (Chicago: S. J. Clarke, 1927), 212.

17. Walter H. Case, *Long Beach Community Book* (Long Beach, CA: Arthur H. Cawston, 1948), 81.

18. Auguste Rollier, "Heliotherapy: Its Therapeutic, Prophylactic and Social Value," *American Journal of Nursing* 27, no. 10 (October 1927): 823.

19. "Nude Bathing Will Be Next," *Los Angeles Times*, July 20, 1930, 1; "Physicians Design Home of Health," *New York Times*, May 25, 1930.

20. *Whither Honolulu? A Memorandum on Park and City Planning* (Honolulu: Honolulu City and County Board, 1938), republished in Lewis Mumford, *City Development: Studies in Disintegration and Renewal* (New York: Harcourt, Brace, 1945), 124–125.

21. Ronald A. Davidson and J. Nicholas Entrikin, "The Los Angeles Coast as a Public Place," *Geographical Review* 95, no. 4 (October 2005): 581.

22. Joanne Meyerowitz, "Sexual Geography and Gender Economy: The Furnished Room Districts of Chicago, 1890–1930," *Gender and History* 2 (September 1990): 274–297; Frank Mort, "The Sexual Geography of the City," *Blackwell Companion to the City* (London: Wiley-Blackwell, 2000), 307–314.

23. Eric Schaefer and Eithne Johnson, "Quarantined! A Case Study of Boston's Combat Zone," in *Hop on Pop: The Politics and Pleasures of Popular Culture*, ed. Henry Jenkins, Tara McPherson, and Jane Shattuc (Durham, NC: Duke University Press, 2002), 431.

24. The public interest in nude beaches, and academic interest in their sexual and sociological significance, was recorded in the 1970s. See Douglas, Rasmussen, and Flanagan, *The Nude Beach*; William E. Hartman, Marilyn Fithian, and Donald Johnson, *Nudist Society: The Controversial Study of the Clothes-Free Naturist Movement in America* (Los Angeles: Elysium Growth Press, 1970; rev. and updated by Iris Bancroft, 1991).

25. "In the Beginning," *Bare in Mind: A Nudist News Service*, January 1979, 16.

26. Jayne Bernard, "Sunbathing in Southern California: An Historical Overview," in *The Westerners Brand Book, 16*, ed. Raymund F. Wood (Los Angeles: Westerners Los Angeles Corral, 1982), 39.

27. Ibid.

28. Cec Cinder, *The Nudist Idea* (Riverside, CA: Ultraviolet Press, 1998), 588–589.

29. For more on the politics of nudity within the American counterculture and other groups around the world, see Timothy Miller, *The Hippies and American Values* (Knoxville: University of Tennessee Press, 1991), 59–62; Philip Carr-Gomm, *A Brief History of Nakedness* (London: Reaktion Books, 2010).

30. Cinder, *The Nudist Idea*, 591.

31. Ibid., 593.

32. "Committee for Free Beaches," quoted in Cinder, *The Nudist Idea*, 593.

33. Darrell Tarver, quoted in Jefferson Poland, "Committee for Free Beaches," in *Sex Marchers*, ed. Jefferson Poland and Sam Sloan (Los Angeles: Elysium, 1968), 80.

34. Ibid., 81–82.

35. Cinder, *The Nudist Idea*, 594.

36. Poland, "Committee for Free Beaches," 85.

37. Cinder, *The Nudist Idea*, 596.

38. Beachfront Newsletters 1–3 (1973–1974), Free Beach Collection, Department of Special Collections, Pomona Public Library, Pomona, California; Sarah Schrank, "Naked Houses: The Architecture of Nudism and the Rethinking of the American Suburbs," *Journal of Urban History* 38, no. 4 (July 2012), 648–649; "County Left Bare-Asses; Court Voids Nudist Law," *The Advocate* 2, no. 8 (August 1968): 2.

39. Neal Blum, chairman of public relations and education, American Sunbathing Association, letter to Ed Lange, September 2, 1968; Ed Lange, committee chairman, American Sunbathing Association, letter to William Penn Mott, director, Department of Parks and Recreation, Sacramento, California, March 20, 1969, Elysium Papers, Private Collection, Southern California Naturist Association Archives, Moorpark, California.

40. Steve Kline, "Deputies Trying to Get the Goods on Nude Bathers," *Los Angeles Times*, August 19, 1971, 1.

41. Ibid.

42. "Nudist Free Beach," *Bare in Mind*, April 1972, p. 2, Elysium Papers, Private Collection, Southern California Naturist Association Archives, Moorpark, California.

43. Dewey Schurman, "Nude Bathing Is Becoming Popular Pastime for Some," *Santa Barbara News-Press*, October 1971, A-12, Elysium Papers, Private Collection, Southern California Naturist Association Archives, Moorpark, California.

44. Tom Kleveland, "Nudism, Noise: An Analogy," *Santa Barbara News-Press*, April 5, 1972, B-1, Elysium Papers, Private Collection, Southern California Naturist Association Archives, Moorpark, California.

45. Dennis Craig Smith, "Freeing the American Beaches" *Human Quest*, vol. 1 (Los Angeles: Elysium Growth Press, 1975), 54. Pomona Public Library Free Beach Collection.

46. Jackie Davison, "Free Beach Crackdown," *Los Angeles Free Press*, May 5, 1972, n.p., Elysium Papers, Private Collection, Southern California Naturist Association Archives, Moorpark, California.

47. Earth Institute, "Free Beach Defense Strategy," 1972, Elysium Papers, Private Collection, Southern California Naturist Association Archives, Moorpark, California.

48. Schurman, "Nude Bathing Is Becoming Popular Pastime for Some."

49. Ibid.; M. G. Eschner, "Nude Beach Raid," *Los Angeles Times*, April 26, 1972, D6.

50. Davison, "Free Beach Crackdown."

51. Elder, *Free Beaches*, 85.

52. Ibid.; Declaration of Gerald Franklin, attorney at law, April 13, 1972, Elysium Papers, Private Collection, Southern California Naturist Association Archives, Moorpark, California.

53. Sharon Millern, "Nude Bathing Regulation Gets Supervisors' Approval," *Santa Barbara News-Press*, September 17, 1973, B1, clipping, Free Beach Collection, Department of Special Collections, Pomona Public Library, Pomona, California.

54. Cinder, *The Nudist Idea*, 596.

55. Allen Baylis, "What Every Naturist Should Know About California Laws Regarding Nudity," *Nude and Natural* 26, no. 4 (Summer 2007): 75; California Penal Code Section 314–318.6.

56. "But at a Secluded Beach, Court Oks Nude Sunbathing," *Los Angeles Times*, June 14, 1972, A3.

57. Pat Bryant, "Courts Look Other Way at Topless Swimsuits," *Los Angeles Times*, July 27, 1972.

58. Cinder, *The Nudist Idea*, 598; "Arrests of Nudes on Beach to Continue Despite Court Ruling," *Los Angeles Times*, June 15, 1972.

59. "Beachfront USA and the Inevitable Nude Beach," *Beachfront USA Newsletter*, n.d., Pomona Public Library Free Beach Collection, Pomona, California.

60. Cinder, *The Nudist Idea*, 604; "Arrests to Continue for Beach Nudity," *Los Angeles Times*, August 24, 1972, 1; Myrna Oliver, "Court Plea to Allow Public on Beach Used by Nudists Fails," *Los Angeles Times*, September 13, 1972, A3.

61. "Los Angeles: Beachfront USA," *News Bulletin*, August 1976, Free Beach Collection, Department of Special Collections, Pomona Public Library, Pomona, California.

62. Doug Smith, "Summer '72: Nude Impact at Beaches," *Los Angeles Times*, October 1, 1972.

63. See Sarah Schrank, *Art and the City: Civic Imagination and Cultural Authority in Los Angeles* (Philadelphia: University of Pennsylvania Press, 2009), 107–114.

64. See Shelly McKenzie, *Getting Physical: The Rise of Fitness Culture in America* (Lawrence: University Press of Kansas, 2013), 14–53.

65. Jonathan Black, *Making the American Body: The Remarkable Saga of the Men and Women Whose Feats, Feuds, and Passions Shaped Fitness History* (Lincoln: University of Nebraska Press, 2013), 39.

66. Doug Smith, "Summer '72: Nude Impact at Beaches," *Los Angeles Times*, October 1, 1972, WS6.

67. Doug Smith, "Nude Bathers Plan Battle for Beach in Venice," *Los Angeles Times*, March 9, 1972.

68. Ibid.

69. Cec Cinder, "Free Beach Venice 88," *A Publication of the Institute for Nudist Studies*, November 1985, 10, Southern California Naturist Association Archives. See also Gerald Faris, "Malibu Claustrophobia: Nude Bathers 'Hemmed In,'" *Los Angeles Times*, September 13, 1973, WS1.

70. Cinder, "Free Beach Venice 88."

71. "'Nude Zone' Plan Wins Approval of City Council Unit," *Los Angeles Times*, June 28, 1974, D1.

72. Henry Walton, "The Venice Beach Experience," *Beachfront Newsletter* (October–December 1974): 1, Free Beach Collection, Department of Special Collections, Pomona Public Library, Pomona, California.

73. Ibid.; "Nude Sunbathing at Venice Beach," *Los Angeles Times*, June 30, 1974, 10–12.

74. Paul G. Lowenberg, Beachfront USA Board of Directors, letter to Councilwoman Pat Russell, July 12, 1974, Council File No. 606057, Los Angeles City Archives.

75. Lawrence M. Tabat, letter to Councilwoman Pat Russell, July 22, 1974, Council File No. 606057, Los Angeles City Archives.

76. Monica Gray, letter to the editor, *Los Angeles Times*, June 30, 1974, 12.

77. Charles T. Powers, "Beach Nudity: Anatomy of a Phenomenon," *Los Angeles Times*, July 4, 1974, F1.

78. J. Edward Gibbons, letter to Councilwoman Pat Russell, July 26, 1974, Council File No. 606057, Los Angeles City Archives.

79. Ibid.

80. Myrna Oliver, "Nude Clubs Fail to Win Theater Status," *Los Angeles Times*, July 13, 1973.

81. Erwin Baker, "City Council Votes 12-1 to Ban Beach Nudity," *Los Angeles Times*, July 12, 1974, 3; "LA Bans Nude Body in Racks," *The Advocate*, June 5, 1974.

82. Dorothy Townsend, "Council Panel Votes to Ban Street Sales of Smutty Material," *Los Angeles Times*, March 8, 1974; Myrna Oliver, "Suit Challenges City Ban on Nude Photos Visible in Newsracks," *Los Angeles Times*, May 30, 1974; "LA Bans Nude Body in Racks," *The Advocate*, June 5, 1974.

83. Erwin Baker, "'Stroller' Strips, Council Follows with Nudity Ban," *Los Angeles Times*, July 12, 1974, A1; Gary Mussell, "1974: How Venice Beach Almost Became Legally Nude," *Southern California Naturist Association Newsletter* 14, no. 5 (May 2015): 11.

84. Walton, "The Venice Beach Experience"; Baker, "City Council Votes 12-1 to Ban Beach Nudity"; William Farr, "Nude Not Lewd—Only Disruptive," *Los Angeles Times*, October 4, 1974.

85. Councilman David Cunningham, press release, July 18, 1974, David Cunningham Papers, Los Angeles City Archives, File No. B-608, "Nude Beaches."

86. Ibid.

87. Ibid.

88. Baker, "City Council Votes 12-1 to Ban Beach Nudity."

89. Mussell, "1974: How Venice Beach Almost Became Legally Nude."

90. "The 1974 Los Angeles City Ordinance and the 1975 *Eckl v. Davis* Case," Court of Appeal of California, Second Appellate District, Division Three, Civ. No. 44984, September 30, 1975, Court Documents.

91. "Court Upholds City's Ban on Beach Nudity," *Los Angeles Times*, October 1, 1975, 3.

92. Alan Citron, "A Cover-Up in Venice: Nude Sunbathers Ordered to Dress for the Occasion," *Los Angeles Times*, June 22, 1986, WS1.

93. Julie Bagby, "Nude Activists Busted at California 'Beach Walk,'" *The Bulletin*, October 1986, 11, Free Beach Collection, Department of Special Collections, Pomona Public Library, Pomona, California; "Dave and Suzy Arrested," *Sidelights (from the Glen Eden Sun Club)*, vol. 23, no. 10, October 1986, 1, Elysium Papers, Private Collection, Southern California Naturist Association Archives, Moorpark, California.

94. Phillipp Gollner, "Court Upholds Law That Bans Venice Beach Nudity," *Daily News*, September 15, 1992, repr. *Journal of the Senses* 101 (1992): 17, Elysium Papers, Private Collection, Southern California Naturist Association Archives, Moorpark, California.

95. Jane Weisman Stein, "Black's Beach: A Gawk in the Sun," *Los Angeles Times*, August 5, 1975, E1.

96. Ibid., E4.

97. Ibid.

98. Ibid.

99. "Park Officials Ask Supervisors to End Plan for Nude Beaches," *San Diego Union*, October 30, 1975, B4.

100. Roger Showley, "Nudes Use Beaches in County," *San Diego Union*, November 11, 1975, B1.

101. Stein, "Black's Beach: A Gawk in the Sun."

102. Ibid.

103. For a detailed history of the racial and sexual politics of Save Our Children, see Gillian Frank's excellent essay, "'The Civil Rights of Parents': Race and Conservative Politics in Anita Bryant's Campaign Against Gay Rights in 1970s Florida," *Journal of the History of Sexuality* 22, no. 1 (January 2013): 126–160.

104. Dale Fetherling, "All Eyes on Nude Beach: Survival at Stake in Tuesday Election," *Los Angeles Times*, September 18, 1977, B1.

105. "Nudism Opposed," *San Diego Union*, November 4, 1975, B5; Fetherling, "All Eyes on Nude Beach: Survival at Stake in Tuesday Election," B7.

106. Robert Kistler, "Voters Reject Nude Beach in San Diego," *Los Angeles Times*, September 21, 1977, B1; "Nude Beaches Repealed," *Los Angeles Times*, October 5, 1977, A1.

107. Charles Finley, "47,000 Nudists Celebrate Black's Beach Fourth Birthday," *Beachhead (Bare in Mind)*, July 1978, 7, Elysium Papers, Private Collection, Southern California Naturist Association Archives, Moorpark, California; Nancy Skelton, "Law Turns Head on Black's Beach Party," *Los Angeles Times*, May 29, 1978, C1.

108. Finley, "47,000 Nudists Celebrate Black's Beach Fourth Birthday."

109. "Nude Beach Backers File Petitions for Ballot Measure," *Los Angeles Times*, August 17, 1978, E3; Nancy Ray, "Nude Beach Issue Fails to Qualify for Spot on Ballot," *Los Angeles Times*, September 12, 1978, A5.

110. Nancy Ray, "Nude Beach Obscures Peril of Cliffs," *Los Angeles Times*, April 21, 1980, C1; Nancy Ray, "San Diego Moves to Build Stairs to Black's Beach," *Los Angeles Times*, May 30, 1980, A1; Miles Corwin, "Section of Black's Beach Closed for Safety," *Los Angeles Times*, April 3, 1982, A1; Sharon Spivak, "Unstable Cliff Poses Danger on City Beach," *La Jolla Light*, June 10, 1982, A1, Free Beach Collection, Department of Special Collections, Pomona Public Library, Pomona, California; Cheryl Yockey, "City Council Panel Urges Closing of Black's Beach," *Los Angeles Times*, June 10, 1982, A1; Cheryl Yockey, "Danger Lurks Along Paths at Black's Beach," *Los Angeles Times*, June 14, 1982, A1; Scott Harris, "Nude Beach Loses Its Lifeguards," *Los Angeles Times*, April 16, 1983, A1; Barry M. Horstman, "Black's Beach Is Denuded of Guards, Too," *Los Angeles Times*, May 29, 1983, A1; Paula Parker, "Drowning Brings Call for Lifeguards at Black's Beach," *Los Angeles Times*, June 21, 1983, A1; Ted Vollmer, "Lifeguards Will Return to Black's Beach," *Los Angeles Times*, July 2, 1983, A13.

111. California State Park Rangers Association, "The Cahill Memo and Its Effect on Enforcing CCR 4322 'Nudity' in California State Parks."

112. Mark Storey, "The History of the Naturist Society," *Nude and Natural* 28, no. 3 (Spring 2009): 22.

113. Ibid.

114. Jackie Davison, "Welcome to National Nude Beach Day," *Journal of the Senses* (Fall 1976): 10.

115. National Capital Beachfront, "Quiet, Relaxed Observance of National Nude Days

Planned for July 11 and 12," *The Capital Sun*, July–August 1981, 1, Free Beach Collection, Department of Special Collections, Pomona Public Library, Pomona, California.

116. Diane Coutu, "Crew Dynamites Hazardous Cliff at Nude Beach," *Los Angeles Times*, September 8, 1978, B3 and B22.

117. Robert W. Stewart, "Land Falling: Nude Beach Poses Peril to Ecology," *Los Angeles Times*, August 22, 1982, WS10.

118. Richard O'Reilly, "Nude Beach's Fate Restudied," *Los Angeles Times*, September 18, 1980, A14.

119. Clothing Optional Society, "Proposals for Pirates Cove—Big Dume Beach Area," submitted to E. Charles Fullerton, director, State of California Department of Fish and Game, Elysium Papers, Private Collection, Southern California Naturist Association Archives, Moorpark, California.

120. Claire Spiegel, "Nude Sunbathers Won't Lose Their Beach to Seals," *Los Angeles Times*, June 19, 1980, A3; Sid Bernstein, "L.A. Board Acts on Nude Beach Issues," *Los Angeles Times*, September 3, 1980, A6; Stewart, "Land Falling: Nude Beach Poses Peril to Ecology," WS1.

121. Nicole Szulc and Robert Knowles, "Nudists Get the Word: Pirate's Cove Closed," *Los Angeles Examiner*, August 29, 1980, clipping, Free Beach Collection, Department of Special Collections, Pomona Public Library, Pomona, California.

122. Stewart, "Land Falling: Nude Beach Poses Peril to Ecology," WS1.

123. Nancy Graham, "2nd Nudity Trial Judge Ousted: 200 Malibu Beach Bathers Continue to Jam Docket," *Los Angeles Times*, September 3, 1981, A1; Nancy Graham, "Delays Protested in Nude Bathing Cases," *Los Angeles Times*, October 1, 1981, A1.

124. Stewart, "Land Falling: Nude Beach Poses Peril to Ecology."

125. Storey, "The History of the Naturist Society," 22.

126. Ibid.

127. Ibid., 23.

128. "Card-Carrying Nudists Are 'Conservatives' by Today's Buff Bathing Rules," *Los Angeles Herald-Examiner*, August 13, 1972, clipping, Elysium Papers, Private Collection, Southern California Naturist Association Archives, Moorpark, California.

129. "The Great California Cover-Up: State Beach Nudity Proposal Is Rejected," *Los Angeles Herald Examiner*, June 1, 1979; "Nude Bathers Get No State Beaches," *San Francisco Chronicle*, June 1, 1979, clippings, Free Beach Documentation Center, Oshkosh, Wisconsin; Carol Gulotta, "Don't Look Now, Nudist Beaches Eyed," *Los Angeles Herald Examiner*, August 16, 1979, Free Beach Collection, Department of Special Collections, Pomona Public Library, Pomona, California.

130. Carl Ingram, "Brown Throws Cold Water on Nude Beaches Proposal," *Los Angeles Times*, April 21, 1979, C1.

131. Ibid.

132. David Irving, "California Parks Nude Beaches Plan Shelved," *Sun* 79, clipping, Free Beach Collection, Department of Special Collections, Pomona Public Library, Pomona, California.

133. Deputy Director for Operations Jack V. Harrison, letter to the Western Sunbathing Association, Inc., June 14, 1988; "NAC to Naturists: 'We've Got Your Back,'" *Nude and Natural Newsletter*, May 2011, 1–2.

134. *Naturist Action Committee v. California State Department Parks and Recreation*, Case #G040929, Filed June 25, 2009, Elysium Papers, Private Collection, Southern California Naturist Association Archives, Moorpark, California.

135. "NAC to Naturists: 'We've Got Your Back,'" *Nude and Natural Newsletter*, May 2011, 1–2.

136. Cape Cod Free the Free Beach Committee Manifesto, "Background on Truro's Federal Ban on the Free Beach," *Green Mountain Quarterly* 4 (August 1976): 39, Free Beach Collection, Department of Special Collections, Pomona Public Library, Pomona, California.

137. Eugene Callen, cited in Storey, "The History of the Naturist Society," 32.

138. "Freedom of Beach," *Green Mountain Quarterly* 4 (August 1976): 83, Free Beach Collection, Department of Special Collections, Pomona Public Library, Pomona, California.

139. Ibid.

140. "Freedom of Beach," August 8, 1976, Bulletin, Free Beach Collection, Department of Special Collections, Pomona Public Library, Pomona, California.

141. "Parading the Beauties," *Clothed with the Sun* 2, no. 4 (February 1983): n.p., Department of Special Collections, California Case, Pomona Public Library, Pomona, California.

142. Mollie Moore-Sullivan, "For Women: Beat the Blues, Try Nude Recreation," *California Nudist*, Fall 1989, Elysium Papers, Private Collection, Southern California Naturist Association Archives, Moorpark, California.

143. "From the Writings of Eugene Callen," *Green Mountain Quarterly* 4 (August 1976): 32, Free Beach Collection, Department of Special Collections, Pomona Public Library, Pomona, California.

144. Ibid., 23–24. See *The Newsletter* published by the Naturist Action Committee, The Naturist Society, and the Naturist Education Foundation.

145. Herb Seal, "Family Group-Identification Within Nudist Movement in Oregon and Northern California: A Selected Study of Forty Nudist Families" (master's thesis, San Francisco State College, 1960); Sandra June Robinson, "Nudism: The Bare Facts" (master's thesis, San Jose State College, 1967); Manfred F. DeMartino, *The New Female Sexuality: The Sexual Practices and Experiences of Social Nudists, "Potential" Nudists, and Lesbians* (New York: Julian Press, 1969).

146. See Bryant Paul, Daniel Linz, and Bradley J. Shafer, "Government Regulation of 'Adult' Businesses Through Zoning and Anti-Nudity Ordinances: Debunking the Legal Myth of Secondary Effects," *Communication Law and Policy* 6, no. 2 (Spring 2001).

147. Randall Grometstein, "Wrongful Conviction and Moral Panic: National and International Perspectives on Organized Child Sexual Abuse," in *Wrongful Conviction: International Perspectives on Miscarriages of Justice*, ed. C. Ronald Huff and Martin Killias (Philadelphia: Temple University Press, 2008).

148. See Paul Okami, Richard Olmstead, Paul R. Abramson, and Laura Pendleton, "Early Childhood Exposure to Parental Nudity and Scenes of Parental Sexuality ('Primal Scenes'): An 18-Year Longitudinal Study of Outcome," *Archives of Sexual Behavior* 27, no. 4 (1998).

149. Richard Mason, "Less Baxandall: The Man and His Legacy," *Nude and Natural* 28, no. 3 (Spring 2009): 21.

150. Brian Hoffman, *Naked: A Cultural History of Nudism* (New York: New York University Press, 2015), 242–244.

151. Ibid., 245.

152. Robert T. Page, general counsel, American Sunbathing Association, "New Public Awareness: Organized Nudists and Child Pornography" (paper delivered to the ASA Park Management Conference, Las Vegas, Nevada, December 8, 1985), Elysium Papers, Private Collection, Southern California Naturist Association Archives, Moorpark, California.

153. Ibid., 21.

154. Ibid.

155. Marc Santora, "This Summer, Fire Island Isn't the Place to Bare All," *New York Times*, February 28, 2013, A20.

CHAPTER 6

1. For a compelling argument about the relationship between branding and authenticity, see Sarah Banet-Weiser, *Authentic™: The Politics of Ambivalence in a Brand Culture* (New York: New York University Press, 2012).

2. There is a large online repository of articles and blogs on the shift in how women's magazines represent female bodies. See, for example, Martha Ross, "Fashion, Politics, and Feminism: Women's Magazines Find New Winning Formula," *Mercury News*, February 21, 2017.

3. Dove Self-Esteem Project, online site.

4. See, for example, Connie Sobczak, *Embody: Learning to Love Your Unique Body (and Quiet That Critical Voice!)* (Carlsbad, CA: Gürze Books, 2014).

5. "There's Another World . . . Behind the Skinny-Dipping Scene," promotional pamphlet, Western Sunbathing Association, n.d., ca. 1980s, Pomona Public Library Free Beach Collection, Pomona, California.

6. *Southern California Naturist Association Newsletter*, June 2017, 9; July 2017, 6.

7. *Southern California Naturist Association Newsletter*, July 2016, 2–3.

8. Rolf Holbach, "SCNA Looking for More Volunteers as Club Expands into New Areas," *Southern California Naturist Association Newsletter* 17, no. 5 (May 2018): 1.

9. *Natural and Nude Yoga Techniques*, dir. Optik Dave, 64 mins., 2005.

10. Tara Stiles, *Slim Calm Sexy Yoga: 210 Proven Yoga Moves for Mind/Body Bliss* (New York: Rodale Books, 2010); Lizette Alvarez, "Rebel Yoga," *New York Times*, January 21, 2011; YogaDork, "Tara Stiles Launches 'Slim, Calm, Sexy' Yoga to Acclaim, Insult, Revolt," August 31, 2011, online site.

11. Judith Hanson Lasater, letter to the editor, *Yoga Journal*, September 2010.

12. Joseph S. Alter, "Yoga and Fetishism: Reflections on Marxist Social Theory," *Journal of the Royal Anthropological Institute* 12, no. 4 (December 2006): 764.

13. Ibid.

14. Philip Carr-Gomm, *A Brief History of Nakedness* (London: Reaktion Books, 2010); David Gordon White, *Sinister Yogis* (Chicago: University of Chicago Press, 2009).

15. James Mallinson, "Yogis in Mughal India," in *Yoga: The Art of Transformation*, ed. Molly Emma Aitken and Debra Diamond (Washington, DC: Arthur M. Sackler Gallery, Smithsonian Institution, 2013), 76.

16. White, *Sinister Yogis*.

17. See White, *Sinister Yogis*; Sarah Strauss, *Positioning Yoga: Balancing Acts Across Cultures* (New York: Berg, 2005).

18. Carr-Gomm, *Brief History of Nakedness*, 58.

19. Marguerite Agniel, "The Mental Element in Our Physical Well-Being," *The Nudist: Sunshine and Health* 7, no. 6 (June 1938): 18–21.

20. Elizabeth De Michelis, *A History of Modern Yoga: Patañjali and Western Esotericism* (London: Continuum, 2004); Mark Singleton, *Yoga Body: The Origins of Modern Posture Practice* (Oxford: Oxford University Press, 2010); Stefanie Syman, *The Subtle Body: The Story of Yoga in America* (New York: Farrar, Straus, and Giroux, 2010).

21. See Philip Goldberg, *American Veda: From Emerson and the Beatles to Yoga and Meditation—How Indian Spirituality Changed the West* (New York: Harmony Books, 2010).

22. See Goldberg, *American Veda*; Robert Love, *The Great Oom: The Improbable Birth of Yoga in America* (New York: Viking, 2010).

23. Michelle Goldberg, *The Goddess Pose: The Audacious Life of Indra Devi, the Woman Who Helped Bring Yoga to the West* (New York: Knopf, 2015).

24. Shelly McKenzie, *Getting Physical: The Rise of Fitness Culture in America* (Lawrence: University Press of Kansas, 2013).

25. Advertisement for the Insight School, Evanston, Illinois, *Sunshine and Health* 29, no. 1 (January 1960): 3.

26. *Sunshine and Health* 30, no. 4 (April 1961): 23; *Nude Living* 1, no. 6 (April 1962), Richard and Dion Neutra Papers, Box 1476, Folder 14, Department of Special Collections, Charles Young Research Library, University of California, Los Angeles.

27. Malcolm Leigh, *Naked Yoga* (New York: New American Library, 1972); *Naked Yoga*, dir. Paul Corsden, 24 mins., 1974.

28. Elysium Institute, "Ongoing Seminars," *Journal of the Senses* 67 (Spring 1984): 26–42, Elysium Papers, Private Collection, Southern California Naturist Association Archives, Moorpark, California.

29. Ibid., 36.

30. Chris Shilling, *The Body in Culture, Technology, and Society* (London: Sage, 2005), 35–37.

31. There is a growing feminist literature that addresses the potential of yoga for female empowerment and emotional, as well as physical, healing. See Carol A. Horton and Roseanne Harvey, eds., *21st Century Yoga: Culture, Politics, and Practice* (Chicago: Kleio Books, 2012); Melanie Klein and Anna Guest-Jelley, eds., *Yoga and Body Image: 25 Personal Stories About Beauty, Bravery, and Loving Your Body* (Woodbury, MN: Llewellyn, 2014); Carol A. Horton, *Yoga PhD: Integrating the Life of the Mind and the Wisdom of the Body* (Chicago: Kleio Books, 2012).

32. Bold and Naked Studio, online site accessed July 5, 2015.

33. Ibid.

34. Bold and Naked Blog, accessed July 28, 2015.

35. Bold and Naked website, accessed September 16, 2017.

36. Ibid.

37. For more on the commodification of the body and the commodity fetish, see Jon Stratton, *The Desirable Body: Cultural Fetishism and the Erotics of Consumption* (Urbana: University of Illinois Press, 1996), 25–57.

38. Sheila Jeffreys, *Beauty and Misogyny: Harmful Cultural Practices in the West* (London: Routledge, 2005), 5–10.

39. Testimonials as to women's liberated experience within nudist culture are plentiful but become especially articulate in the 1980s, in the wake of second wave feminism's greatest wins and losses. A nice example is Mollie Moore-Sullivan, "For Women: Beat the Blues,

Try Nude Recreation," *California Naturist*, Fall 1989, 1, Free Beach Collection, Department of Special Collections, Pomona Public Library, Pomona, California.

40. Female guests at a nudist resort I visited in Palm Springs, California, were happy to talk to me about their experiences in nudist culture over many years. They emphasized that no matter how old, overweight, or different from accepted body norms they might feel in the clothed world, the nudist world produced a sense of body satisfaction and joy unattainable anywhere else.

41. *Yoke Magazine* 2: Balance, 2014. Cover image.

42. Katrina "Rainsong" Messenger, *R.A.W Nude Yoga: Celebrating the Human Body Temple* (Phoenix, AZ: Bridgewood Press, 2013), 8.

43. Ibid., 9.

44. Megan Leigh, interview by Naked Yoga Alliance, June 5, 2015, online site accessed July 1, 2015.

45. See Alter, "Yoga and Fetishism." Also J. L. Masson, "Sex and Yoga: Psychoanalysis and the Indian Religious Experience," *Journal of Indian Philosophy* 2, no. 3 (March–June 1974): 307–320.

46. *The World's Best Nude Beaches and Resorts* (Bristol, UK: Lifestyle Press, 2007), 4.

47. Mark Storey, "The Naturist Society: A Brief History," *N: The Magazine of Naturist Living* 19, no. 3 (Spring 2000), online version.

48. Ibid.

49. Ibid.

50. Ibid.

51. "Nudists on Cruises: The Right to Bare Arms, Legs, and Other Body Parts," *The Economist*, July 5, 2014.

52. Lisa Coleman and Matt Rees, "Naked Appeal," *Forbes*, October 12, 1992, 138.

53. "Clothes-Free Cruise Goes Mainstream," *Journal of the Senses* 96 (Summer 1991): cover page, Elysium Papers, Private Collection, Southern California Naturist Association, Moorpark, California.

54. Coleman and Rees, "Naked Appeal."

55. "Nudists on Cruises: The Right to Bare Arms, Legs, and Other Body Parts," *The Economist*, July 5, 2014.

56. Ibid.

57. Richard Cantave, "Black Nudists: Embracing the Skin You're In with the Black Naturists Association," *Griots Republic*, October 6, 2017, online site accessed May 11, 2018.

58. Ibid.

59. Douglas Belkin, "Wearing Only a Smile, Nudists Seek Out the Young and the Naked," *Wall Street Journal*, May 2, 2011.

60. Molly Oswaks, "A New Generation of Nudists Is Rethinking au Naturel," *Playboy*, April 21, 2015.

61. Ibid.

62. "*Playboy* in Popular Culture," *New York Times*, October 12, 2015.

63. Derek Hawkins, "After a Nudity-Free Year, *Playboy* Will Again Run Pictures of Naked Women," *Washington Post*, February 14, 2017.

64. Ellen E. Woodall, "The American Nudist Movement: From Cooperative to Capital, the Song Remains the Same," *Journal of Popular Culture* 36 (November 2002): 264–284.

65. Ashley Powers, "A Naked Grab for Money?" *Los Angeles Times*, May 30, 2012; "Palm Springs Nudist Resort May Face Legal Challenge over 'No Children' Policy," accessed April 5, 2012, mydesert.com; Brian Hoffman, *Naked: A Cultural History of American Nudism* (New York: New York University Press, 2015), 258.

EPILOGUE

1. Kevin O'Keefe, "The Life, Death, and Legacy of the Oscar Streaker," *The Advocate*, March 26, 2014.

2. William Farr, "Council Streaker Gets 4 Months; Spurns Probation," *Los Angeles Times*, October 30, 1974.

3. O'Keefe, "Life, Death, and Legacy of the Oscar Streaker."

4. "Robert Opel's Fey-Way Studios," online site accessed September 18, 2017.

5. "Oscar Night Streaker Shot to Death in S.F. Sex Shop," *Los Angeles Times*, July 9, 1979, A1.

6. Bill Kirkpatrick, "'It Beats Rocks and Tear Gas': Streaking and Cultural Politics in the Post-Vietnam Era," *Journal of Popular Culture* 43, no. 5 (2010): 1023–1024.

7. See Kirkpatrick, "'It Beats Rocks and Tear Gas.'"

8. For a discussion of the anxiety prompted by naked bodies moving through urban space, see political theorist Davina Cooper's essay "Theorising Nudist Equality: An Encounter Between Political Fantasy and Public Appearance," *Antipode* 43, no. 2 (2011): 326–357. Cooper argues that it is "contact between body and place that unsettles. Beyond the fear of what touch carries is an anxiety simply about touch itself. Despite naturism's claim to build hardier bodies, naked bodies are seen as vulnerable. This is not simply fear that, in a densely thronged urban space, incidental physical intimacy may occur without clothing's protective divider. It is also a reading of the urban, as itself figuratively touching—and debilitating through touching—as the unnatural life of cities imprints upon and diminishes bodies" (346).

9. Jennifer Picht, "Guide to the World Naked Bike Ride in NYC," *TimeOut New York*, May 5, 2016, accessed September 19, 2016.

10. Nudism, as articulated by political theorist Davina Cooper, "makes banal that which gets fetishized elsewhere." Davina Cooper, *Everyday Utopias: The Conceptual Life of Promising Spaces* (Durham, NC: Duke University Press, 2014), 82.

11. Phil Macnaghten and John Urry, "Bodies of Nature: Introduction," *Body and Society* 6, nos. 3–4 (2000): 2.

12. As Macnaghten and Urry put it, "bodies in nature are thus subject to novel, complex and contradictory opportunities both of escape, freedom and 'bodily naturalness' and of being constrained by modes of bodily surveillance, regulation, and monitoring." Ibid., 3.

13. Sarah Jaquette Ray, *The Ecological Other: Environmental Exclusion in American Culture* (Tucson: University of Arizona Press, 2013).

14. David Bell and Ruth Holliday, "Naked as Nature Intended," *Body and Society* 6, nos. 3–4 (2000): 130.

15. Ivan A. Brovont, "Prejudice Exhibitionist," *Natural Herald*, April 1950, 9, Robert J. Young Collection, Wolfsonian-Florida International University Rare Book and Special Collections Library, Miami Beach, Florida.

16. The conflation of sexually objectified women with soon-to-be butchered animals evokes the vegetarian feminist criticism of Carol J. Adams. Adams, in her groundbreaking work, *The Sexual Politics of Meat*, has convincingly argued against the troubling ease with which misogynistic societal norms objectify the bodies of animals and women to the point of marginalization, violence, and murder. Carol J. Adams, *The Sexual Politics of Meat: A Feminist-Vegetarian Critical Theory* (New York: Continuum, 1990).

17. Deborah Acosta, "Free the Nipple?" *New York Times* [video], January 26, 2016, online site accessed October 3, 2016.

18. See www.GoTopless.org and www.rael.org.

19. In *Naked Politics: Nudity, Political Action, and the Rhetoric of the Body* (Lanham: Lexington Books, 2012), Brett Lunceford includes a discussion of Facebook's role in the lactivist debate, as both the platform for breastfeeding spectacle and an arbiter of "appropriate nudity."

20. Ibid., 65.

21. Acosta, "Free the Nipple?"

22. See the work of Bernice L. Hausman, "Things (Not) to Do with Breasts in Public: Maternal Embodiment and the Biocultural Politics of Infant Feeding," *New Literary History* 38, no. 3 (Summer 2007): 479–504; Jessica Martucci, "Why Breastfeeding? Natural Motherhood in Post-War America," *Journal of Women's History* 27, no. 2 (Summer 2015): 110–133; Cindy A. Stearns, "The Work of Breastfeeding," *Women's Studies Quarterly* 37, nos. 3–4 (Fall–Winter 2009): 63–80.

23. Mia Fineman, "Naked Ambition: Why Doesn't Spencer Tunick Get Any Respect?" *Slate*, January 16, 2008, online site accessed September 22, 2017.

24. Spencer Tunick Website, online site accessed September 22, 2017.

25. The Spencer Tunick Experience, online site accessed September 22, 2017.

26. Fineman, "Naked Ambition."

27. Ibid.

28. Donald M. Lowe, *The Body in Late-Capitalist USA* (Durham, NC: Duke University Press, 1995), 133.

29. Ruth Barcan, *Nudity: A Cultural Anatomy* (Oxford: Berg, 2004), 3. Barcan revisits this point on page 280.

INDEX

Page numbers in italics refer to figures.

ACKNOWLEDGMENTS

I have been lucky, over the course of writing this book, to receive the generous support of many institutions, colleagues, friends, and family members. One might think that writing a history of nudity would raise some eyebrows, even hackles, but nobody even blinked; instead, I have been overwhelmed by how helpful people have been, encouraged by their enthusiasm for the project, and deeply touched by their patience as I circulated the roughest of drafts and subjected many to verbal treatises on everything from nudist architecture to the domestic fetishism of hot tubs.

Fellowships from the Huntington Library, the Haynes Foundation, and the Wolfsonian-Florida International University funded much of the early research for *Free and Natural: Nudity and the American Cult of the Body*. I am especially grateful to California State University, Long Beach's College of Liberal Arts for supporting this project with sabbatical leaves and Research, Scholarly, and Creative Activities awards, which reduced my teaching load and allowed me much-needed time to research and write. A President's Award for Outstanding Faculty Achievement provided encouragement as I completed the book and I am grateful to President Jane Close Conoley and Dean David Wallace for so generously supporting my scholarship and pedagogy.

Portions of *Free and Natural* have appeared elsewhere. Many thanks to the Canadian Centre for Architecture for including my essay, "Sunbathing in Suburbia: Health, Fashion and the Built Environment," in the exhibition catalogue, *Imperfect Health: The Medicalization of Architecture* (edited by Giovanna Borasi and Mirko Zardini, 2012), and for publishing my essay's French translation. Many ideas and images from that essay appear here. Chapter 2 is a version of an article that originally appeared in the *Journal of Urban History*, and which was nominated by the journal's editors for the Urban History Association's 2012 Best Article Award. Parts of Chapter 6 first appeared in my essay "Naked Yoga and the Sexualization of Asana," in *Yoga, The Body, and Embodied Social Change: An Intersectional Feminist Analysis*, edited by Beth

Berila, Melanie Klein, and Chelsea Jackson Roberts (Lanham, MD: Roman and Littlefield, 2016). Sections of the introduction were originally published in the journal *Modern American History*, published by Cambridge University Press. All this material has been reprinted with permission.

A critically important part of this project was finding appropriate images to illustrate the free and natural lifestyle and to secure permission to reproduce them. I would like to thank the following people and institutions for their help: Caroline Dagbert and Stéphane Aleixandre, Canadian Centre for Architecture; Vanessa Davis, Gerald Davis Estate; Stéphane Deschênes, Bare Oaks Family Naturist Park; Terri Garst and Kurt Thum, Los Angeles Public Library; Gary Mussell, Southern California Naturist Association; Carol Myers, San Diego History Center; and Amy Silverman, Lynton Gardiner, Silvia Ros, and Larry Wiggins, the Wolfsonian-Florida International University.

This book would have been impossible to write without either the help of participants in naked living experiments, or the specialty archival collections that document the free and natural lifestyle. Many, many thanks to Gary Mussell, Patty Fitzgibbons, and Rolf Holbach of the Southern California Naturist Association for granting me access to the Elysium papers and for hours of their time answering my questions. Thank you to Stéphane Deschênes of the Bare Oaks Family Naturist Park for the delightful interview and subsequent podcast. Thank you to the staffs of the Pomona Public Library Free Beach Collection, the Palm Springs Historical Society, and the Palm Desert Historical Society. Thanks, too, to the nude yogis of the Love Dome, Venice Beach, California. I would also like to extend my gratitude to the yoga community of Long Beach, which spreads free and natural living and good vibes throughout Southern California. The teachers, students, and healers of Yoga108 Studio, Purple Yoga, Glow Hot Yoga, Yogalution, Go Inward, Kava Yoga, Sacred Roots, and Long Beach Meditation have supported me with community, calm, and some mean vinyasa.

Brilliant readers shaped this book. My editors, Peggy Shaffer and Robert Lockhart, have been steadfast in their support and have lent their keen eyes to fine-tuning my manuscript from the very beginning. Phoebe S. K. Young and Whitney Strub offered extraordinarily insightful comments and smart analytical strategies that have been essential to the revisions. Bernice Schrank painstakingly read each chapter, polishing my prose and sharpening my arguments along the way. Eileen Luhr read an early draft of the book and challenged me to further develop my lines of inquiry.

My colleagues at California State University, Long Beach, have been simply wonderful. They have attended my talks, fed me, and offered the warmest greetings on the most difficult of days. Many heartfelt thanks to Elyse Blankley, Patricia Cleary, Jane Dabel, Kathleen Divito, Ali İğmen, Tim Keirn, Marie Kelleher, Eileen Luhr, Caitlin Murdock, Jessica Zacher Pandya, Mihir Pandya, Pamela Roberts, David Shafer, Sean Smith, Amy Bentley-Smith, Michiko Takeuchi, Oliver Wang, and Hugh Wilford.

A special debt of gratitude is to be paid to Liz Brown, Sharon Mizota, Lisa Jane Persky, and Joy Press, for creating the smartest, funniest, and warmest literary circle in Los Angeles. Didem Ekici deserves special thanks for encouraging my study of the body's relationship to the built environment and for collaborating with me on an edited volume of collected essays. Merry Ovnick, my colleague and editor at *Southern California Quarterly*, has been the most supportive of friends and an enthusiastic fan of this project. William Deverell has been one of my most important mentors and has always encouraged my study of the Southland.

I would like to thank Sarah Banet-Weiser for her warmth and humor as we worked together at *American Quarterly*. Marni Zatzman was years ahead of me in exploring free and natural living and I am grateful for our thirty-year friendship. I am forever thankful that Lori Seay and I met in 1994 at Mary Jane's, the late, great hippie health food store in St. John's, Newfoundland. We have long shared the experience of traveling from the West Coast to Atlantic Canada and built the friendship of a lifetime along the way. Gus Munem is an exemplar of loyalty, love, patience, and punk rock. Thank you for being on my team.

My family always has been my most significant source of love and encouragement. My parents, Bill and Bernice, have supported me through everything life has kicked my way. Their intelligence, humor, integrity, and devotion to each other inspire me every day. My brother, Joe, is my staunchest ally and I am delighted by the loving family he has created with his wife, Amaya, and my two adorably rambunctious nieces, Bibiana and Kate. It is my sincerest hope that they inherit a society in which they can be as free and natural as they so choose. My sister, Rachel, has always had my back and is the smartest, funniest, and most beautiful woman I know. Together with my brother-in-law, Andrew, she has provided help, support, and laughs when I needed them most. I love you all so much.